Bryn Mawr Greek Commentaries

Sophocles
Oidipous Tyrannos

Jeffrey Rusten

Thomas Library, Bryn Mawr College
Bryn Mawr, Pennsylvania

Copyright © 1990 Jeffrey Rusten

Manufactured in the United States of America

Printed and distributed by

The Department of Greek
Thomas Library
Bryn Mawr College
Bryn Mawr, PA 19010

ISBN 0-929524-67-5

For Gilbert Rose

SERIES PREFACE

These lexical and grammatical notes are meant not as a full-scale commentary but as a clear and concise aid to the beginning student. The editors have been told to resist their critical impulses and to say only what will help the student read the text. Our commentaries, then, are the beginning of the interpretative process, not the end.

We expect that the student will know the basic Attic declensions and conjugations, basic grammar (the common functions of cases and moods; the common types of clauses and conditions), and how to use a dictionary. In general we have tried to avoid duplication of material easily extractable from the lexicon, but we have provided help with odd verb forms, and, recognizing that endless page-flipping can be counter-productive, we have provided the occasional bonus of assistance with uncommon vocabulary. The bibliography lists a few books in English that have proved useful as secondary reading.

Production of these commentaries has been made possible by a generous grant from the Division of Education Programs, the National Endowment for the Humanities.

Copy for this volume was prepared at Cornell University, Department of Classics.

Richard Hamilton
General Editor

Gregory W. Dickerson
Associate Editor

Gilbert P. Rose
Associate Editor

VOLUME PREFACE

A 19th-century schoolmaster is said to have commended to his students a play of Sophocles as "a veritable treasure-house of grammatical peculiarities" (quoted by Gilbert Highet, *The Classical Tradition* [Oxford 1949] 494). In offering help with the grammar of *Oidipous Tyrannos* I hope I shall not appeal to that sort of approach, but to those who wish, even at an early stage, to read one of the works which justifies learning ancient Greek in the first place.

The text is my own, but it almost always agrees with the Oxford Classical Text of Sir Hugh Lloyd-Jones and N. G. Wilson (Oxford 1990); divergences are noted in Appendix I. I have learned much from the edition with commentary by R. D. Dawe (Cambridge 1982) which offers acute analysis and vigorous and witty argument; but I think that at least some students will want help in reading the play at a more elementary level, and with less attention to textual criticism and emendation.

I also believe that a commentary for beginners should be more extensive, rather than abbreviated; thus my frequent references to other notes on the play (Jebb, Dawe, Lloyd-Jones and Wilson) and advanced grammatical works (Denniston, Moorhouse, Smyth, on occasion even Kühner-Gerth and Bruhn's *Anhang*) are meant to summarize and draw attention to the authoritative aid offered by these books rather than terrify the reader.

Two sections with "Textual Notes" and "Topics for Discussion" offer suggestions for those who wish to go further, in one direction or another; references to secondary literature not in English, excluded by the BMC series guidelines, are usually given only there.

I have been fortunate in having colleagues at Cornell (Frederick Ahl, Gordon Kirkwood, Pietro Pucci) and elsewhere (Patricia Easterling, Sir Hugh Lloyd-Jones, William Merritt Sale, Ruth Scodel, Bernd Seidensticker) who taught me much about the play—although I would not necessarily wish to implicate them in my conclusions. Richard Hamilton in particular provided unfailing enthusiasm and encouragement.

Gilbert Rose was especially generous with his time, correcting or querying virtually every note of a preliminary version, which led to countless revisions and improvements. I have taken the liberty of dedicating these notes to him, not only because of his extravagant contribution to them, but also because he exemplifies the kind of conscientious and imaginative teacher who I hope will find them useful.

Errors great and small doubtless remain; I would be grateful if students and teachers would pass on to me whatever they find.

November 24, 1990   Jeffrey Rusten
                                                                      Dept. of Classics
                                                                  Goldwin Smith 120
                                                                   Cornell University
                                                                  Ithaca, NY, 14853
                                                        (jsr@crux1.cit.cornell.edu)

In this reprint I have been able to correct errors and misinterpretations (uncovered especially by William Race and Richard Hamilton), and make the relative length of the two volumes more manageable with different typefaces, and by moving the two appendixes of the first printing to the introduction of the first volume.

October 26, 1991   J. R.

CONTENTS

page

Series Preface	v
Volume Preface	vii
Abbreviations and Symbols	xi
The Structure and Meters of *Oidipous Tyrannos*	1
Textual Notes and Divergences from the *Oxford Classical Text*	5
Topics for Discussion	9
ΣΟΦΟΚΛΕΟΥΣ ΟΙΔΙΠΟΥΣ ΤΥΡΑΝΝΟΣ	13
Commentary	59
Grammatical Index	131

ABBREVIATIONS AND SYMBOLS

Bruhn	Ewald Bruhn's *Anhang* (= Appendix), vol. 8 of the Sophocles edition of F. W. Schneidewin and A. Nauck (Berlin 1899). Cited by paragraphs.
D	R. D. Dawe, Sophocles, *Oedipus Rex* (Cambridge 1982).
Dale	Dale, *Metrical Analyses of Tragic Choruses* (Bulletin of the Institute of Classical Studies, University of London, Supplement Volume 21, 3 fascicles, 1971-1983).
Dawe, *Studies*	R. D. Dawe, *Studies on the Text of Sophocles* vol. 1 (Leiden 1973).
GP	J. D. Denniston, *The Greek Particles* (2nd ed., Oxford 1954).
J	R. C. Jebb, *Sophocles, The Plays and Fragments*, Part I: *Oedipus Tyrannus* (2nd ed., Cambridge 1887).
K-G	Kühner-Gerth, *Ausführliche Grammatik der griechischen Sprache* II:*Satzlehre* (3rd ed., 2 vols., Hannover 1898). Cited by volume and page.
Lewis	R. G. Lewis, "The Procedural Basis of *Oedipus Tyrannus*," *Greek, Roman and Byzantine Studies* 30 (1989) 41-66.
lit.	"literally."
LJ-W	H. Lloyd-Jones and N. G. Wilson, *Sophoclea: Studies on the Text of Sophocles* (Oxford 1990).
LSJ	H. J. Liddell and R. Scott, *A Greek-English Lexicon*, 9th ed. rev. by H. Stuart Jones (Oxford 1925-1940).
M	A. C. Moorhouse, *The Syntax of Sophocles* (*Mnemosyne* Supplement Volume 75, Leiden 1982). Cited by page.
MT	W. W. Goodwin, *Syntax of the Moods and Tenses of the Greek Verb* (London 1889). Cited by paragraph.
O	Oidipous
OCT	*Sophoclis Fabulae*, ed. H. Lloyd-Jones and N. G. Wilson (Oxford Classical Texts, Oxford 1990).
sc.	"understand, supply" (from Lat. *scilicet*)
S	H. W. Smyth, *Greek Grammar* (2nd ed. revised by G. Messing, Cambridge Mass. 1956). Cited by paragraph.
κτλ.	καὶ τὰ λοιπά (= "*et cetera*")
<	"is from" (in the commentary only).
<>	encloses words inserted by editorial conjecture (to be added in translation).

Abbreviations and Symbols

[καί] encloses words deleted by editorial conjecture (to be ignored in translation).

† designates words (or encloses phrases) considered unintelligible because of textual corruption.

When several meanings of a word are given, the one *italicized* is the one appropriate to the current passage.

THE STRUCTURE AND METERS OF *OIDIPOUS TYRANNOS*

The parts of a Greek tragedy are defined by the <u>exits and entrances</u> of the three actors (playing various parts) and the chorus, and the alternation of <u>recited speech (dialogue) and song (lyric)</u>.[1] The meters of lyric are much more elusive, and their details are beyond the scope of a beginners' commentary;[2] but the meter of dialogue is mostly iambic trimeter, which follows regular rules.

DISTRIBUTION OF PARTS

Actor I: Oidipous
Actor II: Priest (1-150), Teiresias (316-462), Iokaste (634-862, 911-1072), Shepherd (1125-1185), Messenger from the Palace (1223-1530).
Actor III: Kreon (87-150, 513-677), Messenger from Corinth (924-1185), Kreon (1422-1530).

Exits and entrances are indicated in English in the text. The stage allowed three possible directions for these: 1) the palace (a central door); 2) offstage to or from the city of Thebes; 3) offstage to or from the country (Delphi, Corinth, Mt. Kithaeron).[3]

NAMES OF STRUCTURAL DIVISIONS[4]

πρόλογος (lit. 'preliminary talk') dialogue: anything (sometimes a lengthy scene, sometimes a single speech) that precedes the entry of the chorus.

---

[1] Oliver Taplin, *The Stagecraft of Aeschylus* (Oxford 1977) 49-60.
[2] On the dialect and style of tragic lyric see the introductory note to lines 151-215. For their meters, in addition to West and Raven (note 5 below), see A. M. Dale, *The Lyric Metres of Greek Drama* (Cambridge, second edition 1968) and her posthumously published *Metrical Analyses of Tragic Choruses* (Bulletin of the Institute of Classical Studies, University of London, Supplement Volume 21 [three parts, 1971-1983]).
[3] On details of staging in *Oidipous Tyrannos* see Oliver Taplin, "Sophocles in his Theater," in *Sophocle* (ed. J. de Romilly, Fondation Hardt Entretiens vol. 29, Geneva 1983) 155-183 and David Seale, *Vision and Stagecraft in Sophocles* (London 1982) 113-143.
[4] Most of the terms are derived from Aristotle, *Poetics*, chapter 12.

πάροδος ('entry from the side') lyric: the entry of the chorus, usually first chanting in *anapaests*, then singing (and dancing) in the metrically matching pattern of *strophe* ('turning') and *antistrophe* ('counter-turning').

ἐπεισόδιον (perhaps 'additional entrance') dialogue: the spoken dialogue sections (which advance the plot) between songs of the chorus.

στάσιμον ('stationary song,' as opposed to πάροδος and ἔξοδος) lyric: any song (consisting of at least one *strophe* and matching *antistrophe*) by the chorus after its entrance.

ἔξοδος ('exit') dialogue: the concluding section of the tragedy (after which there is no further chorus song).

Other types of scenes:

ἀγγελία ('report') dialogue: a messenger-speech describing at length what has happened offstage.

κομμός ('breast-beating') lyric: a shared lament between chorus and actor(s).

στιχομυθία ('speech by the line') dialogue: rapid exchanges consisting of one or two lines each between two characters with frequent interruption, sespecially in interrogations or arguments.

THE STRUCTURE OF *OIDIPOUS TYRANNOS*
(the number of episodes and stasima can vary from play to play)

Prologue (dialogue): 1-150
    Parodos (chorus): 151-215
Episode I (dialogue): 216-462
    Stasimon I (chorus): 463-512
Episode II: 513-862 (with a lyric *kommos*, 649-696)
    Stasimon II: 863-910
Episode III: 911-1085
    Stasimon III: 1086-1109
Episode IV: 1110-1185
    Stasimon IV : 1186-1221
Exodos (dialogue): 1222-1530 (with a lyric *kommos*, 1297-1368)

IAMBIC TRIMETER[5]

I. Metrical quantities: A syllable is *long* either (i) by nature, if it contains a long vowel or diphthong; or (ii) by position, if it is followed by two consonants (χ, ψ, ξ count as two). All other syllables are *short*.

II. Mute + liquid: An exception to the rule above is that in tragedy, a mute consonant (π, β, φ, κ, γ, χ, τ, δ, θ) followed by a liquid (λ, μ, ν, ρ) sometimes (usually in the middle of a word) makes position, sometimes (usually at word-boundary) does not: e.g., Κάδμου (—), but πᾶσι κλεινός (‒᷾ ‒᷾), τίνι τρόπῳ (᷾᷾ ᷾‒). The variation is illustrated by τέκνα, ‒᷾ in line 1, but ᷾᷾ in line 6.[6]

III. Iambic trimeter: The standard meter of tragic dialogue is a line consisting roughly of six iambic feet (short + long syllable, ᷾‒) but called trimeter, because it has just three repeated units, called *metra* ("×" indicates a syllable that may be *either* long *or* short):

×‒᷾‒ ×‒᷾‒ ×‒᷾‒

Note how far this verse may stray from being simply "six iambs": the first syllable of each metron may be either long or short; in addition, the last syllable in the line is considered long, regardless of quantity, because of the pause before the following verse, so that the third metron could really be described as ×‒᷾×. E.g., line 6 (ἀγὼ δικαιῶν μὴ παρ' ἀγγέλων, τέκνα) has the pattern ‒‒᷾‒ ‒‒᷾‒ ᷾‒᷾᷾.

IV. Resolution: Additional freedom is allowed by the possibility of resolution, the replacement of any long syllable in this scheme (× or ‒) by a double-short (᷾᷾). E.g., line 10 (πρὸ τῶνδε φωνεῖν· τίνι τρόπῳ καθέστατε) has the pattern ᷾‒᷾‒ ‒᷾᷾᷾‒ ᷾‒᷾᷾, and line 20 (ἀγοραῖσι θακεῖ, πρός τε Παλλάδος διπλοῖς) is ᷾᷾‒᷾‒ ‒‒᷾‒ ᷾‒᷾‒.[7]

---

[5] The most authoritative account is M. L. West, *Greek Metre* (Oxford 1982), and a simplified version is available in his *Introduction to Greek Metre* (Oxford 1987); but both relate tragic meters to those of earlier poetry, and must be read in their entirety. Easier to dip into for occasional information on tragedy is D. S. Raven, *Greek Metre: An Introduction* (London 1962).
[6] For details see West, *Greek Metre* 16-17.
[7] See West, *Greek Metre* 85 n. 27 for finer distinctions than can be drawn here.

V. Changes in quantity: Finally, when two syllables are not separated by a consonant, either the first may be shortened if long (*correption*) or they may both be pronounced as one long syllable (*synizesis*).[8] E.g., line 13 (εἴην τοιάνδε μὴ‿οὐ κατοικτίρων ἕδραν) has the pattern --ᴗ-ᴗ-ᴗ- --ᴗ-, with -οι- in τοιάνδε shortened by correption, and μὴ οὐ combined by synizesis.

VI. The Caesura: Sense-pauses (word- or phrase-end) within the line tend to occur *within* the metra. These are called caesurae, and are most common in two positions: (i) the "penthemimeral" (lit. "at the fifth half-foot"), e.g. line 16 βωμοῖσι τοῖς σοῖς, οἱ μὲν οὐδέπω μακρὰν (--ᴗ- -:-ᴗ- ᴗ-ᴗ-); or (ii) the "hepthemimeral" (lit. "at the seventh half-foot"), e.g. line 11 δείσαντες ἢ στέρξαντες; ὡς θέλοντος ἄν (--ᴗ- --ᴗ:- ᴗ-ᴗᴗ).

OTHER DIALOGUE METERS

Also appearing in dialogue is the **trochaic tetrameter** (lines 1515-1530 in this play). It is usually described as consisting of seven and one-half trochaic feet (-ᴗ) or four metra, but in fact it is identical to the iambic trimeter preceded by -ᴗ-:

Trochaic tetrameter: -ᴗ- x-ᴗ- x-ᴗ- x-ᴗ-
Iambic trimeter: x-ᴗ- x-ᴗ- x-ᴗ-

Except for this addition, roughly the same rules apply to the tetrameter as to the trimeter.

Anapaestic dimeters, traditionally suited for marching songs and usually recited by the chorus as it enters or leaves the stage (*parodos* and *exodos*), are not used for this purpose in *Oidipous Tyrannos*.[9]

---

[8] West, *Greek Metre* 12 prefers the term *synekphonesis*.
[9] Although there is a brief anapestic series within the *kommos*, 1297-1306.

TEXTUAL NOTES, AND DIVERGENCES FROM THE OXFORD CLASSICAL TEXT

I have noted only major divergences (not, e.g., details of orthography or punctuation). Information on manuscripts and authors of conjectures should be sought from LJ-W and the critical apparatus of the *OCT*.

10 (στέρξαντες) Dawe's emendation to στέργοντες is not absolutely necessary, as the tenses of the participle do not always indicate strictly relative time, see M 212. If emendations are in order, a more probable one might be στέρξοντες, "in order to make a request" (see LSJ as cited in the commentary) or "resolved to endure."

18 (ἱερεύς) So Bentley (adopted by *OCT*), for ἱερεῖς of the manuscripts; not all the old men can be priests, and only this one is mentioned; the assimilation to the plural after βαρεῖς is a likely error.

(οἱ δ' ἔτ') Several manuscripts have either οἱ δέ τ' or οἵδ' ἔτ'. It is better to retain the δέ (see the structural diagram in the commentary) than to interpret it as οἵδε τ' (so Dawe and *OCT*).

20-1 The identification of these Theban sites creates numerous difficulties, on which see Sarantis Symeonoglou, *The Topography of Thebes* (Princeton 1985): 1) the main agora was on the central hill called the *Kadmeia*, a second may have been to the northwest (Symeonoglou 137-8); 2) the temple of Athena was that of *Onka*; no other is known (Symeonoglou 130); 3) "at the prophetic ash of Ismenos" seems to designate the oracular sanctuary of Apollo Ismenios to the southeast of the city (Symeonoglou 132-3, 236-9), but there was also one of Apollo σπόδιος (where the altar was made of the ashes of sacrificial victims) on the Kadmeia itself (Symeonoglou 129-130, 184)—unless, as some have thought, the two are the same.

51 ἀνόρθωσον closes the thought by repeating the word (46) which began it, a common practice. Dawe is wrong to follow Ritter in suggesting the line be deleted.

60 (νοσεῖτε πάντες) *OCT* follows Barrett in placing a stop after these words; but many of the examples of καί = "and yet" cited by *GP* 292 are continuous.

161 Blaydes' αἰτῶ for ἰώ (adopted by *OCT*) is unneccessary; for this type of anacoluthon (although not in lyric, as LJ-W note) see K-

G II.108-9. (For Ιώ + (προ)φάνητε cf. *Antigone* 1149, *Ajax* 694.)

161-2 For the temple of Artemis *Eukleia* at Thebes see Symeonoglou (cited on 20-1) 135-6.

174 (άλλον...άλλῳ) άλλον...άλλᾳ *OCT*, but cf. K-G I.444.

216-75 Many scholars have attempted to produce an exact correspondence with legal procedure and fewer shifts in thought by transposing, deleting or postulating lacunae, but few have agreed; see most recently Alan Griffiths, "Oedipus' Proclamation to the Thebans," *Studies in Honour of T. B. L. Webster* (ed. J.H. Betts, J. T. Hooker and J. R. Green, Bristol 1986) vol. 1, 130-133; Dawe, *Studies* I 221-226, LJ-W 85-6. The best of these is Wecklein's deletion of 246-251 (adopted by *OCT*), which produces good sense. Without it, lines 233-243 would seem to be a curse not on the murderer, but on some potential informant who keeps silent; the latter is perhaps possible legally (see Lewis, "Procedural Basis" 56), but subsequent allusions to 238-41 (350-1, 818-9, 1381-3) show the former must be meant.

220 (αὐτός) *OCT* prefers αὐτό.

293 (δρῶντ') It is tempting to retain the manuscript reading ἰδόντ' as a contrast to ἐλέχθη and ἤκουσα, yet that is perhaps why it was corrupted to this form in the first place; it is clear from 295-6 that O and the chorus are discussing the murderer, not an eyewitness.

463 (εἶπε) The conjecture ᾖδε (*OCT*) is attractive, but it should not be deduced from the variant reading εἶδε, which attempts to supply a verb of perception for the participle (for εἶπε with participle see K-G II.72).

478 (ὁ ταῦρος) LJ-W have explained this reading: Rudolf Kassel, *Rheinisches Museum* 116 (1973) 109-112 showed how often proverbial comparisons are evoked in Greek without ὡς (e.g., Kratinos fr. 56 Kassel-Austin, ὁ δ' ὄνος ὕεται, "he's an ass in the rain [who doesn't react]"). Passages describing the proverbial solitary "herd-scorning" (ἀτιμαγέλης) bull are collected by Gow on Theocritus 9.5.

510 (τῶν ἀπό) Most manuscripts have τῷ ("therefore") ἀπό, but hiatus (vowel at both word-end and word-beginning) is strictly avoided in tragedy. *OCT* and LJ-W prefer the conjecture τώς (= οὕτως), but a papyrus and one ancient commentator seem to have read τῶν.

516-7 LJ-W find φέρον alone in 517 intolerable, and in *OCT* prefer the conjecture δοκεῖ τι for νομίζει in 516.

523 τάχ' ἂν δ', found in a papyrus, is adopted by LJ-W and *OCT*; but it is not an improvement, and may have been inserted by someone who did not understand the typically adversative force of ἀλλά...μὲν δή (*GP* 394).

659 The easier (and less likely) reading φυγήν is not necessary; for such a variation cf. Thuc. 2.40.2 οὐ τοὺς λόγους...βλάβην ἡγούμενοι, ἀλλὰ μὴ προδιδαχθῆναι.

742 Dawe and *OCT* prefer μέλας, evidently assuming that it indicates *black hair*, but a glance at LSJ μέλας I, or the index to R. Foerster, *Scriptores Physiognomici Grace et Latini* (2 vols., Leipzig 1893) shows that without further specification it would refer to the color of eyes or skin (either "brown-eyed" or "dark-complexioned").

891 (ἕξεται) *OCT* follows Dawe in printing the conjecture θίξεται.

894 (†ἔρξεταιt) *OCT* print the conjecture τεύξεται (and would have preferred Erfurdt's ἀμύνων also), "which man will succeed in warding off the arrows of passion from his soul?"

1134-5 LJ-W are right to assume a lacuna here, as the anacoluthon is more serious than others cited with it at *GP* 369 n. 1: not only is ἐγώ missing a verb, but so is τὸν Κιθαιρῶνος τόπον. An alternative solution would be to delete 1134-5; but they seem an unlikely interpolation.

1167 *OCT* prints the manuscript reading γεννημάτων and marks it corrupt, but LJ-W prefer the conjecture ἐκ δωμάτων.

1337 *OCT* prints the conjecture βλεπτὸν ἦν, but it is argued against (rightly) in LJ-W.

1463 *OCT* marks ἠμή as corrupt.

1446 (προτρέψομαι) LJ-W argue (rightly) for this reading, but *OCT* prints the variant προστρέψομαι.

1471 (τί φημι;) *OCT* gives the correct accentuation for the first time; the alternative (if τι is indefinite rather than interrogative) would be τὶ φημί; (see Kühner-Blass, *Ausführliche Grammatik der griechischen Sprache* part I [*Elementar- und Formenlehre*] 1.345); but all current editions (J, D, Schneidewin-Nauck) print the impossible τί φημί;

1505 (περιίδῃς) *OCT* prefers a different conjecture, πάτερ, ἴδῃς.

1514 (ὑμᾶς κυρῆσαι) *OCT*'s ἡμᾶς κυρῆσαι must be a misprint.

TOPICS FOR DISCUSSION

Oedipus the King is one of a few privileged works (like *Hamlet* or the *Iliad*) where interpretation also becomes an exercise in self-expression: the more intently we examine it, the more we find reflected our own preoccupations and enthusiasms. This is by no means a defect, but it suggests we cannot put "the play itself" into one compartment, and our own and others' reactions to it into another. Since sexuality, personality disorder, political leadership, individual freedom, and theodicy have all been cast as its central character, I hope readers of the grammatical commentary will also keep in mind from the outset the great variety of approaches to this play, of which this is a sampling:

I. Previous accounts of the story of Oidipous

1. How has Sophocles altered (or selected from) the legends of O known from epic, and from Aeschylus' *Oidipous* (which won first prize, as Sophocles' did *not*)? For Homer see *Odyssey* 11.271-280; for the epic *Thebais* and *Oidipodeia* see Malcolm Davies, *The Epic Cycle* (Bristol 1989) 19-29; for Aeschylus' *Laios* and *Oidipous* see G. O. Hutchinson's introd. to his edition of Aeschylus, *Septem contra Thebas* (Oxford 1985) xvii-xxx, and Stefan Radt, *Tragicorum Graecorum Fragmenta* vol. 3: Aeschylus (Göttingen 1985) pp. 231-2, 287-8 and 434.

II. Date and Circumstances of Sophocles' Production

1. For its defeat in the competition (by Philokles) see Stefan Radt, *Tragicorum Graecorum Fragmenta* vol. 4: Sophocles (Göttingen 1977) p. 50.

2. Do aspects of the play allude to contemporary events? See O. Longo, *Edipo e Nicia* (Padua 1975); V. Ehrenberg, *Sophocles and Pericles* (Oxford 1954); B. M. Knox, "The Date of the Oedipus Tyrannus of Sophocles" in *Word and Action: Essays on the Ancient Theater* (Baltimore 1979) 112-124.

3. What was the standing of the Delphic oracle at this time? See Jean Defradas, *Les thèmes de la propaganda delphique* (Paris 1954).

4. What are the political implications of the word τύραννος to describe Oedipus? To what extent is the play a political power-struggle? See B. M. Knox, "Why is Oedipus called 'tyrannus'?" in *Word and Action: Essays on the Ancient Theater* (Baltimore 1979) 87-95; Diego Lanza, *Il tiranno e il suo pubblico* (Turin 1977) 141ff; Lewis, "Procedural Basis" (with comparisons to the investigation of Alcibiades in 415 B. C.); J.-P. Vernant, "The Lame Tyrant: From Oedipus to Periander," *Myth and Tragedy in Ancient Greece* (tr. Janet Lloyd, New York, 1988) 207-236.

III. The Plot

1. The chorus is on stage all the time, to hear and observe everything; how much does it understand, and what influence does it have? This is particularly problematical in the second stasimon (see introductory note on 863-910). See R. Burton, *The Chorus in Sophocles' Tragedies* (Oxford 1980) 138-185; Ruth Scodel, "Hybris in the Second Stasimon of the *Oedipus Rex*," *Classical Philology* 76 (1982) 214-223, and C. Carey, "The Second Stasimon of Sophocles' *Oedipus Tyrannus*," *Journal of Hellenic Studies* 106 (1986) 175-179.

2. How is the development of the plot illustrative of the best kind of tragedy? (Especially in the third episode, see the introductory note on 911-1085). See Aristotle, *Poetics*, chapter 11 and 13; Jean-Pierre Vernant, "Ambiguity and Reversal: on the Enigmatic Structure of *Oedipus Rex* ," in *Myth and Tragedy in Ancient Greece* (tr. Janet Lloyd, New York 1988) 113-140.

3. The detective-story: How good is the evidence that O really killed Laius? Are there any loose ends left, or inconsistencies in the evidence presented? See Tycho von Wilamowitz-Moellendorff, *Die dramatische Technik des Sophokles* (Berlin 1917) 69-88; Sandor Goodhart, "ληστὰς ἔφασκε: Oedipus and Laius' Many Murderers," *Diacritics* 8:1 (spring 1978) 55-71; Jonathan Culler, *The Pursuit of Signs* (Ithaca 1981) 174; Frederick M. Ahl, *Evidence and Self-Conviction in Sophocles' Oedipus* (forthcoming Ithaca 1991).

IV. Final Judgments

1. O's self-blinding. Why does he not commit suicide, as his words at 1183 lead us to expect? Is blindness for him a penance, a strategy for distancing himself from his guilt, or a form of self-castration? See

Georges Devereux, "The self-blinding of Oidipous in Sophokles' *Oidipous Tyrannos*," *Journal of Hellenic Studies* 93 (1973) 36-49; R. G. A. Buxton, "Blindness and Limits: Sophocles and the Logic of Myth," *Journal of Hellenic Studies* 100 (1980) 24-5.

2. Does the inconclusive final scene prepare us for a sequel? See Deborah Roberts, "Sophoclean Endings: Another Story," *Arethusa* 21 (1988) 183-4; Bernd Seidensticker, "Bezeihungen zwischen den Oedipusdramen des Sophokles," *Hermes* 100 (1972) 255-273.

3. Does O change at the play's conclusion? Has he reached some new insight about himself or the gods? Or is he, despite his humiliation, as domineering as ever? See M. Davies, "The End of Sophocles' O. T.," *Hermes* 110 (1982) 268-279, Oliver Taplin, "Sophocles in his Theater," in *Sophocle* (ed. J. de Romilly, Fondation Hardt Entretiens vol. 29, Geneva 1983), Pietro Pucci, *Oedipus and the Fabrication of Man* (forthcoming).

4. Is O the most guilty of mankind, or the most victimized? How important is this question (and our estimate of the gods' justice) for the understanding of the play? See E. R. Dodds, "On Misunderstanding the *Oedipus Rex*," in Eric Segal (ed.), *Oxford Readings in Greek Tragedy* (Oxford 1983) 177-188, and David Hester, "Oedipus and Jonah," *Proceedings of the Cambridge Philological Society* 203 (1977) 32-61.

V. Oidipous as psychological and anthropological paradigm

To what extent is O's story not that of a unique individual, but:

1. A case-study in the sexual drive and intrafamilial aggression of male children? See Peter Rudnytsky, *Freud and Oedipus* (New York 1987) and (for an attack on this approach) J.-P. Vernant, "Oedipus Without the Complex," in *Myth and Tragedy in Ancient Greece* (tr. Janet Lloyd, New York 1988) 85-112.

2. An example of a breakthrough in self-awareness achieved through Freudian analysis? See Cynthia Chase, "Oedipal Textuality: Reading Freud's Reading of *Oedipus*," *Diacritics* 9.1 (Spring 1979) 54-78.

3. A 'test-case' for the applicability of any theory of myth to the data for ancient Greece? See René Girard, "Oedipus and the Surrogate Victim," *Violence and the Sacred* (1977) 68-88; Claude Lévi-Strauss, "The Structural Study of Myth," in *Structural Anthropology* (tr. C. Jacobsen and B. G. Schoepf, New York 1963) 206-231; Terence Turner, "Oedipus: Time and Structure in Narrative Form," in Robert F. Spencer (ed.), *Forms of Symbolic Action* (Seattle 1969) 26-68.

ΟΙΔΙΠΟΥΣ ΤΥΡΑΝΝΟΣ

[A priest leads in a group of suppliants, who sit outside the palace. O enters from within.]
ΟΙΔΙΠΟΥΣ
  ὦ τέκνα, Κάδμου τοῦ πάλαι νέα τροφή,
  τίνας ποθ' ἕδρας τάσδε μοι θοάζετε
  ἱκτηρίοις κλάδοισιν ἐξεστεμμένοι;
  πόλις δ' ὁμοῦ μὲν θυμιαμάτων γέμει,
  ὁμοῦ δὲ παιάνων τε καὶ στεναγμάτων· 5
  ἁγὼ δικαιῶν μὴ παρ' ἀγγέλων, τέκνα,
  ἄλλων ἀκούειν αὐτὸς ὧδ' ἐλήλυθα,
  ὁ πᾶσι κλεινὸς Οἰδίπους καλούμενος.
    ἀλλ', ὦ γεραιέ, φράζ', ἐπεὶ πρέπων ἔφυς
  πρὸ τῶνδε φωνεῖν· τίνι τρόπῳ καθέστατε, 10
  δείσαντες ἢ στέρξαντες; ὡς θέλοντος ἂν
  ἐμοῦ προσαρκεῖν πᾶν· δυσάλγητος γὰρ ἂν
  εἴην τοιάνδε μὴ οὐ κατοικτίρων ἕδραν.
ΙΕΡΕΥΣ
  ἀλλ', ὦ κρατύνων Οἰδίπους χώρας ἐμῆς,
  ὁρᾷς μὲν ἡμᾶς ἡλίκοι προσήμεθα 15
  βωμοῖσι τοῖς σοῖς, οἱ μὲν οὐδέπω μακρὰν
  πτέσθαι σθένοντες, οἱ δὲ σὺν γήρᾳ βαρεῖς
  (ἱερεὺς ἐγὼ μὲν Ζηνός), οἱ δ' ἔτ' ἠθέων
  λεκτοί· τὸ δ' ἄλλο φῦλον ἐξεστεμμένον
  ἀγοραῖσι θακεῖ, πρός τε Παλλάδος διπλοῖς 20
  ναοῖς, ἐπ' Ἰσμηνοῦ τε μαντείᾳ σποδῷ.
    πόλις γάρ, ὥσπερ καὐτὸς εἰσορᾷς, ἄγαν
  ἤδη σαλεύει, κἀνακουφίσαι κάρα

βυθῶν ἔτ' οὐχ οἵα τε φοινίου σάλου,
φθίνουσα μὲν κάλυξιν ἐγκάρποις χθονός, 25
φθίνουσα δ' ἀγέλαις βουνόμοις τόκοισί τε
ἀγόνοις γυναικῶν· ἐν δ' ὁ πυρφόρος θεὸς
σκήψας ἐλαύνει, λοιμὸς ἔχθιστος, πόλιν,
ὑφ' οὗ κενοῦται δῶμα Καδμεῖον, μέλας δ'
Ἅιδης στεναγμοῖς καὶ γόοις πλουτίζεται. 30
θεοῖσι μέν νυν οὐκ ἰσούμενόν σ' ἐγὼ
οὐδ' οἵδε παῖδες ἑζόμεσθ' ἐφέστιοι,
ἀνδρῶν δὲ πρῶτον ἔν τε συμφοραῖς βίου
κρίνοντες ἔν τε δαιμόνων ξυναλλαγαῖς,
ὅς γ' ἐξέλυσας ἄστυ Καδμεῖον μολὼν 35
σκληρᾶς ἀοιδοῦ δασμὸν ὃν παρείχομεν,
καὶ ταῦθ' ὑφ' ἡμῶν οὐδὲν ἐξειδὼς πλέον
οὐδ' ἐκδιδαχθείς, ἀλλὰ προσθήκῃ θεοῦ
λέγῃ νομίζῃ θ' ἡμὶν ὀρθῶσαι βίον.
νῦν δ', ὦ κράτιστον πᾶσιν Οἰδίπου κάρα, 40
ἱκετεύομέν σε πάντες οἵδε πρόστροποι
ἀλκήν τιν' εὑρεῖν ἡμίν, εἴτε του θεῶν
φήμην ἀκούσας εἴτ' ἀπ' ἀνδρὸς οἶσθά που·
ὡς τοῖσιν ἐμπείροισι καὶ τὰς ξυμφορὰς
ζώσας ὁρῶ μάλιστα τῶν βουλευμάτων. 45
ἴθ', ὦ βροτῶν ἄριστ', ἀνόρθωσον πόλιν·
ἴθ', εὐλαβήθηθ'· ὡς σὲ νῦν μὲν ἥδε γῆ
σωτῆρα κλῄζει τῆς πάρος προθυμίας,
ἀρχῆς δὲ τῆς σῆς μηδαμῶς μεμνήμεθα
στάντες τ' ἐς ὀρθὸν καὶ πεσόντες ὕστερον, 50
ἀλλ' ἀσφαλείᾳ τήνδ' ἀνόρθωσον πόλιν.
ὄρνιθι γὰρ καὶ τὴν τότ' αἰσίῳ τύχην
παρέσχες ἡμῖν, καὶ τὰ νῦν ἴσος γενοῦ·
ὡς, εἴπερ ἄρξεις τῆσδε γῆς ὥσπερ κρατεῖς,
ξὺν ἀνδράσιν κάλλιον ἢ κενῆς κρατεῖν· 55
ὡς οὐδέν ἐστιν οὔτε πύργος οὔτε ναῦς
ἔρημος ἀνδρῶν μὴ ξυνοικούντων ἔσω.
ΟΙ. ὦ παῖδες οἰκτροί, γνωτὰ κοὐκ ἄγνωτά μοι
προσήλθεθ' ἱμείροντες· εὖ γὰρ οἶδ' ὅτι

ΟΙΔΙΠΟΥΣ ΤΥΡΑΝΝΟΣ

νοσεῖτε πάντες, καὶ νοσοῦντες ὡς ἐγὼ 60
οὐκ ἔστιν ὑμῶν ὅστις ἐξ ἴσου νοσεῖ.
τὸ μὲν γὰρ ὑμῶν ἄλγος εἰς ἕν' ἔρχεται
μόνον καθ' αὑτόν, κοὐδέν' ἄλλον, ἡ δ' ἐμὴ
ψυχὴ πόλιν τε κἀμὲ καὶ σ' ὁμοῦ στένει.
ὥστ' οὐχ ὕπνῳ γ' εὕδοντά μ' ἐξεγείρετε· 65
ἀλλ' ἴστε πολλὰ μέν με δακρύσαντα δή,
πολλὰς δ' ὁδοὺς ἐλθόντα φροντίδος πλάνοις·
ἣν δ' εὖ σκοπῶν εὕρισκον ἴασιν μόνην,
ταύτην ἔπραξα· παῖδα γὰρ Μενοικέως
Κρέοντ', ἐμαυτοῦ γαμβρόν, ἐς τὰ Πυθικὰ 70
ἔπεμψα Φοίβου δώμαθ', ὡς πύθοιθ' ὅ τι
δρῶν ἢ τί φωνῶν τήνδε ῥυσαίμην πόλιν.
καί μ' ἦμαρ ἤδη ξυμμετρούμενον χρόνῳ
λυπεῖ τί πράσσει· τοῦ γὰρ εἰκότος πέρα
ἄπεστι πλείω τοῦ καθήκοντος χρόνον. 75
ὅταν δ' ἵκηται, τηνικαῦτ' ἐγὼ κακὸς
μὴ δρῶν ἂν εἴην πάνθ' ὅσ' ἂν δηλοῖ θεός.
[Kreon enters from the country.]
ΙΕ. ἀλλ' εἰς καλὸν σύ τ' εἶπας οἵδε τ' ἀρτίως
Κρέοντα προσστείχοντα σημαίνουσί μοι.
ΟΙ. ὦναξ Ἄπολλον, εἰ γὰρ ἐν τύχῃ γέ τῳ 80
σωτῆρι βαίη λαμπρὸς ὥσπερ ὄμματι.
ΙΕ. ἀλλ' εἰκάσαι μέν, ἡδύς· οὐ γὰρ ἂν κάρα
πολυστεφὴς ὧδ' εἷρπε παγκάρπου δάφνης.
ΟΙ. τάχ' εἰσόμεσθα· ξύμμετρος γὰρ ὡς κλύειν.
ἄναξ, ἐμὸν κήδευμα, παῖ Μενοικέως, 85
τίν' ἡμὶν ἥκεις τοῦ θεοῦ φήμην φέρων;
ΚΡΕΩΝ
ἐσθλήν· λέγω γὰρ καὶ τὰ δύσφορ', εἰ τύχοι
κατ' ὀρθὸν ἐξιόντα, πάντ' ἂν εὐτυχεῖν.
ΟΙ. ἔστιν δὲ ποῖον τοὔπος; οὔτε γὰρ θρασὺς
οὔτ' οὖν προδείσας εἰμὶ τῷ γε νῦν λόγῳ. 90
ΚΡ. εἰ τῶνδε χρῄζεις πλησιαζόντων κλύειν,
ἕτοιμος εἰπεῖν, εἴτε καὶ στείχειν ἔσω.
ΟΙ. ἐς πάντας αὔδα· τῶνδε γὰρ πλέον φέρω

τὸ πένθος ἢ καὶ τῆς ἐμῆς ψυχῆς πέρι.
ΚΡ. λέγοιμ' ἂν οἷ' ἤκουσα τοῦ θεοῦ πάρα. 95
ἄνωγεν ἡμᾶς Φοῖβος ἐμφανῶς, ἄναξ,
μίασμα χώρας ὡς τεθραμμένον χθονὶ
ἐν τῇδ' ἐλαύνειν μηδ' ἀνήκεστον τρέφειν.
ΟΙ. ποίῳ καθαρμῷ; τίς ὁ τρόπος τῆς ξυμφορᾶς;
ΚΡ. ἀνδρηλατοῦντας, ἢ φόνῳ φόνον πάλιν 100
λύοντας, ὡς τόδ' αἷμα χειμάζον πόλιν.
ΟΙ. ποίου γὰρ ἀνδρὸς τήνδε μηνύει τύχην;
ΚΡ. ἦν ἡμίν, ὦναξ, Λάϊός ποθ' ἡγεμὼν
γῆς τῆσδε, πρὶν σὲ τήνδ' ἀπευθύνειν πόλιν.
ΟΙ. ἔξοιδ' ἀκούων· οὐ γὰρ εἰσεῖδόν γέ πω. 105
ΚΡ. τούτου θανόντος νῦν ἐπιστέλλει σαφῶς
τοὺς αὐτοέντας χειρὶ τιμωρεῖν τινας.
ΟΙ. οἱ δ' εἰσὶ ποῦ γῆς; ποῦ τόδ' εὑρεθήσεται
ἴχνος παλαιᾶς δυστέκμαρτον αἰτίας;
ΚΡ. ἐν τῇδ' ἔφασκε γῇ· τὸ δὲ ζητούμενον 110
ἁλωτόν, ἐκφεύγει δὲ τἀμελούμενον.
ΟΙ. πότερα δ' ἐν οἴκοις, ἢ 'ν ἀγροῖς ὁ Λάϊος,
ἢ γῆς ἐπ' ἄλλης τῷδε συμπίπτει φόνῳ;
ΚΡ. θεωρός, ὡς ἔφασκεν, ἐκδημῶν πάλιν
πρὸς οἶκον οὐκέθ' ἵκεθ', ὡς ἀπεστάλη. 115
ΟΙ. οὐδ' ἄγγελός τις οὐδὲ συμπράκτωρ ὁδοῦ
κατεῖδ' ὅτου τις ἐκμαθὼν ἐχρήσατ' ἄν;
ΚΡ. θνῄσκουσι γάρ, πλὴν εἷς τις ὃς φόβῳ φυγὼν
ὧν εἶδε πλὴν ἓν οὐδὲν εἶχ' εἰδὼς φράσαι.
ΟΙ. τὸ ποῖον; ἓν γὰρ πόλλ' ἂν ἐξεύροι μαθεῖν, 120
ἀρχὴν βραχεῖαν εἰ λάβοιμεν ἐλπίδος.
ΚΡ. λῃστὰς ἔφασκε συντυχόντας οὐ μιᾷ
ῥώμῃ κτανεῖν νιν, ἀλλὰ σὺν πλήθει χερῶν.
ΟΙ. πῶς οὖν ὁ λῃστής, εἴ τι μὴ ξὺν ἀργύρῳ
ἐπράσσετ' ἐνθένδ', ἐς τόδ' ἂν τόλμης ἔβη; 125
ΚΡ. δοκοῦντα ταῦτ' ἦν· Λαΐου δ' ὀλωλότος
οὐδεὶς ἀρωγὸς ἐν κακοῖς ἐγίγνετο.
ΟΙ. κακὸν δὲ ποῖον ἐμποδὼν τυραννίδος
οὕτω πεσούσης εἶργε τοῦτ' ἐξειδέναι;

ΟΙΔΙΠΟΥΣ ΤΥΡΑΝΝΟΣ 17

ΚΡ. ἡ ποικιλῳδὸς Σφὶγξ τὸ πρὸς ποσὶ σκοπεῖν   130
μεθέντας ἡμᾶς τἀφανῆ προσήγετο.
ΟΙ. ἀλλ' ἐξ ὑπαρχῆς αὖθις αὔτ' ἐγὼ φανῶ·
ἐπαξίως γὰρ Φοῖβος, ἀξίως δὲ σύ
πρὸ τοῦ θανόντος τήνδ' ἔθεσθ' ἐπιστροφήν·
ὥστ' ἐνδίκως ὄψεσθε κἀμὲ σύμμαχον,   135
γῇ τῇδε τιμωροῦντα τῷ θεῷ θ' ἅμα.
ὑπὲρ γὰρ οὐχὶ τῶν ἀπωτέρω φίλων
ἀλλ' αὐτὸς αὑτοῦ τοῦτ' ἀποσκεδῶ μύσος.
ὅστις γὰρ ἦν ἐκεῖνον ὁ κτανὼν τάχ' ἂν
κἄμ' ἂν τοιαύτῃ χειρὶ τιμωρεῖν θέλοι·   140
κείνῳ προσαρκῶν οὖν ἐμαυτὸν ὠφελῶ.
ἀλλ' ὡς τάχιστα, παῖδες, ὑμεῖς μὲν βάθρων
ἵστασθε, τούσδ' ἄραντες ἱκτῆρας κλάδους,
ἄλλος δὲ Κάδμου λαὸν ὧδ' ἀθροιζέτω,
ὡς πᾶν ἐμοῦ δράσοντος· ἢ γὰρ εὐτυχεῖς   145
σὺν τῷ θεῷ φανούμεθ' ἢ πεπτωκότες.
[Exit O into the palace]
ΙΕ. ὦ παῖδες, ἱστώμεσθα· τῶνδε γὰρ χάριν
καὶ δεῦρ' ἔβημεν ὧν ὅδ' ἐξαγγέλλεται.
Φοῖβος δ' ὁ πέμψας τάσδε μαντείας ἅμα
σωτήρ θ' ἵκοιτο καὶ νόσου παυστήριος.   150
[Exeunt priest, suppliants and Kreon to the city.]

ΧΟΡΟΣ
ὦ Διὸς ἀδυεπὲς φάτι, τίς ποτε τᾶς   στρ. α
   πολυχρύσου
Πυθῶνος ἀγλαὰς ἔβας
Θήβας; ἐκτέταμαι φοβερὰν φρένα δείματι
   πάλλων,
ἰήιε Δάλιε Παιάν,
ἀμφὶ σοὶ ἀζόμενος· τί μοι ἢ νέον   155
ἢ περιτελλομέναις ὥραις πάλιν ἐξανύσεις χρέος;
εἰπέ μοι, ὦ χρυσέας τέκνον ἐλπίδος, ἄμβροτε
   Φήμα.

18 ΣΟΦΟΚΛΕΟΥΣ

πρῶτά σε κεκλόμενος, θύγατερ Διός, ἄμβροτ᾽
Ἀθάνα, ἀντ. α
γαιάοχόν τ᾽ ἀδελφεὰν 160
Ἄρτεμιν, ἃ κυκλόεντ᾽ ἀγορᾶς θρόνον εὐκλέα
θάσσει,
καὶ Φοῖβον ἑκαβόλον—ἰώ,
τρισσοὶ ἀλεξίμοροι προφάνητέ μοι,
εἴ ποτε καὶ προτέρας ἄτας ὑπερορνυμένας
πόλει 165
ἠνύσατ᾽ ἐκτοπίαν φλόγα πήματος, ἔλθετε καὶ νῦν.

ὦ πόποι, ἀνάριθμα γὰρ φέρω στρ. β
πήματα· νοσεῖ δέ μοι πρόπας
στόλος, οὐδ᾽ ἔνι φροντίδος ἔγχος 170
ᾧ τις ἀλέξεται· οὔτε γὰρ ἔκγονα
κλυτᾶς χθονὸς αὔξεται οὔτε τόκοισιν
ἰηίων καμάτων ἀνέχουσι γυναῖκες·
ἄλλον δ᾽ ἂν ἄλλῳ προσίδοις ἅπερ εὔπτερον
ὄρνιν 175
κρεῖσσον ἀμαιμακέτου πυρὸς ὄρμενον
ἀκτὰν πρὸς ἑσπέρου θεοῦ.

ὧν πόλις ἀνάριθμος ὄλλυται· ἀντ. β
νηλέα δὲ γένεθλα πρὸς πέδῳ 180
θαναταφόρα κεῖται ἀνοίκτως·
ἐν δ᾽ ἄλοχοι πολιαί τ᾽ ἔπι ματέρες
ἀκτὰν παρὰ βώμιον ἄλλοθεν ἄλλαι
λυγρῶν πόνων ἱκτῆρες ἐπιστενάχουσι. 185
παιὼν δὲ λάμπει στονόεσσά τε γῆρυς ὄμαυλος·
τῶν ὕπερ, ὦ χρυσέα θύγατερ Διός,
εὐῶπα πέμψον ἀλκάν.

Ἀρεά τε τὸν μαλερόν, ὃς στρ. γ
νῦν ἄχαλκος ἀσπίδων 191
φλέγει με περιβόητος ἀντιάζων,
παλίσσυτον δράμημα νωτίσαι πάτρας,

ΟΙΔΙΠΟΥΣ ΤΥΡΑΝΝΟΣ 19

ἔπουρον εἴτ' ἐς μέγαν
θάλαμον Ἀμφιτρίτας, 195
εἴτ' ἐς τὸν ἀπόξενον ὅρμων
Θρήικιον κλύδωνα·
†τελεῖν γάρ εἴ τι νὺξ ἀφῇ,
τοῦτ' ἐπ' ἦμαρ ἔρχεται·†
τόν, ὦ ⟨τᾶν⟩ πυρφόρων 200
ἀστραπᾶν κράτη νέμων,
ὦ Ζεῦ πάτερ, ὑπὸ σῷ φθίσον κεραυνῷ.

Λύκει' ἄναξ, τά τε σὰ χρυ- ἀντ. γ.
σοστρόφων ἀπ' ἀγκυλᾶν
βέλεα θέλοιμ' ἂν ἀδάματ' ἐνδατεῖσθαι 205
ἀρωγὰ προσταθέντα, τάς τε πυρφόρους
Ἀρτέμιδος αἴγλας, ξὺν αἷς
Λύκι' ὄρεα διάσσει·
τὸν χρυσομίτραν τε κικλήσκω,
τᾶσδ' ἐπώνυμον γᾶς, 210
οἰνῶπα Βάκχον, εὔιον
Μαινάδων ὁμόστολον,
πελασθῆναι φλέγοντ'
ἀγλαῶπι ⟨–◡–⟩
πεύκᾳ 'πὶ τὸν ἀπότιμον ἐν θεοῖς θεόν. 215

[Enter O from the palace.]
ΟΙ. αἰτεῖς· ἃ δ' αἰτεῖς, τἄμ' ἐὰν θέλῃς ἔπη
κλύων δέχεσθαι τῇ νόσῳ θ' ὑπηρετεῖν,
ἀλκὴν λάβοις ἂν κἀνακούφισιν κακῶν,
ἁγὼ ξένος μὲν τοῦ λόγου τοῦδ' ἐξερῶ,
ξένος δὲ τοῦ πραχθέντος· οὐ γὰρ ἂν μακρὰν 220
ἴχνευον αὐτός, μὴ οὐκ ἔχων τι σύμβολον,
νῦν δ' (ὕστερος γὰρ ἀστὸς εἰς ἀστοὺς τελῶ)
ὑμῖν προφωνῶ πᾶσι Καδμείοις τάδε·
ὅστις ποθ' ὑμῶν Λάϊον τὸν Λαβδάκου
κάτοιδεν ἀνδρὸς ἐκ τίνος διώλετο, 225

ΣΟΦΟΚΛΕΟΥΣ

τοῦτον κελεύω πάντα σημαίνειν ἐμοί·
κεἰ μὲν φοβεῖται, τοὐπίκλημ' †ὑπεξελὼν†
αὐτὸς κατ' αὑτοῦ· πείσεται γὰρ ἄλλο μὲν
ἀστεργὲς οὐδέν, γῆς δ' ἄπεισιν ἀβλαβής.
εἰ δ' αὖ τις ἄλλον οἶδεν ἢ 'ξ ἄλλης χθονὸς   230
τὸν αὐτόχειρα, μὴ σιωπάτω· τὸ γὰρ
κέρδος τελῶ 'γὼ χἠ χάρις προσκείσεται.
εἰ δ' αὖ σιωπήσεσθε, καί τις ἢ φίλου
δείσας ἀπώσει τοὔπος ἢ χαὑτοῦ τόδε,
ἃκ τῶνδε δράσω, ταῦτα χρὴ κλύειν ἐμοῦ·   235
τὸν ἄνδρ' ἀπαυδῶ τοῦτον, ὅστις ἐστί, γῆς
τῆσδ' ἧς ἐγὼ κράτη τε καὶ θρόνους νέμω
μήτ' εἰσδέχεσθαι μήτε προσφωνεῖν τινα,
μήτ' ἐν θεῶν εὐχαῖσι μήτε θύμασιν
κοινὸν ποιεῖσθαι, μήτε χέρνιβος νέμειν·   240
ὠθεῖν δ' ἀπ' οἴκων πάντας, ὡς μιάσματος
τοῦδ' ἡμὶν ὄντος, ὡς τὸ Πυθικὸν θεοῦ
μαντεῖον ἐξέφηνεν ἀρτίως ἐμοί.
ἐγὼ μὲν οὖν τοιόσδε τῷ τε δαίμονι
τῷ τ' ἀνδρὶ τῷ θανόντι σύμμαχος πέλω·   245
[κατεύχομαι δὲ τὸν δεδρακότ', εἴτε τις
εἷς ὢν λέληθεν εἴτε πλειόνων μέτα,
κακὸν κακῶς νιν ἄμορον ἐκτρῖψαι βίον·
ἐπεύχομαι δ', οἴκοισιν εἰ ξυνέστιος
ἐν τοῖς ἐμοῖς γένοιτ' ἐμοῦ ξυνειδότος,   250
παθεῖν ἅπερ τοῖσδ' ἀρτίως ἠρασάμην.]
ὑμῖν δὲ ταῦτα πάντ' ἐπισκήπτω τελεῖν,
ὑπέρ τ' ἐμαυτοῦ τοῦ θεοῦ τε τῆσδέ τε
γῆς ὧδ' ἀκάρπως κἀθέως ἐφθαρμένης.
οὐδ' εἰ γὰρ ἦν τὸ πρᾶγμα μὴ θεήλατον,   255
ἀκάθαρτον ὑμᾶς εἰκὸς ἦν οὕτως ἐᾶν,
ἀνδρός γ' ἀρίστου βασιλέως ὀλωλότος,
ἀλλ' ἐξερευνᾶν.
    νῦν δ', ἐπεὶ κυρῶ τ' ἐγὼ
ἔχων μὲν ἀρχὰς ἃς ἐκεῖνος εἶχε πρίν,
ἔχων δὲ λέκτρα καὶ γυναῖχ' ὁμόσπορον   260

ΟΙΔΙΠΟΥΣ ΤΥΡΑΝΝΟΣ

κοινῶν τε παίδων κοίν' ἄν, εἰ κείνῳ γένος
μὴ 'δυστύχησεν, ἦν ἄν ἐκπεφυκότα,
νῦν δ' ἐς τὸ κείνου κρᾶτ' ἐνήλαθ' ἡ τύχη·
ἀνθ' ὧν ἐγὼ τάδ', ὡσπερεὶ τοὐμοῦ πατρός,
ὑπερμαχοῦμαι, κἀπὶ πάντ' ἀφίξομαι, 265
ζητῶν τὸν αὐτόχειρα τοῦ φόνου λαβεῖν,
τῷ Λαβδακείῳ παιδὶ Πολυδώρου τε καὶ
τοῦ πρόσθε Κάδμου τοῦ πάλαι τ' Ἀγήνορος·
καὶ ταῦτα τοῖς μὴ δρῶσιν εὔχομαι θεοὺς
μήτ' ἀροτὸν αὐτοῖς γῆς ἀνιέναι τινά, 270
μήτ' οὖν γυναικῶν παῖδας, ἀλλὰ τῷ πότμῳ
τῷ νῦν φθερεῖσθαι κἄτι τοῦδ' ἐχθίονι.
ὑμῖν δὲ τοῖς ἄλλοισι Καδμείοις ὅσοις
τάδ' ἔστ' ἀρέσκονθ' ἥ τε σύμμαχος Δίκη
χοἰ πάντες εὖ ξυνεῖεν εἰσαεὶ θεοί. 275
ΧΟ. ὥσπερ μ' ἀραῖον ἔλαβες, ὧδ', ἄναξ, ἐρῶ·
οὔτ' ἔκτανον γὰρ οὔτε τὸν κτανόντ' ἔχω
δεῖξαι. τὸ δὲ ζήτημα τοῦ πέμψαντος ἦν
Φοίβου τόδ' εἰπεῖν, ὅστις εἴργασταί ποτε.
ΟΙ. δίκαι' ἔλεξας· ἀλλ' ἀναγκάσαι θεοὺς 280
ἂν μὴ θέλωσιν οὐδ' ⟨ἂν⟩ εἷς δύναιτ' ἀνήρ.
ΧΟ. τὰ δεύτερ' ἐκ τῶνδ' ἂν λέγοιμ' ἅ μοι δοκεῖ.
ΟΙ. εἰ καὶ τρίτ' ἔστι, μὴ παρῇς τὸ μὴ οὐ φράσαι.
ΧΟ. ἄνακτ' ἄνακτι ταὔθ' ὁρῶντ' ἐπίσταμαι
μάλιστα Φοίβῳ Τειρεσίαν, παρ' οὗ τις ἂν 285
σκοπῶν τάδ', ὦναξ, ἐκμάθοι σαφέστατα.
ΟΙ. ἀλλ' οὐκ ἐν ἀργοῖς οὐδὲ τοῦτ' ἐπράξαμεν·
ἔπεμψα γὰρ Κρέοντος εἰπόντος διπλοῦς
πομπούς· πάλαι δὲ μὴ παρὼν θαυμάζεται.
ΧΟ. καὶ μὴν τά γ' ἄλλα κωφὰ καὶ παλαί' ἔπη. 290
ΟΙ. τὰ ποῖα ταῦτα; πάντα γὰρ σκοπῶ λόγον.
ΧΟ. θανεῖν ἐλέχθη πρός τινων ὁδοιπόρων.
ΟΙ. ἤκουσα κἀγώ· τὸν δὲ δρῶντ' οὐδεὶς ὁρᾷ.
ΧΟ. ἀλλ' εἴ τι μὲν δὴ δείματός γ' ἔχει μέρος,
τὰς σὰς ἀκούων οὐ μενεῖ τοιάσδ' ἀράς. 295
ΟΙ. ᾧ μή 'στι δρῶντι τάρβος, οὐδ' ἔπος φοβεῖ.

ΣΟΦΟΚΛΕΟΥΣ

[Enter Teiresias from the city.]
ΧΟ. ἀλλ' οὑξελέγξων νιν πάρεστιν· οἵδε γὰρ
τὸν θεῖον ἤδη μάντιν ὧδ' ἄγουσιν, ᾧ
τἀληθὲς ἐμπέφυκεν ἀνθρώπων μόνῳ.
ΟΙ. ὢ πάντα νωμῶν Τειρεσία, διδακτά τε 300
ἄρρητά τ' οὐράνιά τε καὶ χθονοστιβῆ,
πόλιν μέν, εἰ καὶ μὴ βλέπεις, φρονεῖς δ' ὅμως
οἵᾳ νόσῳ σύνεστιν· ἧς σὲ προστάτην
σωτῆρά τ', ὦναξ, μοῦνον ἐξευρίσκομεν.
Φοῖβος γάρ, εἰ καὶ μὴ κλύεις τῶν ἀγγέλων, 305
πέμψασιν ἡμῖν ἀντέπεμψεν, ἔκλυσιν
μόνην ἂν ἐλθεῖν τοῦδε τοῦ νοσήματος,
εἰ τοὺς κτανόντας Λάϊον μαθόντες εὖ
κτείναιμεν ἢ γῆς φυγάδας ἐκπεμψαίμεθα.
σὺ δ' οὖν φθονήσας μήτ' ἀπ' οἰωνῶν φάτιν, 310
μήτ' εἴ τιν' ἄλλην μαντικῆς ἔχεις ὁδόν,
ῥῦσαι σεαυτὸν καὶ πόλιν, ῥῦσαι δ' ἐμέ,
ῥῦσαι δὲ πᾶν μίασμα τοῦ τεθνηκότος·
ἐν σοὶ γὰρ ἐσμεν· ἄνδρα δ' ὠφελεῖν ἀφ' ὧν
ἔχοι τε καὶ δύναιτο κάλλιστος πόνων. 315
ΤΕΙΡΕΣΙΑΣ
φεῦ φεῦ, φρονεῖν ὡς δεινὸν ἔνθα μὴ τέλη
λύῃ φρονοῦντι· ταῦτα γὰρ καλῶς ἐγὼ
εἰδὼς διώλεσ'· οὐ γὰρ ἂν δεῦρ' ἱκόμην.
ΟΙ. τί δ' ἔστιν; ὡς ἄθυμος εἰσελήλυθας.
ΤΕ. ἄφες μ' ἐς οἴκους· ῥᾷστα γὰρ τὸ σόν τε σὺ 320
κἀγὼ διοίσω τοὐμόν, ἢν ἐμοὶ πίθῃ.
ΟΙ. οὔτ' ἔννομ' εἶπας οὔτε προσφιλῆ πόλει
τῇδ' ἥ σ' ἔθρεψε, τήνδ' ἀποστερῶν φάτιν.
ΤΕ. ὁρῶ γὰρ οὐδὲ σοὶ τὸ σὸν φώνημ' ἰὸν
πρὸς καιρόν· ὡς οὖν μηδ' ἐγὼ ταὐτὸν πάθω... 325
ΟΙ. μή, πρὸς θεῶν, φρονῶν γ' ἀποστραφῇς ἐπεὶ
πάντες σε προσκυνοῦμεν οἵδ' ἱκτήριοι.
ΤΕ. πάντες γὰρ οὐ φρονεῖτ'· ἐγὼ δ' οὐ μή ποτε
τἄμ', ὡς ἂν εἴπω μὴ τὰ σ', ἐκφήνω κακά.

ΟΙΔΙΠΟΥΣ ΤΥΡΑΝΝΟΣ

ΟΙ. τί φῄς; ξυνειδὼς οὐ φράσεις, ἀλλ' ἐννοεῖς 330
ἡμᾶς προδοῦναι καὶ καταφθεῖραι πόλιν;
ΤΕ. ἐγὼ οὔτ' ἐμαυτὸν οὔτε σ' ἀλγυνῶ· τί ταῦτ'
ἄλλως ἐλέγχεις; οὐ γὰρ ἂν πύθοιό μου.
ΟΙ. οὐκ, ὦ κακῶν κάκιστε, καὶ γὰρ ἂν πέτρου
φύσιν σύ γ' ὀργάνειας, ἐξερεῖς ποτε, 335
ἀλλ' ὧδ' ἄτεγκτος κἀτελεύτητος φανῇ;
ΤΕ. ὀργὴν ἐμέμψω τὴν ἐμήν, τὴν σὴν δ' ὁμοῦ
ναίουσαν οὐ κατεῖδες, ἀλλ' ἐμὲ ψέγεις.
ΟΙ. τίς γὰρ τοιαῦτ' ἂν οὐκ ἂν ὀργίζοιτ' ἔπη
κλύων ἃ νῦν σὺ τήνδ' ἀτιμάζεις πόλιν; 340
ΤΕ. ἥξει γὰρ αὐτά, κἂν ἐγὼ σιγῇ στέγω.
ΟΙ. οὐκοῦν ἅ γ' ἥξει καὶ σὲ χρὴ λέγειν ἐμοί.
ΤΕ. οὐκ ἂν πέρα φράσαιμι· πρὸς τάδ', εἰ θέλεις,
θυμοῦ δι' ὀργῆς ἥτις ἀγριωτάτη.
ΟΙ. καὶ μὴν παρήσω γ' οὐδέν, ὡς ὀργῆς ἔχω, 345
ἅπερ ξυνίημ'. ἴσθι γὰρ δοκῶν ἐμοὶ
καὶ ξυμφυτεῦσαι τοὔργον, εἰργάσθαι θ', ὅσον
μὴ χερσὶ καίνων· εἰ δ' ἐτύγχανες βλέπων,
καὶ τοὔργον ἂν σοῦ τοῦτ' ἔφην εἶναι μόνου.
ΤΕ. ἄληθες; ἐννέπω σὲ τῷ κηρύγματι 350
ᾧπερ προεῖπας ἐμμένειν, κἀφ' ἡμέρας
τῆς νῦν προσαυδᾶν μήτε τούσδε μήτ' ἐμέ,
ὡς ὄντι γῆς τῆσδ' ἀνοσίῳ μιάστορι.
ΟΙ. οὕτως ἀναιδῶς ἐξεκίνησας τόδε
τὸ ῥῆμα; καὶ ποῦ τοῦτο φεύξεσθαι δοκεῖς; 355
ΤΕ. πέφευγα· τἀληθὲς γὰρ ἰσχῦον τρέφω.
ΟΙ. πρὸς τοῦ διδαχθείς; οὐ γὰρ ἔκ γε τῆς τέχνης.
ΤΕ. πρὸς σοῦ· σὺ γάρ μ' ἄκοντα προὔτρεψω λέγειν.
ΟΙ. ποῖον λόγον; λέγ' αὖθις, ὡς μᾶλλον μάθω.
ΤΕ. οὐχὶ ξυνῆκας πρόσθεν; ἢ 'κπειρᾷ λέγων; 360
ΟΙ. οὐχ ὥστε γ' εἰπεῖν γνωστόν· ἀλλ' αὖθις φράσον.
ΤΕ. φονέα σέ φημι τἀνδρὸς οὗ ζητεῖς κυρεῖν.
ΟΙ. ἀλλ' οὔ τι χαίρων δίς γε πημονὰς ἐρεῖς.
ΤΕ. εἴπω τι δῆτα κἄλλ', ἵν' ὀργίζῃ πλέον;
ΟΙ. ὅσον γε χρῄζεις· ὡς μάτην εἰρήσεται. 365

ΣΟΦΟΚΛΕΟΥΣ

ΤΕ. λεληθέναι σέ φημι σὺν τοῖς φιλτάτοις
αἴσχισθ' ὁμιλοῦντ', οὐδ' ὁρᾶν ἵν' εἶ κακοῦ.
ΟΙ. ἦ καὶ γεγηθὼς ταῦτ' ἀεὶ λέξειν δοκεῖς;
ΤΕ. εἴπερ τί γ' ἔστι τῆς ἀληθείας σθένος.
ΟΙ. ἀλλ' ἔστι, πλὴν σοί· σοὶ δὲ τοῦτ' οὐκ ἔστ', ἐπεὶ 370
τυφλὸς τά τ' ὦτα τόν τε νοῦν τά τ' ὄμματ' εἶ.
ΤΕ. σὺ δ' ἄθλιός γε ταῦτ' ὀνειδίζων ἃ σοὶ
οὐδεὶς ὃς οὐχὶ τῶνδ' ὀνειδιεῖ τάχα.
ΟΙ. μιᾶς τρέφῃ πρὸς νυκτός, ὥστε μήτ' ἐμὲ
μήτ' ἄλλον ὅστις φῶς ὁρᾷ βλάψαι ποτ' ἄν. 375
ΤΕ. οὐ γάρ σε μοῖρα πρός γε μοῦ πεσεῖν, ἐπεὶ
ἱκανὸς Ἀπόλλων, ᾧ τάδ' ἐκπρᾶξαι μέλει.
ΟΙ. Κρέοντος ἢ σοῦ ταῦτα τἀξευρήματα;
ΤΕ. Κρέων δέ σοι πῆμ' οὐδέν, ἀλλ' αὐτὸς σὺ σοί.
ΟΙ. ὦ πλοῦτε καὶ τυραννὶ καὶ τέχνη τέχνης 380
ὑπερφέρουσα τῷ πολυζήλῳ βίῳ,
ὅσος παρ' ὑμῖν ὁ φθόνος φυλάσσεται,
εἰ τῆσδέ γ' ἀρχῆς οὕνεχ', ἣν ἐμοὶ πόλις
δωρητόν, οὐκ αἰτητόν, εἰσεχείρισεν,
ταύτης Κρέων ὁ πιστός, οὑξ ἀρχῆς φίλος, 385
λάθρᾳ μ' ὑπελθὼν ἐκβαλεῖν ἱμείρεται,
ὑφεὶς μάγον τοιόνδε μηχανορράφον,
δόλιον ἀγύρτην, ὅστις ἐν τοῖς κέρδεσιν
μόνον δέδορκε, τὴν τέχνην δ' ἔφυ τυφλός.
ἐπεί, φέρ' εἰπέ, ποῦ σὺ μάντις εἶ σαφής; 390
πῶς οὐχ, ὅθ' ἡ ῥαψῳδὸς ἐνθάδ' ἦν κύων,
ηὔδας τι τοῖσδ' ἀστοῖσιν ἐκλυτήριον;
καίτοι τό γ' αἴνιγμ' οὐχὶ τοὐπιόντος ἦν
ἀνδρὸς διειπεῖν, ἀλλὰ μαντείας ἔδει·
ἣν οὔτ' ἀπ' οἰωνῶν σὺ προὐφάνης ἔχων 395
οὔτ' ἐκ θεῶν του γνωτόν· ἀλλ' ἐγὼ μολών,
ὁ μηδὲν εἰδὼς Οἰδίπους, ἔπαυσά νιν,
γνώμῃ κυρήσας οὐδ' ἀπ' οἰωνῶν μαθών·
ὃν δὴ σὺ πειρᾷς ἐκβαλεῖν, δοκῶν θρόνοις
παραστατήσειν τοῖς Κρεοντείοις πέλας. 400
κλαίων δοκεῖς μοι καὶ σὺ χὼ συνθεὶς τάδε

ΟΙΔΙΠΟΥΣ ΤΥΡΑΝΝΟΣ 25

ἀγηλατήσειν· εἰ δὲ μὴ 'δόκεις γέρων
εἶναι, παθὼν ἔγνως ἂν οἷά περ φρονεῖς.
ΧΟ. ἡμῖν μὲν εἰκάζουσι καὶ τὰ τοῦδ' ἔπη
ὀργῇ λελέχθαι καὶ τὰ σ', Οἰδίπου, δοκεῖ. 405
δεῖ δ' οὐ τοιούτων ἀλλ,' ὅπως τὰ τοῦ θεοῦ
μαντεῖ' ἄριστα λύσομεν, τόδε σκοπεῖν.
ΤΕ. εἰ καὶ τυραννεῖς, ἐξισωτέον τὸ γοῦν
ἴσ' ἀντιλέξαι· τοῦδε γὰρ κἀγὼ κρατῶ·
οὐ γάρ τι σοὶ ζῶ δοῦλος, ἀλλὰ Λοξίᾳ, 410
ὥστ' οὐ Κρέοντος προστάτου γεγράψομαι.
λέγω δ', ἐπειδὴ καὶ τυφλόν μ' ὠνείδισας·
σὺ καὶ δέδορκας κοὐ βλέπεις ἵν' εἶ κακοῦ,
οὐδ' ἔνθα ναίεις, οὐδ' ὅτων οἰκεῖς μέτα.
ἆρ' οἶσθ' ἀφ' ὧν εἶ; καὶ λέληθας ἐχθρὸς ὢν 415
τοῖς σοῖσιν αὐτοῦ νέρθε κἀπὶ γῆς ἄνω.
καί σ' ἀμφιπλὴξ μητρός τε καὶ τοῦ σοῦ πατρὸς
ἐλᾷ ποτ' ἐκ γῆς τῆσδε δεινόπους ἀρά,
βλέποντα νῦν μὲν ὄρθ', ἔπειτα δὲ σκότον.
βοῆς δὲ τῆς σῆς ποῖος οὐκ ἔσται λιμήν, 420
ποῖος Κιθαιρὼν οὐχὶ σύμφωνος τάχα,
ὅταν καταίσθῃ τὸν ὑμέναιον ὃν δόμοις
ἄνορμον εἰσέπλευσας εὐπλοίας τυχών;
ἄλλων δὲ πλῆθος οὐκ ἐπαισθάνῃ κακῶν
ἅ σ' ἐξισώσει σοί τε καὶ τοῖς σοῖς τέκνοις. 425
πρὸς ταῦτα καὶ Κρέοντα καὶ τοὐμὸν στόμα
προπηλάκιζε· σοῦ γὰρ οὐκ ἔστιν βροτῶν
κάκιον ὅστις ἐκτριβήσεταί ποτε.
ΟΙ. ἦ ταῦτα δῆτ' ἀνεκτὰ πρὸς τούτου κλύειν;
οὐκ εἰς ὄλεθρον; οὐχὶ θᾶσσον; οὐ πάλιν 430
ἄψορρος οἴκων τῶνδ' ἀποστραφεὶς ἄπει;
ΤΕ. οὐδ' ἱκόμην ἔγωγ' ἄν, εἰ σὺ μὴ 'κάλεις.
ΟΙ. οὐ γάρ τί σ' ᾔδη μῶρα φωνήσοντ', ἐπεὶ
σχολῇ σ' ἂν οἴκους τοὺς ἐμοὺς ἐστειλάμην.
ΤΕ. ἡμεῖς τοιοίδ' ἔφυμεν, ὡς μὲν σοὶ δοκεῖ, 435
μῶροι, γονεῦσι δ' οἵ σ' ἔφυσαν, ἔμφρονες.
ΟΙ. ποίοισι; μεῖνον· τίς δέ μ' ἐκφύει βροτῶν;

ΣΟΦΟΚΛΕΟΥΣ

ΤΕ. ἥδ' ἡμέρα φύσει σε καὶ διαφθερεῖ.
ΟΙ. ὡς πάντ' ἄγαν αἰνικτὰ κἀσαφῆ λέγεις.
ΤΕ. οὔκουν σὺ ταῦτ' ἄριστος εὑρίσκειν ἔφυς; 440
ΟΙ. τοιαῦτ' ὀνείδιζ' οἷς ἔμ' εὑρήσεις μέγαν.
ΤΕ. αὕτη γε μέντοι σ' ἡ τύχη διώλεσεν.
ΟΙ. ἀλλ' εἰ πόλιν τήνδ' ἐξέσωσ', οὔ μοι μέλει.
ΤΕ. ἄπειμι τοίνυν· καὶ σύ, παῖ, κόμιζέ με.
ΟΙ. κομιζέτω δῆθ'· ὡς παρὼν σύ γ' ἐμποδὼν 445
ὀχλεῖς, συθείς τ' ἂν οὐκ ἂν ἀλγύναις πλέον.
[Exit O into the palace.]
ΤΕ. εἰπὼν ἄπειμ' ὧν οὕνεκ' ἦλθον, οὐ τὸ σὸν
δείσας πρόσωπον· οὐ γὰρ ἔσθ' ὅπου μ' ὀλεῖς.
λέγω δέ σοι· τὸν ἄνδρα τοῦτον, ὃν πάλαι
ζητεῖς ἀπειλῶν κἀνακηρύσσων φόνον 450
τὸν Λαΐειον, οὗτός ἐστιν ἐνθάδε,
ξένος λόγῳ μέτοικος· εἶτα δ' ἐγγενὴς
φανήσεται Θηβαῖος, οὐδ' ἡσθήσεται
τῇ ξυμφορᾷ· τυφλὸς γὰρ ἐκ δεδορκότος
καὶ πτωχὸς ἀντὶ πλουσίου ξένην ἔπι 455
σκήπτρῳ προδεικνὺς γαῖαν ἐμπορεύσεται.
φανήσεται δὲ παισὶ τοῖς αὑτοῦ ξυνὼν
ἀδελφὸς αὑτὸς καὶ πατήρ, κἀξ ἧς ἔφυ
γυναικὸς υἱὸς καὶ πόσις, καὶ τοῦ πατρὸς
ὁμόσπορός τε καὶ φονεύς. καὶ ταῦτ' ἰὼν 460
εἴσω λογίζου· κἂν λάβῃς ἐψευσμένον,
φάσκειν ἔμ' ἤδη μαντικῇ μηδὲν φρονεῖν.
[Exit T to the city.]

ΧΟ. τίς ὅντιν' ἁ θεσπιέπει- στρ. α
α Δελφὶς εἶπε πέτρα
ἄρρητ' ἀρρήτων τελέσαν- 465
τα φοινίαισι χερσίν;
ὥρα νιν ἀελλάδων
ἵππων σθεναρώτερον
φυγᾷ πόδα νωμᾶν·
ἔνοπλος γὰρ ἐπ' αὐτὸν ἐπενθρῴσκει

πυρὶ καὶ στεροπαῖς ὁ Διὸς γενέτας, 470
δειναὶ δ' ἅμ' ἕπονται
Κῆρες ἀναπλάκητοι.

ἔλαμψε γὰρ τοῦ νιφόεν- ἀντ. α
τος ἀρτίως φανεῖσα
φήμα Παρνασοῦ τὸν ἄδη- 475
λον ἄνδρα πάντ' ἰχνεύειν·
φοιτᾷ γὰρ ὑπ' ἀγρίαν
ὕλαν ἀνά τ' ἄντρα καὶ
πετραῖος ὁ ταῦρος,
μέλεος μελέῳ ποδὶ χηρεύων,
τὰ μεσόμφαλα γᾶς ἀπονοσφίζων 480
μαντεῖα· τὰ δ' αἰεὶ
ζῶντα περιποτᾶται.

δεινὰ μὲ νῦν, δεινὰ ταράσσει στρ. β
σοφὸς οἰωνοθέτας,
οὔτε δοκοῦντ' οὔτ' ἀποφάσκονθ'· 485
ὅ τι λέξω δ' ἀπορῶ·
πέτομαι δ' ἐλπίσιν οὔτ' ἐνθάδ' ὁρῶν οὔτ' ὀπίσω.
τί γὰρ ἢ Λαβδακίδαις
ἢ τῷ Πολύβου νεῖ- 490
κος ἔκειτ'; οὔτε πάροιθέν
ποτ' ἔγωγ' οὔτε τὰ νῦν πω
ἔμαθον πρὸς ὅτου δὴ
βασάνῳ ⟨–⏑⏑–⟩
ἐπὶ τὰν ἐπίδαμον
φάτιν εἶμ' Οἰδιπόδα Λαβδακίδαις 495
ἐπίκουρος ἀδήλων θανάτων.

ἀλλ' ὁ μὲν οὖν Ζεὺς ὅ τ' Ἀπόλλων ἀντ. β
ξυνετοὶ καὶ τὰ βροτῶν
εἰδότες· ἀνδρῶν δ' ὅτι μάντις

28   ΣΟΦΟΚΛΕΟΥΣ

πλέον ἢ 'γὼ φέρεται, 500
κρίσις οὐκ ἔστιν ἀληθής.
σοφίᾳ δ' ἂν σοφίαν
παραμείψειεν ἀνήρ,
ἀλλ' οὔποτ' ἔγωγ' ἄν,
πρὶν ἴδοιμ' ὀρθὸν ἔπος, μεμ- 505
φομένων ἂν καταφαίην.
φανερὰ γὰρ ἐπ' αὐτῷ
πτερόεσσ' ἦλθε κόρα
ποτέ, καὶ σοφὸς ὤφθη
βασάνῳ θ' ἁδύπολις· τῷ ἀπ' ἐμᾶς 510
φρενὸς οὔποτ' ὀφλήσει κακίαν.

[Enter Kreon from the city.]
ΚΡ. ἄνδρες πολῖται, δείν' ἔπη πεπυσμένος
κατηγορεῖν μου τὸν τύραννον Οἰδίπουν,
πάρειμ' ἀτλητῶν. εἰ γὰρ ἐν ταῖς ξυμφοραῖς 515
ταῖς νῦν νομίζει πρός γ' ἐμοῦ πεπονθέναι
λόγοισιν εἴτ' ἔργοισιν εἰς βλάβην φέρον,
οὔτοι βίου μοι τοῦ μακραίωνος πόθος,
φέροντι τήνδε βάξιν. οὐ γὰρ εἰς ἁπλοῦν
ἡ ζημία μοι τοῦ λόγου τούτου φέρει, 520
ἀλλ' ἐς μέγιστον, εἰ κακὸς μὲν ἐν πόλει,
κακὸς δὲ πρὸς σοῦ καὶ φίλων κεκλήσομαι.
ΧΟ. ἀλλ' ἦλθε μὲν δὴ τοῦτο τοὔνειδος, τάχ' ἂν δ'
ὀργῇ βιασθὲν μᾶλλον ἢ γνώμῃ φρενῶν.
ΚΡ. τοὔπος δ' ἐφάνθη ταῖς ἐμαῖς γνώμαις ὅτι 525
πεισθεὶς ὁ μάντις τοὺς λόγους ψευδεῖς λέγοι;
ΧΟ. ηὐδᾶτο μὲν τάδ', οἶδα δ' οὐ γνώμῃ τίνι.
ΚΡ. ἐξ ὀμμάτων δ' ὀρθῶν τε κἀπ' ὀρθῆς φρενὸς
κατηγορεῖτο τοὐπίκλημα τοῦτό μου;
[Enter O from the palace.]
ΧΟ. οὐκ οἶδ'· ἃ γὰρ δρῶσ' οἱ κρατοῦντες οὐχ ὁρῶ. 530
[αὐτὸς δ' ὅδ' ἤδη δωμάτων ἔξω περᾷ.]
ΟΙ. οὗτος σύ, πῶς δεῦρ' ἦλθες; ἦ τοσόνδ' ἔχεις
τόλμης πρόσωπον ὥστε τὰς ἐμὰς στέγας

ΟΙΔΙΠΟΥΣ ΤΥΡΑΝΝΟΣ

ἵκου, φονεὺς ὢν τοῦδε τἀνδρὸς ἐμφανῶς
ληστής τ' ἐναργὴς τῆς ἐμῆς τυραννίδος; 535
φέρ' εἰπὲ πρὸς θεῶν, δειλίαν ἢ μωρίαν
ἰδών τιν' ἔν μοι ταῦτ' ἐβουλεύσω ποεῖν;
ἢ τοὔργον ὡς οὐ γνωριοῖμί σου τόδε
δόλῳ προσέρπον, κοὐκ ἀλεξοίμην μαθών;
ἆρ' οὐχὶ μῶρόν ἐστι τοὐγχείρημά σου, 540
ἄνευ τε πλούτου καὶ φίλων τυραννίδα
θηρᾶν, ὃ πλήθει χρήμασίν θ' ἁλίσκεται;
ΚΡ. οἶσθ' ὡς πόησον; ἀντὶ τῶν εἰρημένων
ἴσ' ἀντάκουσον, κᾆτα κρῖν' αὐτὸς μαθών.
ΟΙ. λέγειν σὺ δεινός, μανθάνειν δ' ἐγὼ κακὸς 545
σοῦ· δυσμενῆ γὰρ καὶ βαρύν σ' εὕρηκ' ἐμοί.
ΚΡ. τοῦτ' αὐτὸ νῦν μου πρῶτ' ἄκουσον ὡς ἐρῶ.
ΟΙ. τοῦτ' αὐτὸ μή μοι φράζ' ὅπως οὐκ εἶ κακός.
ΚΡ. εἴ τοι νομίζεις κτῆμα τὴν αὐθαδίαν
εἶναί τι τοῦ νοῦ χωρίς, οὐκ ὀρθῶς φρονεῖς. 550
ΟΙ. εἴ τοι νομίζεις ἄνδρα συγγενῆ κακῶς
δρῶν οὐχ ὑφέξειν τὴν δίκην, οὐκ εὖ φρονεῖς.
ΚΡ. ξύμφημί σοι ταῦτ' ἔνδικ' εἰρῆσθαι· τὸ δὲ
πάθημ' ὁποῖον φὴς παθεῖν δίδασκέ με.
ΟΙ. ἔπειθες, ἢ οὐκ ἔπειθες ὡς χρείη μ' ἐπὶ 555
τὸν σεμνόμαντιν ἄνδρα πέμψασθαί τινα;
ΚΡ. καὶ νῦν ἔθ' αὑτός εἰμι τῷ βουλεύματι.
ΟΙ. πόσον τιν' ἤδη δῆθ' ὁ Λάϊος χρόνον—
ΚΡ. δέδρακε ποῖον ἔργον; οὐ γὰρ ἐννοῶ.
ΟΙ. ἄφαντος ἔρρει θανασίμῳ χειρώματι; 560
ΚΡ. μακροὶ παλαιοί τ' ἂν μετρηθεῖεν χρόνοι.
ΟΙ. τότ' οὖν ὁ μάντις οὗτος ἦν ἐν τῇ τέχνῃ;
ΚΡ. σοφός γ' ὁμοίως κἀξ ἴσου τιμώμενος.
ΟΙ. ἐμνήσατ' οὖν ἐμοῦ τι τῷ τότ' ἐν χρόνῳ;
ΚΡ. οὔκουν ἐμοῦ γ' ἑστῶτος οὐδαμοῦ πέλας. 565
ΟΙ. ἀλλ' οὐκ ἔρευναν τοῦ κανόντος ἔσχετε;
ΚΡ. παρέσχομεν, πῶς δ' οὐχί; κοὐκ ἠκούσαμεν—
ΟΙ. πῶς οὖν τόθ' οὗτος ὁ σοφὸς οὐκ ηὔδα τάδε;
ΚΡ. οὐκ οἶδ'· ἐφ' οἷς γὰρ μὴ φρονῶ σιγᾶν φιλῶ.

ΣΟΦΟΚΛΕΟΥΣ

ΟΙ. τοσόνδε γ' οΙσθα καὶ λέγοις ἂν εὖ φρονῶν— 570
ΚΡ. ποῖον τόδ'; εἰ γὰρ οἶδά γ', οὐκ ἀρνήσομαι.
ΟΙ. ὁθούνεκ', εἰ μὴ σοὶ ξυνῆλθε, τὰς ἐμὰς
οὐκ ἄν ποτ' εἶπεν Λαΐου διαφθοράς.
ΚΡ. εἰ μὲν λέγει τάδ', αὐτὸς οἶσθ'· ἐγὼ δὲ σοῦ
μαθεῖν δικαιῶ ταῦθ' ἅπερ κἀμοῦ σὺ νῦν. 575
ΟΙ. ἐκμάνθαν'· οὐ γὰρ δὴ φονεὺς ἁλώσομαι.
ΚΡ. τί δῆτ'; ἀδελφὴν τὴν ἐμὴν γήμας ἔχεις;
ΟΙ. ἄρνησις οὐκ ἔνεστιν ὧν ἀνιστορεῖς.
ΚΡ. ἄρχεις δ' ἐκείνῃ ταὐτὰ γῆς ἴσον νέμων;
ΟΙ. ἂν ᾗ θέλουσα πάντ' ἐμοῦ κομίζεται. 580
ΚΡ. οὔκουν ἰσοῦμαι σφῷν ἐγὼ δυοῖν τρίτος;
ΟΙ. ἐνταῦθα γὰρ δὴ καὶ κακὸς φαίνῃ φίλος.
ΚΡ. οὔκ, εἰ διδοίης γ' ὡς ἐγὼ σαυτῷ λόγον.
σκέψαι δὲ τοῦτο πρῶτον, εἴ τιν' ἂν δοκεῖς
ἄρχειν ἑλέσθαι ξὺν φόβοισι μᾶλλον ἢ 585
ἄτρεστον εὕδοντ', εἰ τά γ' αὔθ' ἕξει κράτη.
ἐγὼ μὲν οὖν οὔτ' αὐτὸς ἱμείρων ἔφυν
τύραννος εἶναι μᾶλλον ἢ τύραννα δρᾶν,
οὔτ' ἄλλος ὅστις σωφρονεῖν ἐπίσταται.
νῦν μὲν γὰρ ἐκ σοῦ πάντ' ἄνευ φόβου φέρω· 590
εἰ δ' αὐτὸς ἦρχον, πολλὰ κἂν ἄκων ἔδρων.
πῶς δῆτ' ἐμοὶ τυραννὶς ἡδίων ἔχειν
ἀρχῆς ἀλύπου καὶ δυναστείας ἔφυ;
οὔπω τοσοῦτον ἠπατημένος κυρῶ
ὥστ' ἄλλα χρῄζειν ἢ τὰ σὺν κέρδει καλά. 595
νῦν πᾶσι χαίρω, νῦν με πᾶς ἀσπάζεται,
νῦν οἱ σέθεν χρῄζοντες ἐκκαλοῦσί με·
τὸ γὰρ τυχεῖν αὐτοῖσι πᾶν ἐνταῦθ' ἔνι.
πῶς δῆτ' ἐγὼ κεῖν' ἂν λάβοιμ' ἀφεὶς τάδε;
[οὐκ ἂν γένοιτο νοῦς κακὸς καλῶς φρονῶν.] 600
ἀλλ' οὔτ' ἐραστὴς τῆσδε τῆς γνώμης ἔφυν,
οὔτ' ἂν μετ' ἄλλου δρῶντος ἂν τλαίην ποτέ.
καὶ τῶνδ' ἔλεγχον, τοῦτο μὲν Πυθώδ' ἰών,
πεύθου τὰ χρησθέντ' εἰ σαφῶς ἤγγειλά σοι·
τοῦτ' ἄλλ', ἐάν με τῷ τερασκόπῳ λάβῃς 605

ΟΙΔΙΠΟΥΣ ΤΥΡΑΝΝΟΣ 31

κοινῇ τι βουλεύσαντα, μή μ' ἁπλῇ κτάνῃς
ψήφῳ, διπλῇ δέ, τῇ τ' ἐμῇ καὶ σῇ, λαβών,
γνώμῃ δ' ἀδήλῳ μή με χωρὶς αἰτιῶ.
οὐ γὰρ δίκαιον οὔτε τοὺς κακοὺς μάτην
χρηστοὺς νομίζειν οὔτε τοὺς χρηστοὺς κακούς. 610
φίλον γὰρ ἐσθλὸν ἐκβαλεῖν ἴσον λέγω
καὶ τὸν παρ' αὑτῷ βίοτον, ὃν πλεῖστον φιλεῖ.
ἀλλ' ἐν χρόνῳ γνώσῃ τάδ' ἀσφαλῶς, ἐπεὶ
χρόνος δίκαιον ἄνδρα δείκνυσιν μόνος·
κακὸν δὲ κἂν ἐν ἡμέρᾳ γνοίης μιᾷ. 615
ΧΟ. καλῶς ἔλεξεν εὐλαβουμένῳ πεσεῖν,
ἄναξ· φρονεῖν γὰρ οἱ ταχεῖς οὐκ ἀσφαλεῖς.
ΟΙ. ὅταν ταχύς τις οὑπιβουλεύων λάθρᾳ
χωρῇ, ταχὺν δεῖ κἀμὲ βουλεύειν πάλιν.
εἰ δ' ἡσυχάζων προσμενῶ, τὰ τοῦδε μὲν 620
πεπραγμέν' ἔσται, τἀμὰ δ' ἡμαρτημένα.
ΚΡ. τί δῆτα χρῄζεις; ἦ με γῆς ἔξω βαλεῖν;
ΟΙ. ἥκιστα· θνῄσκειν, οὐ φυγεῖν σε βούλομαι,
⟨..⟩
ΚΡ. ὅταν προδείξῃς οἷόν ἐστι τὸ φθονεῖν.
⟨..⟩
ΟΙ. ὡς οὐχ ὑπείξων οὐδὲ πιστεύσων λέγεις; 625
ΚΡ. οὐ γὰρ φρονοῦντά σ' εὖ βλέπω.
      ΟΙ. τὸ γοῦν ἐμόν.
ΚΡ. ἀλλ' ἐξ ἴσου δεῖ κἀμόν.
      ΟΙ. ἀλλ' ἔφυς κακός.
ΚΡ. εἰ δὲ ξυνίης μηδέν;
      ΟΙ. ἀρκτέον γ' ὅμως.
ΚΡ. οὔτοι κακῶς γ' ἄρχοντος.
      ΟΙ. ὦ πόλις, πόλις.
ΚΡ. κἀμοὶ πόλεως μέτεστιν, οὐχὶ σοὶ μόνῳ. 630
ΧΟ. παύσασθ', ἄνακτες· καιρίαν δ' ὑμῖν ὁρῶ
τήνδ' ἐκ δόμων στείχουσαν Ἰοκάστην, μεθ' ἧς
τὸ νῦν παρεστὸς νεῖκος εὖ θέσθαι χρεών.
[Enter Iokaste from the palace.]
ΙΟΚΑΣΤΗ

τί τὴν ἄβουλον, ὦ ταλαίπωροι, στάσιν
γλώσσης ἐπήρασθ', οὐδ' ἐπαισχύνεσθε γῆς 635
οὕτω νοσούσης ἴδια κινοῦντες κακά;
οὐκ εἶ σύ τ' οἴκους σύ τε, Κρέων, τὰς σὰς στέγας,
καὶ μὴ τὸ μηδὲν ἄλγος εἰς μέγ' οἴσετε;
ΚΡ. ὅμαιμε, δεινά μ' Οἰδίπους, ὁ σὸς πόσις,
δρᾶσαι δικαιοῖ, †δυοῖν ἀποκρίνας κακοῖν,† 640
ἢ γῆς ἀπῶσαι πατρίδος ἢ κτεῖναι λαβών.
ΟΙ. ξύμφημι· δρῶντα γάρ νιν, ὦ γύναι, κακῶς
εἴληφα τοὐμὸν σῶμα σὺν τέχνῃ κακῇ.
ΚΡ. μὴ νῦν ὀναίμην, ἀλλ' ἀραῖος, εἴ σέ τι
δέδρακ', ὀλοίμην, ὧν ἐπαιτιᾷ με δρᾶν. 645
ΙΟ. ὦ πρὸς θεῶν πίστευσον, Οἰδίπους, τάδε,
μάλιστα μὲν τόνδ' ὅρκον αἰδεσθεὶς θεῶν,
ἔπειτα κἀμὲ τούσδε θ' οἳ πάρεισί σοι.

ΧΟ. πιθοῦ θελήσας φρονή- στρ.
σας τ', ἄναξ, λίσσομαι— 650
ΟΙ. τί σοι θέλεις δῆτ' εἰκάθω;
ΧΟ. τὸν οὔτε πρὶν νήπιον
νῦν τ' ἐν ὅρκῳ μέγαν καταίδεσαι.
ΟΙ. οἶσθ' οὖν ἃ χρῄζεις;
      ΧΟ. οἶδα.
         ΟΙ. φράζε δὴ τί φῄς.
ΧΟ. τὸν ἐναγῆ φίλον μήποτε σ' αἰτίᾳ 656
σὺν ἀφανεῖ λόγων ἄτιμον βαλεῖν.
ΟΙ. εὖ νυν ἐπίστω, ταῦθ' ὅταν ζητῇς, ἐμοὶ
ζητῶν ὄλεθρον ἢ φυγεῖν ἐκ τῆσδε γῆς.
ΧΟ. οὐ τὸν πάντων θεῶν θεὸν πρόμον 660
Ἅλιον· ἐπεὶ ἄθεος ἄφιλος ὅ τι πύματον
ὀλοίμαν, φρόνησιν εἰ τάνδ' ἔχω.
ἀλλά μοι δυσμόρῳ γᾶ φθίνου- 665
σα τρύχει καρδίαν, τάδ' εἰ κακοῖς
προσάψει τοῖς πάλαι τὰ πρὸς σφῷν.

ΟΙ. ὁ δ' οὖν ἴτω, κεἰ χρή με παντελῶς θανεῖν

ΟΙΔΙΠΟΥΣ ΤΥΡΑΝΝΟΣ 33

ἢ γῆς ἄτιμον τῆσδ' ἀπωσθῆναι βίᾳ· 670
τὸ γὰρ σόν, οὐ τὸ τοῦδ', ἐποικτίρω στόμα
ἐλεινόν· οὗτος δ' ἔνθ' ἂν ᾖ στυγήσεται.
ΚΡ. στυγνὸς μὲν εἴκων δῆλος εἶ, βαρὺς δ' ὅταν
θυμοῦ περάσῃς· αἱ δὲ τοιαῦται φύσεις
αὐταῖς δικαίως εἰσὶν ἄλγισται φέρειν. 675
ΟΙ. οὔκουν μ' ἐάσεις κἀκτὸς εἶ;
ΚΡ. πορεύσομαι,
σοῦ μὲν τυχὼν ἀγνῶτος, ἐν δὲ τοῖσδε σῶς.
[Exit Kr. to the city.]

ΧΟ. γύναι, τί μέλλεις κομί- ἀντ.
ζειν δόμων τόνδ' ἔσω;
ΙΟ. μαθοῦσά γ' ἥτις ἡ τύχη. 680
ΧΟ. δόκησις ἀγνὼς λόγων
ἦλθε, δάπτει δὲ καὶ τὸ μὴ 'νδίκον.
ΙΟ. ἀμφοῖν ἀπ' αὐτοῖν;
ΧΟ. ναίχι.
ΙΟ. καὶ τίς ἦν λόγος;
ΧΟ. ἅλις ἔμοιγ', ἅλις, γᾶς προνοουμένῳ, 685
φαίνεται ἔνθ' ἔληξεν, αὐτοῦ μένειν.
ΟΙ. ὁρᾷς ἵν' ἥκεις, ἀγαθὸς ὢν γνώμην ἀνήρ,
τοὐμὸν παριεὶς καὶ καταμβλύνων κέαρ;
ΧΟ. ὦναξ, εἶπον μὲν οὐχ ἅπαξ μόνον,
ἴσθι δὲ παραφρόνιμον, ἄπορον ἐπὶ φρόνιμα 690
πεφάνθαι μ' ἄν, εἴ σ ἐνοσφίζομαν,
ὅς γ' ἐμὰν γᾶν φίλαν ἐν πόνοις
ἀλύουσαν κατ' ὀρθὸν οὔρισας· 695
τὰ νῦν δ' εὔπομπος αὖ γένοιο.

ΙΟ. πρὸς θεῶν δίδαξον κἄμ', ἄναξ, ὅτου ποτὲ
μῆνιν τοσήνδε πράγματος στήσας ἔχεις.
ΟΙ. ἐρῶ· σὲ γὰρ τῶνδ' ἐς πλέον, γύναι, σέβω· 700
Κρέοντος, οἷά μοι βεβουλευκὼς ἔχει.
ΙΟ. λέγ', εἰ σαφῶς τὸ νεῖκος ἐγκαλῶν ἐρεῖς.
ΟΙ. φονέα μέ φησι Λαΐου καθεστάναι.

ΙΟ. αὐτὸς ξυνειδὼς ἢ μαθὼν ἄλλου πάρα;
ΟΙ. μάντιν μὲν οὖν κακοῦργον εἰσπέμψας, ἐπεὶ 705
τό γ' εἰς ἑαυτὸν πᾶν ἐλευθεροῖ στόμα.
ΙΟ. σύ νυν ἀφεὶς σεαυτὸν ὧν λέγεις πέρι
ἐμοῦ 'πάκουσον καὶ μάθ' οὕνεκ' ἐστί σοι
βρότειον οὐδὲν μαντικῆς ἔχον τέχνης·
φανῶ δέ σοι σημεῖα τῶνδε σύντομα· 710
χρησμὸς γὰρ ἦλθε Λαΐῳ ποτ', οὐκ ἐρῶ
Φοίβου γ' ἀπ' αὐτοῦ, τῶν δ' ὑπηρετῶν ἄπο,
ὡς αὐτὸν ἥξοι μοῖρα πρὸς παιδὸς θανεῖν
ὅστις γένοιτ' ἐμοῦ τε κἀκείνου πάρα.
καὶ τὸν μέν, ὥσπερ γ' ἡ φάτις, ξένοι ποτὲ 715
λῃσταὶ φονεύουσ' ἐν τριπλαῖς ἁμαξιτοῖς·
παιδὸς δὲ βλάστας οὐ διέσχον ἡμέραι
τρεῖς, καί νιν ἄρθρα κεῖνος ἐνζεύξας ποδοῖν
ἔρριψεν ἄλλων χερσὶν εἰς ἄβατον ὄρος.
κἀνταῦθ' Ἀπόλλων οὔτ' ἐκεῖνον ἤνυσεν 720
φονέα γενέσθαι πατρός, οὔτε Λάϊον—
τὸ δεινὸν οὑφοβεῖτο—πρὸς παιδὸς θανεῖν.
τοιαῦτα φῆμαι μαντικαὶ διώρισαν,
ὧν ἐντρέπου σὺ μηδέν· ὧν γὰρ ἂν θεὸς
χρείαν ἐρευνᾷ, ῥᾳδίως αὐτὸς φανεῖ. 725
ΟΙ. οἷόν μ' ἀκούσαντ' ἀρτίως ἔχει, γύναι,
ψυχῆς πλάνημα κἀνακίνησις φρενῶν.
ΙΟ. ποίας μερίμνης τοῦθ' ὑποστραφεὶς λέγεις;
ΟΙ. ἔδοξ' ἀκοῦσαι σοῦ τόδ', ὡς ὁ Λάϊος
κατασφαγείη πρὸς τριπλαῖς ἁμαξιτοῖς. 730
ΙΟ. ηὐδᾶτο γὰρ ταῦτ'· οὐδέ πω λήξαντ' ἔχει.
ΟΙ. καὶ ποῦ 'σθ' ὁ χῶρος οὗτος, οὗ τόδ' ἦν πάθος;
ΙΟ. Φωκὶς μὲν ἡ γῆ κλῄζεται, σχιστὴ δ' ὁδὸς
ἐς ταὐτὸ Δελφῶν κἀπὸ Δαυλίας ἄγει.
ΟΙ. καὶ τίς χρόνος τοῖσδ' ἐστὶν οὑξεληλυθώς; 735
ΙΟ. σχεδόν τι πρόσθεν ἢ σὺ τῆσδ' ἔχων χθονὸς
ἀρχὴν ἐφαίνου, τοῦτ' ἐκηρύχθη πόλει.
ΟΙ. ὦ Ζεῦ, τί μου δρᾶσαι βεβούλευσαι πέρι;
ΙΟ. τί δ' ἐστί σοι τοῦτ', Οἰδίπους, ἐνθύμιον;

ΟΙΔΙΠΟΥΣ ΤΥΡΑΝΝΟΣ 35

ΟΙ. μήπω μ' ἐρώτα· τὸν δὲ Λάϊον φύσιν 740
τίν' εἷρπε φράζε, τίνα δ' ἀκμὴν ἥβης ἔχων;
ΙΟ. μέγας, χνοάζων ἄρτι λευκανθὲς κάρα,
μορφῆς δὲ τῆς σῆς οὐκ ἀπεστάτει πολύ.
ΟΙ. οἴμοι τάλας· ἔοικ' ἐμαυτὸν εἰς ἀρὰς
δεινὰς προβάλλων ἀρτίως οὐκ εἰδέναι. 745
ΙΟ. πῶς φής; ὀκνῶ τοι πρὸς σ' ἀποσκοποῦσ', ἄναξ.
ΟΙ. δεινῶς ἀθυμῶ μὴ βλέπων ὁ μάντις ᾖ.
δείξεις δὲ μᾶλλον, ἢν ἓν ἐξείπῃς ἔτι.
ΙΟ. καὶ μὴν ὀκνῶ μέν, ἃ δ' ἂν ἔρῃ μαθοῦσ' ἐρῶ.
ΟΙ. πότερον ἐχώρει βαιός, ἢ πολλοὺς ἔχων 750
ἄνδρας λοχίτας, οἷ' ἀνὴρ ἀρχηγέτης;
ΙΟ. πέντ' ἦσαν οἱ ξύμπαντες, ἐν δ' αὐτοῖσιν ἦν
κῆρυξ· ἀπήνη δ' ἦγε Λάϊον μία.
ΟΙ. αἰαῖ, τάδ' ἤδη διαφανῆ. τίς ἦν ποτε
ὁ τούσδε λέξας τοὺς λόγους ὑμῖν, γύναι; 755
ΙΟ. οἰκεύς τις ὅσπερ ἵκετ' ἐκσωθεὶς μόνος.
ΟΙ. ἦ κἀν δόμοισι τυγχάνει τὰ νῦν παρών;
ΙΟ. οὐ δῆτ'· ἀφ' οὗ γὰρ κεῖθεν ἦλθε καὶ κράτη
σέ τ' εἶδ' ἔχοντα Λάϊόν τ' ὀλωλότα,
ἐξικέτευσε τῆς ἐμῆς χειρὸς θιγὼν 760
ἀγρούς σφε πέμψαι κἀπὶ ποιμνίων νομάς,
ὡς πλεῖστον εἴη τοῦδ' ἄποπτος ἄστεως.
κἄπεμψ' ἐγώ νιν· ἄξιος γὰρ οἷ' ἀνὴρ
δοῦλος φέρειν ἦν τῆσδε καὶ μείζω χάριν.
ΟΙ. πῶς ἂν μόλοι δῆθ' ἡμὶν ἐν τάχει πάλιν; 765
ΙΟ. πάρεστιν. ἀλλὰ πρὸς τί τοῦτ' ἐφίεσαι;
ΟΙ. δέδοικ' ἐμαυτόν, ὦ γύναι, μὴ πόλλ' ἄγαν
εἰρημέν' ᾖ μοι, δι' ἅ νιν εἰσιδεῖν θέλω.
ΙΟ. ἀλλ' ἵξεται μέν· ἀξία δέ που μαθεῖν
κἀγὼ τά γ' ἐν σοὶ δυσφόρως ἔχοντ', ἄναξ. 770
ΟΙ. κοὺ μὴ στερηθῇς γ', ἐς τοσοῦτον ἐλπίδων
ἐμοῦ βεβῶτος· τῷ γὰρ ἂν καὶ κρείσσονι
λέξαιμ' ἂν ἢ σοὶ διὰ τύχης τοιᾶσδ' ἰών;
ἐμοὶ πατὴρ μὲν Πόλυβος ἦν Κορίνθιος,
μήτηρ δὲ Μερόπη Δωρίς. ἡγόμην δ' ἀνὴρ 775

ἀστῶν μέγιστος τῶν ἐκεῖ, πρίν μοι τύχη
τοιάδ' ἐπέστη, θαυμάσαι μὲν ἀξία,
σπουδῆς γε μέντοι τῆς ἐμῆς οὐκ ἀξία.
ἀνὴρ γὰρ ἐν δείπνοις μ' ὑπερπλησθεὶς μέθης
καλεῖ παρ' οἴνῳ πλαστὸς ὡς εἴην πατρί. 780
κἀγὼ βαρυνθεὶς τὴν μὲν οὖσαν ἡμέραν
μόλις κατέσχον, θἀτέρᾳ δ' ἰὼν πέλας
μητρὸς πατρός τ' ἤλεγχον· οἱ δὲ δυσφόρως
τοὔνειδος ἦγον τῷ μεθέντι τὸν λόγον.
κἀγὼ τὰ μὲν κείνοιν ἐτερπόμην, ὅμως δ' 785
ἔκνιζέ μ' αἰεὶ τοῦθ'· ὑφεῖρπε γὰρ πολύ.
λάθρᾳ δὲ μητρὸς καὶ πατρὸς πορεύομαι
Πυθώδε, καί μ' ὁ Φοῖβος ὧν μὲν ἱκόμην
ἄτιμον ἐξέπεμψεν, ἄλλα δ' ἀθλίῳ
καὶ δεινὰ καὶ δύστηνα προὔφάνη λέγων, 790
ὡς μητρὶ μὲν χρείη με μιχθῆναι, γένος δ'
ἄτλητον ἀνθρώποισι δηλώσοιμ' ὁρᾶν,
φονεὺς δ' ἐσοίμην τοῦ φυτεύσαντος πατρός.
κἀγὼ 'πακούσας ταῦτα τὴν Κορινθίαν
ἄστροις τὸ λοιπὸν τεκμαρούμενος χθόνα 795
ἔφευγον, ἔνθα μήποτ' ὀψοίμην κακῶν
χρησμῶν ὀνείδη τῶν ἐμῶν τελούμενα.
στείχων δ' ἱκνοῦμαι τούσδε τοὺς χώρους ἐν οἷς
σὺ τὸν τύραννον τοῦτον ὄλλυσθαι λέγεις.
καί σοι, γύναι, τἀληθὲς ἐξερῶ. τριπλῆς 800
ὅτ' ἦ κελεύθου τῆσδ' ὁδοιπορῶν πέλας,
ἐνταῦθά μοι κῆρύξ τε κἀπὶ πωλικῆς
ἀνὴρ ἀπήνης ἐμβεβώς, οἷον σὺ φής,
ξυνηντίαζον· κἀξ ὁδοῦ μ' ὅ θ' ἡγεμὼν
αὐτός θ' ὁ πρέσβυς πρὸς βίαν ἠλαυνέτην. 805
κἀγὼ τὸν ἐκτρέποντα, τὸν τροχηλάτην,
παίω δι' ὀργῆς· καί μ' ὁ πρέσβυς, ὡς ὁρᾷ,
ὄχους παραστείχοντα τηρήσας, μέσον
κάρα διπλοῖς κέντροισί μου καθίκετο.
οὐ μὴν ἴσην γ' ἔτεισεν, ἀλλὰ συντόμως 810
σκήπτρῳ τυπεὶς ἐκ τῆσδε χειρὸς ὕπτιος

ΟΙΔΙΠΟΥΣ ΤΥΡΑΝΝΟΣ 37

μέσης ἀπήνης εὐθὺς ἐκκυλίνδεται·
κτείνω δὲ τοὺς ξύμπαντας. εἰ δὲ τῷ ξένῳ
τούτῳ προσήκει Λαΐῳ τι συγγενές,
τίς τοῦδέ γ' ἀνδρὸς νῦν ἔτ' ἀθλιώτερος; 815
τίς ἐχθροδαίμων μᾶλλον ἂν γένοιτ' ἀνήρ;
ᾧ μὴ ξένων ἔξεστι μηδ' ἀστῶν τινα
δόμοις δέχεσθαι, μηδὲ προσφωνεῖν τινα,
ὠθεῖν δ' ἀπ' οἴκων. καὶ τάδ' οὔτις ἄλλος ἦν
ἢ 'γὼ 'π' ἐμαυτῷ τάσδ' ἀρὰς ὁ προστιθείς. 820
λέχη δὲ τοῦ θανόντος ἐν χεροῖν ἐμαῖν
χραίνω, δι' ὧνπερ ὤλετ'. ἆρ' ἔφυν κακός,
ἆρ' οὐχὶ πᾶς ἄναγνος, εἴ με χρὴ φυγεῖν,
καί μοι φυγόντι μῆστι τοὺς ἐμοὺς ἰδεῖν
μήτ' ἐμβατεῦσαι πατρίδος, ἢ γάμοις με δεῖ 825
μητρὸς ζυγῆναι καὶ πατέρα κατακτανεῖν,
Πόλυβον, ὅς ἐξέθρεψε κἀξέφυσέ με;
ἆρ' οὐκ ἀπ' ὠμοῦ ταῦτα δαίμονός τις ἂν
κρίνων ἐπ' ἀνδρὶ τῷδ' ἂν ὀρθοίη λόγον;
μὴ δῆτα, μὴ δῆτ', ὦ θεῶν ἁγνὸν σέβας, 830
ἴδοιμι ταύτην ἡμέραν, ἀλλ' ἐκ βροτῶν
βαίην ἄφαντος πρόσθεν ἢ τοιάνδ' ἰδεῖν
κηλῖδ' ἐμαυτῷ συμφορᾶς ἀφιγμένην.
ΧΟ. ἡμῖν μέν, ὦναξ, ταῦτ' ὀκνήρ'· ἕως δ' ἂν οὖν
πρὸς τοῦ παρόντος ἐκμάθῃς, ἔχ' ἐλπίδα. 835
ΟΙ. καὶ μὴν τοσοῦτόν γ' ἐστί μοι τῆς ἐλπίδος,
τὸν ἄνδρα, τὸν βοτῆρα, προσμεῖναι μόνον.
ΙΟ. πεφασμένου δὲ τίς ποθ' ἡ προθυμία;
ΟΙ. ἐγώ διδάξω σ'· ἢν γὰρ εὑρεθῇ λέγων
σοὶ ταῦτ', ἔγωγ' ἂν ἐκπεφευγοίην πάθος. 840
ΙΟ. ποῖον δέ μου περισσὸν ἤκουσας λόγον;
ΟΙ. λῃστὰς ἔφασκες αὐτὸν ἄνδρας ἐννέπειν
ὥς νιν κατακτείνειαν. εἰ μὲν οὖν ἔτι
λέξει τὸν αὐτὸν ἀριθμόν, οὐκ ἐγὼ 'κτανον·
οὐ γὰρ γένοιτ' ἂν εἷς γε τοῖς πολλοῖς ἴσος· 845
εἰ δ' ἄνδρ' ἕν' οἰόζωνον αὐδήσει, σαφῶς
τοῦτ' ἐστὶν ἤδη τοὔργον εἰς ἐμὲ ῥέπον.

ΙΟ. ἀλλ' ὡς φανέν γε τοὔπος ὧδ' ἐπίστασο,
κοὔκ ἔστιν αὐτῷ τοῦτό γ' ἐκβαλεῖν πάλιν·
πόλις γὰρ ἤκουσ', οὐκ ἐγὼ μόνη, τάδε.
εἰ δ' οὖν τι κἀκτρέποιτο τοῦ πρόσθεν λόγου, 850
οὔτοι ποτ', ὦναξ, τόν γε Λαΐου φόνον
φανεῖ δικαίως ὀρθόν, ὅν γε Λοξίας
διεῖπε χρῆναι παιδὸς ἐξ ἐμοῦ θανεῖν.
καίτοι νιν οὐ κεῖνός γ' ὁ δύστηνός ποτε 855
κατέκταν', ἀλλ' αὐτὸς πάροιθεν ὤλετο.
ὥστ' οὐχὶ μαντείας γ' ἂν οὔτε τῇδ' ἐγὼ
βλέψαιμ' ἂν οὕνεκ' οὔτε τῇδ' ἂν ὕστερον.
ΟΙ. καλῶς νομίζεις. ἀλλ' ὅμως τὸν ἐργάτην
πέμψον τινὰ στελοῦντα, μηδὲ τοῦτ' ἀφῇς. 860
ΙΟ. πέμψω ταχύνασ'· ἀλλ' ἴωμεν ἐς δόμους·
οὐδὲν γὰρ ἂν πράξαιμ' ἂν ὧν οὔ σοι φίλον.
[Exeunt Iokaste and O into the palace.]

ΧΟ. εἴ μοι ξυνείη φέροντι μοῖρα τὰν   στρ. α
εὔσεπτον ἁγνείαν λόγων
ἔργων τε πάντων, ὧν νόμοι πρόκεινται 865
ὑψίποδες, οὐρανίᾳ 'ν
αἰθέρι τεκνωθέντες, ὧν Ὄλυμπος
πατὴρ μόνος, οὐδέ νιν
θνατὰ φύσις ἀνέρων
ἔτικτεν, οὐδὲ μήποτε λά-
θα κατακοιμάσῃ· 870
μέγας ἐν τούτοις θεός, οὐδὲ γηράσκει.

ὕβρις φυτεύει τύραννον· ὕβρις, εἰ   ἀντ. α
πολλῶν ὑπερπλησθῇ μάταν
ἃ μὴ 'πίκαιρα μηδὲ συμφέροντα, 875
ἀκρότατα γεῖσ' ἀναβᾶσ'
ἀπότομον ὤρουσεν εἰς ἀνάγκαν,
ἔνθ' οὐ ποδὶ χρησίμῳ
χρῆται. τὸ καλῶς δ' ἔχον
πόλει πάλαισμα μήποτε λῦ- 880

σαι θεὸν αἰτοῦμαι·
θεὸν οὐ λήξω ποτὲ προστάταν ἴσχων.

εἰ δέ τις ὑπέροπτα χερσὶν   στρ. β
ἢ λόγῳ πορεύεται,
Δίκας ἀφόβητος, οὐδὲ   885
δαιμόνων ἕδη σέβων,
κακά νιν ἕλοιτο μοῖρα,
δυσπότμου χάριν χλιδᾶς,
εἰ μὴ τὸ κέρδος κερδανεῖ δικαίως
καὶ τῶν ἀσέπτων ἔρξεται,   890
ἢ τῶν ἀθίκτων ἕξεται ματᾴζων.
τίς ἔτι ποτ' ἐν τοῖσδ' ἀνὴρ θυμοῦ βέλη
†ἔρξεται† ψυχᾶς ἀμύνειν;
εἰ γὰρ αἱ τοιαίδε πράξεις τίμιαι,   895
τί δεῖ με χορεύειν;

οὐκέτι τὸν ἄθικτον εἶμι   ἀντ. β
γᾶς ἐπ' ὀμφαλὸν σέβων,
οὐδ' ἐς τὸν Ἀβαῖσι ναόν,   900
οὐδὲ τὰν Ὀλυμπίαν,
εἰ μὴ τάδε χειρόδεικτα
πᾶσιν ἁρμόσει βροτοῖς.
ἀλλ', ὦ κρατύνων, εἴπερ ὄρθ' ἀκούεις,
Ζεῦ, πάντ' ἀνάσσων, μὴ λάθοι
σὲ τάν τε σὰν ἀθάνατον αἰὲν ἀρχάν.   905
φθίνοντα γὰρ ⟨–◡–×⟩ Λαΐου
θέσφατ' ἐξαιροῦσιν ἤδη,
κοὐδαμοῦ τιμαῖς Ἀπόλλων ἐμφανής·
ἔρρει δὲ τὰ θεῖα.   910

[Enter Iokaste from the palace.]
10. χώρας ἄνακτες, δόξα μοι παρεστάθη
ναοὺς ἱκέσθαι δαιμόνων, τάδ' ἐν χεροῖν
στέφη λαβούσῃ κἀπιθυμιάματα.
ὑψοῦ γὰρ αἴρει θυμὸν Οἰδίπους ἄγαν

ΣΟΦΟΚΛΕΟΥΣ

λύπαισι παντοίαισιν, οὐδ' ὁποῖ' ἀνὴρ 915
ἔννους τὰ καινὰ τοῖς πάλαι τεκμαίρεται,
ἀλλ' ἔστι τοῦ λέγοντος, ἢν φόβους λέγῃ.
ὅτ' οὖν παραινοῦσ' οὐδὲν ἐς πλέον ποιῶ,
πρὸς σ', ὦ Λύκει' Ἄπολλον, ἄγχιστος γὰρ εἶ,
ἱκέτις ἀφῖγμαι τοῖσδε σὺν κατεύγμασιν, 920
ὅπως λύσιν τιν' ἡμῖν εὐαγῆ πόρῃς·
ὡς νῦν ὀκνοῦμεν πάντες ἐκπεπληγμένον
κεῖνον βλέποντες ὡς κυβερνήτην νεώς.
[Enter a messenger from the country.]
ΑΓΓΕΛΟΣ
ἆρ' ἂν παρ' ὑμῶν, ὦ ξένοι, μάθοιμ' ὅπου
τὰ τοῦ τυράννου δώματ' ἐστὶν Οἰδίπου; 925
μάλιστα δ' αὐτὸν εἴπατ', εἰ κάτισθ', ὅπου.
ΧΟ. στέγαι μὲν αἵδε, καὐτὸς ἔνδον, ὦ ξένε·
γυνὴ δὲ μήτηρ θ' ἥδε τῶν κείνου τέκνων.
ΑΓ. ἀλλ' ὀλβία τε καὶ ξὺν ὀλβίοις ἀεὶ
γένοιτ', ἐκείνου γ' οὖσα παντελὴς δάμαρ. 930
ΙΟ. αὔτως δὲ καὶ σύ γ', ὦ ξέν'· ἄξιος γὰρ εἶ
τῆς εὐεπείας οὕνεκ'. ἀλλὰ φράζ' ὅτου
χρῄζων ἀφῖξαι χὤ τι σημῆναι θέλων.
ΑΓ. ἀγαθὰ δόμοις τε καὶ πόσει τῷ σῷ, γύναι.
ΙΟ. τὰ ποῖα ταῦτα; παρὰ τίνος δ' ἀφιγμένος; 935
ΑΓ. ἐκ τῆς Κορίνθου. τὸ δ' ἔπος οὑξερῶ—τάχα
ἥδοιο μέν, πῶς δ' οὐκ ἄν; ἀσχάλλοις δ' ἴσως.
ΙΟ. τί δ' ἔστι; ποίαν δύναμιν ὧδ' ἔχει διπλῆν;
ΑΓ. τύραννον αὐτὸν οὑπιχώριοι χθονὸς
τῆς Ἰσθμίας στήσουσιν, ὡς ηὐδᾶτ' ἐκεῖ. 940
ΙΟ. τί δ'; οὐχ ὁ πρέσβυς Πόλυβος ἐγκρατὴς ἔτι;
ΑΓ. οὐ δῆτ', ἐπεί νιν θάνατος ἐν τάφοις ἔχει.
ΙΟ. πῶς εἶπας; ἦ τέθνηκε⟨ν Οἰδίπου πατήρ;⟩
ΑΓ. εἰ μὴ λέγω τἀληθές, ἀξιῶ θανεῖν.
ΙΟ. ὦ πρόσπολ', οὐχὶ δεσπότῃ τάδ' ὡς τάχος 945
μολοῦσα λέξεις; ὦ θεῶν μαντεύματα,
ἵν' ἐστέ; τοῦτον Οἰδίπους πάλαι τρέμων
τὸν ἄνδρ' ἔφευγε μὴ κτάνοι, καὶ νῦν ὅδε

ΟΙΔΙΠΟΥΣ ΤΥΡΑΝΝΟΣ

πρὸς τῆς τύχης ὄλωλεν οὐδὲ τοῦδ' ὕπο.
[Enter O from the palace.]
ΟΙ. ὦ φίλτατον γυναικὸς Ἰοκάστης κάρα, 950
τί μ' ἐξεπέμψω δεῦρο τῶνδε δωμάτων;
ΙΟ. ἄκουε τἀνδρὸς τοῦδε, καὶ σκόπει κλύων
τὰ σέμν' ἵν' ἥκει τοῦ θεοῦ μαντεύματα.
ΟΙ. οὗτος δὲ τίς ποτ' ἐστί, καὶ τί μοι λέγει;
ΙΟ. ἐκ τῆς Κορίνθου, πατέρα τὸν σὸν ἀγγελῶν 955
ὡς οὐκέτ' ὄντα Πόλυβον, ἀλλ' ὀλωλότα.
ΟΙ. τί φής, ξέν'; αὐτός μοι σὺ σημήνας γενοῦ.
ΑΓ. εἰ τοῦτο πρῶτον δεῖ μ' ἀπαγγεῖλαι σαφῶς,
εὖ ἴσθ' ἐκεῖνον θανάσιμον βεβηκότα.
ΟΙ. πότερα δόλοισιν; ἢ νόσου ξυναλλαγῇ; 960
ΑΓ. σμικρὰ παλαιὰ σώματ' εὐνάζει ῥοπή.
ΟΙ. νόσοις ὁ τλήμων, ὡς ἔοικεν, ἔφθιτο.
ΑΓ. καὶ τῷ μακρῷ γε συμμετρούμενος χρόνῳ.
ΟΙ. φεῦ φεῦ, τί δῆτ' ἄν, ὦ γύναι, σκοποῖτό τις
τὴν Πυθόμαντιν ἑστίαν, ἢ τοὺς ἄνω 965
κλάζοντας ὄρνις, ὧν ὑφ' ἡγητῶν ἐγὼ
κτανεῖν ἔμελλον πατέρα τὸν ἐμόν; ὁ δὲ θανὼν
κεύθει κάτω δὴ γῆς, ἐγὼ δ' ὅδ' ἐνθάδε
ἄψαυστος ἔγχους—εἴ τι μὴ τὠμῷ πόθῳ
κατέφθιθ'· οὕτω δ' ἂν θανὼν εἴη 'ξ ἐμοῦ. 970
τὰ δ' οὖν παρόντα συλλαβὼν θεσπίσματα
κεῖται παρ' Ἅιδῃ Πόλυβος ἄξι' οὐδενός.
ΙΟ. οὔκουν ἐγώ σοι ταῦτα προὔλεγον πάλαι;
ΟΙ. ηὔδας· ἐγὼ δὲ τῷ φόβῳ παρηγόμην.
ΙΟ. μή νυν ἔτ' αὐτῶν μηδὲν ἐς θυμὸν βάλῃς. 975
ΟΙ. καὶ πῶς τὸ μητρὸς λέκτρον οὐκ ὀκνεῖν με δεῖ;
ΙΟ. τί δ' ἂν φοβοῖτ' ἄνθρωπος, ᾧ τὰ τῆς τύχης
κρατεῖ, πρόνοια δ' ἐστὶν οὐδενὸς σαφής;
εἰκῇ κράτιστον ζῆν, ὅπως δύναιτό τις.
σὺ δ' εἰς τὰ μητρὸς μὴ φοβοῦ νυμφεύματα· 980
πολλοὶ γὰρ ἤδη κἀν ὀνείρασιν βροτῶν
μητρὶ ξυνηυνάσθησαν· ἀλλὰ ταῦθ' ὅτῳ

παρ' οὐδέν ἐστι, ῥᾶστα τὸν βίον φέρει.
ΟΙ. καλῶς ἅπαντα ταῦτ' ἂν ἐξείρητό σοι,
 εἰ μὴ 'κύρει ζῶσ' ἡ τεκοῦσα· νῦν δ' ἐπεὶ 985
 ζῇ, πᾶσ' ἀνάγκη, κεἰ καλῶς λέγεις, ὀκνεῖν.
ΙΟ. καὶ μὴν μέγας ⟨γ'⟩ ὀφθαλμὸς οἱ πατρὸς τάφοι.
ΟΙ. μέγας, ξυνίημ'· ἀλλὰ τῆς ζώσης φόβος.
ΑΓ. ποίας δὲ καὶ γυναικὸς ἐκφοβεῖσθ' ὕπερ;
ΟΙ. Μερόπης, γεραιέ, Πόλυβος ἧς ᾤκει μέτα. 990
ΑΓ. τί δ' ἔστ' ἐκείνης ὑμὶν ἐς φόβον φέρον;
ΟΙ. θεήλατον μάντευμα δεινόν, ὦ ξένε.
ΑΓ. ἦ ῥητόν; ἢ οὐ θεμιστὸν ἄλλον εἰδέναι;
ΟΙ. μάλιστά γ'· εἶπε γάρ με Λοξίας ποτὲ
 χρῆναι μιγῆναι μητρὶ τἠμαυτοῦ, τό τε 995
 πατρῷον αἷμα χερσὶ ταῖς ἐμαῖς ἑλεῖν.
 ὧν οὕνεχ' ἡ Κόρινθος ἐξ ἐμοῦ πάλαι
 μακρὰν ἀπῳκεῖτ'· εὐτυχῶς μέν, ἀλλ' ὅμως
 τὰ τῶν τεκόντων ὄμμαθ' ἥδιστον βλέπειν.
ΑΓ. ἦ γὰρ τάδ' ὀκνῶν κεῖθεν ἦσθ' ἀπόπτολις; 1000
ΟΙ. πατρός γε χρῄζων μὴ φονεὺς εἶναι, γέρον.
ΑΓ. τί δῆτ' ἐγὼ οὐχὶ τοῦδε τοῦ φόβου σ', ἄναξ,
 ἐπείπερ εὔνους ἦλθον, ἐξελυσάμην;
ΟΙ. καὶ μὴν χάριν γ' ἂν ἀξίαν λάβοις ἐμοῦ.
ΑΓ. καὶ μὴν μάλιστα τοῦτ' ἀφικόμην, ὅπως 1005
 σοῦ πρὸς δόμους ἐλθόντος εὖ πράξαιμί τι.
ΟΙ. ἀλλ' οὔποτ' εἶμι τοῖς φυτεύσασιν γ' ὁμοῦ.
ΑΓ. ὦ παῖ, καλῶς εἶ δῆλος οὐκ εἰδὼς τί δρᾷς.
ΟΙ. πῶς, ὦ γεραιέ; πρὸς θεῶν, δίδασκέ με.
ΑΓ. εἰ τῶνδε φεύγεις οὕνεκ' εἰς οἴκους μολεῖν. 1010
ΟΙ. ταρβῶν γε μή μοι Φοῖβος ἐξέλθῃ σαφής.
ΑΓ. ἦ μὴ μίασμα τῶν φυτευσάντων λάβῃς;
ΟΙ. τοῦτ' αὐτό, πρέσβυ, τοῦτό μ' εἰσαεὶ φοβεῖ.
ΑΓ. ἆρ' οἶσθα δῆτα πρὸς δίκης οὐδὲν τρέμων;
ΟΙ. πῶς δ' οὐχί, παῖς γ' εἰ τῶνδε γεννητῶν ἔφυν; 1015
ΑΓ. ὁθούνεκ' ἦν σοι Πόλυβος οὐδὲν ἐν γένει.
ΟΙ. πῶς εἶπας; οὐ γὰρ Πόλυβος ἐξέφυσέ με;
ΑΓ. οὐ μᾶλλον οὐδὲν τοῦδε τἀνδρός, ἀλλ' ἴσον.

ΟΙΔΙΠΟΥΣ ΤΥΡΑΝΝΟΣ 43

ΟΙ. καὶ πῶς ὁ φύσας ἐξ ἴσου τῷ μηδενί;
ΑΓ. ἀλλ' οὔ σ' ἐγείνατ' οὔτ' ἐκεῖνος οὔτ' ἐγώ. 1020
ΟΙ. ἀλλ' ἀντὶ τοῦ δὴ παῖδά μ' ὠνομάζετο;
ΑΓ. δῶρόν ποτ', ἴσθι, τῶν ἐμῶν χειρῶν λαβών.
ΟΙ. κᾆθ' ὧδ' ἀπ' ἄλλης χειρὸς ἔστερξεν μέγα;
ΑΓ. ἡ γὰρ πρὶν αὐτὸν ἐξέπεισ' ἀπαιδία.
ΟΙ. σὺ δ' ἐμπολήσας, ἢ τυχών μ' αὐτῷ δίδως; 1025
ΑΓ. εὑρὼν ναπαίαις ἐν Κιθαιρῶνος πτυχαῖς.
ΟΙ. ὡδοιπόρεις δὲ πρὸς τί τούσδε τοὺς τόπους;
ΑΓ. ἐνταῦθ' ὀρείοις ποιμνίοις ἐπεστάτουν.
ΟΙ. ποιμὴν γὰρ ἦσθα κἀπὶ θητείᾳ πλάνης;
ΑΓ. σοῦ δ', ὦ τέκνον, σωτήρ γε τῷ τότ' ἐν χρόνῳ. 1030
ΟΙ. τί δ' ἄλγος ἴσχοντ' ἐν χεροῖν με λαμβάνεις;
ΑΓ. ποδῶν ἂν ἄρθρα μαρτυρήσειεν τὰ σά.
ΟΙ. οἴμοι, τί τοῦτ' ἀρχαῖον ἐννέπεις κακόν;
ΑΓ. λύω σ' ἔχοντα διατόρους ποδοῖν ἀκμάς.
ΟΙ. δεινόν γ' ὄνειδος σπαργάνων ἀνειλόμην. 1035
ΑΓ. ὥστ' ὠνομάσθης ἐκ τύχης ταύτης ὃς εἶ.
ΟΙ. ὦ πρὸς θεῶν, πρὸς μητρὸς ἢ πατρός; φράσον.
ΑΓ. οὐκ οἶδ'· ὁ δοὺς δὲ ταῦτ' ἐμοῦ λῷον φρονεῖ.
ΟΙ. ἦ γὰρ παρ' ἄλλου μ' ἔλαβες οὐδ' αὐτὸς τυχών;
ΑΓ. οὔκ, ἀλλὰ ποιμὴν ἄλλος ἐκδίδωσί μοι. 1040
ΟΙ. τίς οὗτος; ἦ κάτοισθα δηλῶσαι λόγῳ;
ΑΓ. τῶν Λαΐου δήπου τις ὠνομάζετο.
ΟΙ. ἦ τοῦ τυράννου τῆσδε γῆς πάλαι ποτέ;
ΑΓ. μάλιστα· τούτου τἀνδρὸς οὗτος ἦν βοτήρ.
ΟΙ. ἦ κἄστ' ἔτι ζῶν οὗτος, ὥστ' ἰδεῖν ἐμέ; 1045
ΑΓ. ὑμεῖς γ' ἄριστ' εἰδεῖτ' ἂν οὑπιχώριοι.
ΟΙ. ἔστιν τις ὑμῶν τῶν παρεστώτων πέλας,
ὅστις κάτοιδε τὸν βοτῆρ' ὃν ἐννέπει,
εἴτ' οὖν ἐπ' ἀγρῶν εἴτε κἀνθάδ' εἰσιδών;
σημήναθ', ὡς ὁ καιρὸς ηὑρῆσθαι τάδε. 1050
ΧΟ. οἶμαι μὲν οὐδέν' ἄλλον ἢ τὸν ἐξ ἀγρῶν
ὃν κἀμάτευες πρόσθεν εἰσιδεῖν· ἀτὰρ
ἥδ' ἂν τάδ' οὐχ ἥκιστ' ἂν Ἰοκάστη λέγοι.
ΟΙ. γύναι, νοεῖς ἐκεῖνον, ὅντιν' ἀρτίως

44 ΣΟΦΟΚΛΕΟΥΣ

μολεῖν ἐφιέμεσθα; τόνδ' οὗτος λέγει; 1055
ΙΟ. τί δ' ὄντιν' εἶπε; μηδὲν ἐντραπῇς· τὰ δὲ
ῥηθέντα βούλου μηδὲ μεμνῆσθαι μάτην.
ΟΙ. οὐκ ἂν γένοιτο τοῦθ', ὅπως ἐγὼ λαβὼν
σημεῖα τοιαῦτ' οὐ φανῶ τοὐμὸν γένος.
ΙΟ. μή, πρὸς θεῶν, εἴπερ τι τοῦ σαυτοῦ βίου 1060
κήδῃ, ματεύσῃς τοῦθ'· ἅλις νοσοῦσ' ἐγώ.
ΟΙ. θάρσει· σὺ μὲν γὰρ οὐδ' ἐὰν τρίτης ἐγὼ
μητρὸς φανῶ τρίδουλος, ἐκφανῇ κακή.
ΙΟ. ὅμως πιθοῦ μοι, λίσσομαι· μὴ δρᾶ τάδε.
ΟΙ. οὐκ ἂν πιθοίμην μὴ οὐ τάδ' ἐκμαθεῖν σαφῶς. 1065
ΙΟ. καὶ μὴν φρονοῦσά γ' εὖ τὰ λῷστά σοι λέγω.
ΟΙ. τὰ λῷστα τοίνυν ταῦτά μ' ἀλγύνει πάλαι.
ΙΟ. ὦ δύσποτμ', εἴθε μήποτε γνοίης ὃς εἶ.
ΟΙ. ἄξει τις ἐλθὼν δεῦρο τὸν βοτῆρά μοι;
ταύτην δ' ἐᾶτε πλουσίῳ χαίρειν γένει. 1070
ΙΟ. ἰοὺ ἰού, δύστηνε· τοῦτο γάρ σ' ἔχω
μόνον προσειπεῖν, ἄλλο δ' οὔποθ' ὕστερον.
[Exit Iokaste into the palace.]
ΧΟ. τί ποτε βέβηκεν, Οἰδίπους, ὑπ' ἀγρίας
ᾄξασα λύπης ἡ γυνή; δέδοιχ' ὅπως
μὴ 'κ τῆς σιωπῆς τῆσδ' ἀναρρήξει κακά. 1075
ΟΙ. ὁποῖα χρῄζει ῥηγνύτω· τοὐμὸν δ' ἐγώ,
κεἰ σμικρόν ἐστι, σπέρμ' ἰδεῖν βουλήσομαι.
αὕτη δ' ἴσως, φρονεῖ γὰρ ὡς γυνὴ μέγα,
τὴν δυσγένειαν τὴν ἐμὴν αἰσχύνεται.
ἐγὼ δ' ἐμαυτὸν παῖδα τῆς Τύχης νέμων 1080
τῆς εὖ διδούσης οὐκ ἀτιμασθήσομαι.
τῆς γὰρ πέφυκα μητρός· οἱ δὲ συγγενεῖς
μῆνές με μικρὸν καὶ μέγαν διώρισαν.
τοιόσδε δ' ἐκφὺς οὐκ ἂν ἐξέλθοιμ' ἔτι
ποτ' ἄλλος, ὥστε μὴ 'κμαθεῖν τοὐμὸν γένος. 1085
[O and the messenger remain on stage during the following stasimon.]

ΧΟ. εἴπερ ἐγὼ μάντις εἰ- στρ.

ΟΙΔΙΠΟΥΣ ΤΥΡΑΝΝΟΣ 45

μὶ καὶ κατὰ γνώμαν ἴδρις,
οὐ τὸν Ὀλυμπον ἀπείρων,
ὦ Κιθαιρών, οὐκ ἔσῃ τὰν αὔριον
πανσέληνον μὴ οὐ σέ γε τὸν πατριώταν
   Οἰδίπου   1090
καὶ τροφὸν καὶ ματέρ' αὔξειν,
καὶ χορεύεσθαι πρὸς ἡ-
μῶν, ὡς ἐπίηρα φέροντα   1095
τοῖς ἐμοῖς τυράννοις.
Ἰήϊε Φοῖβε, σοὶ δὲ
ταῦτ' ἀρέστ' εἴη.

τίς σε, τέκνον, τίς σ' ἔτικ-   ἀντ.
τε τῶν μακραιώνων ἄρα
Πανὸς ὀρεσσιβάτα πα-   1100
τρὸς πελασθεῖσ'; ἢ σέ γ' εὐνάτειρά τις
Λοξίου; τῷ γὰρ πλάκες ἀγρόνομοι πᾶσαι
  φίλαι·
εἴθ' ὁ Κυλλάνας ἀνάσσων,
εἴθ' ὁ Βακχεῖος θεὸς   1105
ναίων ἐπ' ἄκρων ὀρέων ⟨σ'⟩ εὕ-
ρημα δέξατ' ἔκ του
Νυμφᾶν ἑλικωπίδων, αἷς
πλεῖστα συμπαίζει.

[Enter a shepherd from the country.]
ΟΙ. εἰ χρή τι κἀμὲ μὴ συναλλάξαντά πω,   1110
    πρέσβεις, σταθμᾶσθαι, τὸν βοτῆρ' ὁρᾶν δοκῶ,
    ὅνπερ πάλαι ζητοῦμεν· ἔν τε γὰρ μακρῷ
    γήρᾳ ξυνᾴδει τῷδε τἀνδρὶ σύμμετρος,
    ἄλλως τε τοὺς ἄγοντας ὥσπερ οἰκέτας
    ἔγνωκ' ἐμαυτοῦ· τῇ δ' ἐπιστήμῃ σύ μου   1115
    προὔχοις τάχ' ἄν που, τὸν βοτῆρ' ἰδὼν πάρος.
ΧΟ. ἔγνωκα γάρ, σάφ' ἴσθι· Λαΐου γὰρ ἦν,
    εἴπερ τις ἄλλος πιστὸς ὡς νομεὺς ἀνήρ.
ΟΙ. σὲ πρῶτ' ἐρωτῶ, τὸν Κορίνθιον ξένον·

46 ΣΟΦΟΚΛΕΟΥΣ

ἢ τόνδε φράζεις; 1120
ΑΓ. τοῦτον, ὅνπερ εἰσορᾷς.
ΟΙ. οὗτος σύ, πρέσβυ, δεῦρό μοι φώνει βλέπων
ὅσ' ἄν σ' ἐρωτῶ. Λαΐου ποτ' ἦσθα σύ;
ΘΕΡΑΠΩΝ
ἢ δοῦλος οὐκ ὠνητός, ἀλλ' οἴκοι τραφείς.
ΟΙ. ἔργον μεριμνῶν ποῖον ἢ βίον τίνα;
ΘΕ. ποίμναις τὰ πλεῖστα τοῦ βίου συνειπόμην. 1125
ΟΙ. χώροις μάλιστα πρὸς τίσιν ξύναυλος ὤν;
ΘΕ. ἦν μὲν Κιθαιρών, ἦν δὲ πρόσχωρος τόπος.
ΟΙ. τὸν ἄνδρα τόνδ' οὖν οἶσθα τῇδέ που μαθών;
ΘΕ. τί χρῆμα δρῶντα; ποῖον ἄνδρα καὶ λέγεις;
ΟΙ. τόνδ' ὃς πάρεστιν· ἢ ξυναλλάξας τί πω; 1130
ΘΕ. οὐχ ὥστε γ' εἰπεῖν ἐν τάχει μνήμης ὕπο.
ΑΓ. κοὐδέν γε θαῦμα, δέσποτ'· ἀλλ' ἐγὼ σαφῶς
ἀγνῶτ' ἀναμνήσω νιν. εὖ γὰρ οἶδ' ὅτι
κάτοιδεν, ἦμος τὸν Κιθαιρῶνος τόπον
ὁ μὲν διπλοῖσι ποιμνίοις, ἐγὼ δ' ἑνὶ 1135
⟨..................⟩
ἐπλησίαζον τῷδε τἀνδρὶ τρεῖς ὅλους
ἐξ ἦρος εἰς ἀρκτοῦρον ἐκμήνους χρόνους·
χειμῶνι δ' ἤδη τἀμά τ' εἰς ἔπαυλ' ἐγὼ
ἤλαυνον, οὗτός τ' εἰς τὰ Λαΐου σταθμά.
λέγω τι τούτων, ἢ οὐ λέγω πεπραγμένον; 1140
ΘΕ. λέγεις ἀληθῆ, καίπερ ἐκ μακροῦ χρόνου.
ΑΓ. φέρ' εἰπὲ νυν, τότ' οἶσθα παῖδά μοί τινα
δούς, ὡς ἐμαυτῷ θρέμμα θρεψαίμην ἐγώ;
ΘΕ. τί δ' ἔστι; πρὸς τί τοῦτο τοὔπος ἱστορεῖς;
ΑΓ. ὅδ' ἐστίν, ὦ τᾶν, κεῖνος ὃς τότ' ἦν νέος. 1145
ΘΕ. οὐκ εἰς ὄλεθρον; οὐ σιωπήσας ἔσῃ;
ΟΙ. ἆ, μὴ κόλαζε, πρέσβυ, τόνδ', ἐπεὶ τὰ σὰ
δεῖται κολαστοῦ μᾶλλον ἢ τὰ τοῦδ' ἔπη.
ΘΕ. τί δ', ὦ φέριστε δεσποτῶν, ἁμαρτάνω;
ΟΙ. οὐκ ἐννέπων τὸν παῖδ' ὃν οὗτος ἱστορεῖ. 1150
ΘΕ. λέγει γὰρ εἰδὼς οὐδέν, ἀλλ' ἄλλως πονεῖ.
ΟΙ. σὺ πρὸς χάριν μὲν οὐκ ἐρεῖς, κλαίων δ' ἐρεῖς.

ΟΙΔΙΠΟΥΣ ΤΥΡΑΝΝΟΣ

ΘΕ. μὴ δῆτα, πρὸς θεῶν, τὸν γέροντά μ' αἰκίσῃ.
ΟΙ. οὐχ ὡς τάχος τις τοῦδ' ἀποστρέψει χέρας;
ΘΕ. δύστηνος, ἀντὶ τοῦ; τί προσχρῄζων μαθεῖν; 1155
ΟΙ. τὸν παῖδ' ἔδωκας τῷδ' ὃν οὗτος ἱστορεῖ;
ΘΕ. ἔδωκ᾿· ὀλέσθαι δ' ὤφελον τῇδ' ἡμέρᾳ.
ΟΙ. ἀλλ' εἰς τόδ' ἥξεις μὴ λέγων γε τοὔνδικον.
ΘΕ. πολλῷ γε μᾶλλον, ἢν φράσω, διόλλυμαι.
ΟΙ. ἀνὴρ ὅδ', ὡς ἔοικεν, ἐς τριβὰς ἐλᾷ. 1160
ΘΕ. οὐ δῆτ' ἔγωγ', ἀλλ' εἶπον ὡς δοίην πάλαι.
ΟΙ. πόθεν λαβών; οἰκεῖον ἢ 'ξ ἄλλου τινός;
ΘΕ. ἐμὸν μὲν οὐκ ἔγωγ', ἐδεξάμην δέ του.
ΟΙ. τίνος πολιτῶν τῶνδε κἀκ ποίας στέγης;
ΘΕ. μὴ πρὸς θεῶν, μή, δέσποθ', ἱστόρει πλέον. 1165
ΟΙ. ὄλωλας, εἴ σε ταῦτ' ἐρήσομαι πάλιν.
ΘΕ. τῶν Λαΐου τοίνυν τις ἦν ἐκ δωμάτων.
ΟΙ. ἦ δοῦλος, ἢ κείνου τις ἐγγενὴς γεγώς;
ΘΕ. οἴμοι, πρὸς αὐτῷ γ' εἰμὶ τῷ δεινῷ λέγειν.
ΟΙ. κἄγωγ' ἀκούειν· ἀλλ' ὅμως ἀκουστέον. 1170
ΘΕ. κείνου γέ τοι δὴ παῖς ἐκλῄζεθ᾿· ἡ δ' ἔσω
κάλλιστ' ἂν εἴποι σὴ γυνὴ τάδ' ὡς ἔχει.
ΟΙ. ἦ γὰρ δίδωσιν ἥδε σοι;
ΘΕ.   μάλιστ', ἄναξ.
ΟΙ. ὡς πρὸς τί χρείας;
ΘΕ.   ὡς ἀναλώσαιμί νιν.
ΟΙ. τεκοῦσα τλήμων; 1175
ΘΕ.   θεσφάτων γ' ὄκνῳ κακῶν.
ΟΙ. ποίων;
ΘΕ.   κτενεῖν νιν τοὺς τεκόντας ἦν λόγος.
ΟΙ. πῶς δῆτ' ἀφῆκας τῷ γέροντι τῷδε σύ;
ΘΕ. κατοικτίσας, ὦ δέσποθ', ὡς ἄλλην χθόνα
δοκῶν ἀποίσειν, αὐτὸς ἔνθεν ἦν· ὁ δὲ
κἄκ' εἰς μέγιστ' ἔσωσεν· εἰ γὰρ οὗτος εἶ 1180
ὅν φησιν οὗτος, ἴσθι δύσποτμος γεγώς.
ΟΙ. ἰοὺ ἰού· τὰ πάντ' ἂν ἐξήκοι σαφῆ.
ὦ φῶς, τελευταῖόν σε προσβλέψαιμι νῦν,
ὅστις πέφασμαι φύς τ' ἀφ' ὧν οὐ χρῆν, ξὺν οἷς τ'

οὐ χρῆν ὁμιλῶν, οὕς τέ μ' οὐκ ἔδει κτανών.   1185
[Exit O to the palace, messenger and shepherd to the country.]

XO. ἰὼ γενεαὶ βροτῶν, στρ. α
ὡς ὑμᾶς ἴσα καὶ τὸ μη-
δὲν ζώσας ἐναριθμῶ.
τίς γάρ, τίς ἀνὴρ πλέον
τᾶς εὐδαιμονίας φέρει   1190
ἢ τοσοῦτον ὅσον δοκεῖν
καὶ δόξαντ' ἀποκλῖναι;
τὸν σόν τοι παράδειγμ' ἔχων,
τὸν σὸν δαίμονα, τὸν σόν, ὦ
τλᾶμον Οἰδιπόδα, βροτῶν   1195
οὐδὲν μακαρίζω·

ὅστις καθ' ὑπερβολὰν ἀντ. α
τοξεύσας ἐκράτησας οὐ
πάντ' εὐδαίμονος ὄλβου,
ὦ Ζεῦ, κατὰ μὲν φθίσας
τὰν γαμψώνυχα παρθένον
χρησμῳδόν, θανάτων δ' ἐμᾷ   1200
χώρᾳ πύργος ἀνέστας·
ἐξ οὗ καὶ βασιλεὺς καλῇ
ἐμὸς καὶ τὰ μέγιστ' ἐτι-
μάθης ταῖς μεγάλαισιν ἐν
Θήβαισιν ἀνάσσων.

τανῦν δ' ἀκούειν τίς ἀθλιώτερος; στρ. β
τίς †ἐν πόνοις, τίς ἄταις ἀγρίαις†   1205
ξύνοικος ἀλλαγᾷ βίου;
ἰὼ κλεινὸν Οἰδίπου κάρα,
ᾧ μέγας λιμὴν
αὑτὸς ἤρκεσεν
παιδὶ καὶ πατρὶ
θαλαμηπόλῳ πεσεῖν,   1210

ΟΙΔΙΠΟΥΣ ΤΥΡΑΝΝΟΣ 49

πῶς ποτε πῶς ποθ' αἱ πατρῷ-
αί σ' ἄλοκες φέρειν, τάλας,
σῖγ' ἐδυνάθησαν ἐς τοσόνδε;

ἐφηῦρέ σ' ἄκονθ' ὁ πάνθ' ὁρῶν χρόνος·   ἀντ. β
δικάζει τὸν ἄγαμον γάμον πάλαι
τεκνοῦντα καὶ τεκνούμενον.   1215
ἰώ, Λαΐειον ⟨ὢ⟩ τέκνον·
εἴθε σ' εἴθ' σε
μήποτ' εἰδόμαν·
ὡς ὀδύρομαι
περίαλλ' ἰὰν χέων
ἐκ στομάτων. τὸ δ' ὀρθὸν εἰ-   1220
πεῖν, ἀνέπνευσά τ' ἐκ σέθεν
καὶ κατεκοίμησα τοὐμὸν ὄμμα.

[Enter a messenger from the palace.]
ΕΞΑΓΓΕΛΟΣ
ὦ γῆς μέγιστα τῆσδ' ἀεὶ τιμώμενοι,
οἷ' ἔργ' ἀκούσεσθ', οἷα δ' εἰσόψεσθ', ὅσον δ'
ἀρεῖσθε πένθος, εἴπερ εὐγενῶς ἔτι   1225
τῶν Λαβδακείων ἐντρέπεσθε δωμάτων.
οἶμαι γὰρ οὔτ' ἂν Ἴστρον οὔτε Φᾶσιν ἂν
νίψαι καθαρμῷ τήνδε τὴν στέγην, ὅσα
κεύθει, τὰ δ' αὐτίκ' εἰς τὸ φῶς φανεῖ κακὰ
ἑκόντα κοὐκ ἄκοντα· τῶν δὲ πημονῶν   1230
μάλιστα λυποῦσ' αἳ φανῶσ' αὐθαίρετοι.
ΧΟ. λείπει μὲν οὐδ' ἃ πρόσθεν ᾔδεμεν τὸ μὴ οὐ
βαρύστον' εἶναι· πρὸς δ' ἐκείνοισιν τί φής;
ΕΞ. ὁ μὲν τάχιστος τῶν λόγων εἰπεῖν τε καὶ
μαθεῖν, τέθνηκε θεῖον Ἰοκάστης κάρα.   1235
ΧΟ. ὦ δυστάλαινα, πρὸς τίνος ποτ' αἰτίας;
ΕΞ. αὐτὴ πρὸς αὑτῆς. τῶν δὲ πραχθέντων τὰ μὲν
ἄλγιστ' ἄπεστιν· ἡ γὰρ ὄψις οὐ πάρα.
ὅμως δ', ὅσον γε κἀν ἐμοὶ μνήμης ἔνι,
πεύσῃ τὰ κείνης ἀθλίας παθήματα.   1240

ΣΟΦΟΚΛΕΟΥΣ

ὅπως γὰρ ὀργῇ χρωμένη παρῆλθ' ἔσω
θυρῶνος, ἵετ' εὐθὺ πρὸς τὰ νυμφικὰ
λέχη, κόμην σπῶσ' ἀμφιδεξίοις ἀκμαῖς.
πύλας δ' ὅπως εἰσῆλθ' ἐπιρράξασ' ἔσω,
καλεῖ τὸν ἤδη Λάϊον πάλαι νεκρόν,   1245
μνήμην παλαιῶν σπερμάτων ἔχουσ', ὑφ' ὧν
θάνοι μὲν αὐτός, τὴν δὲ τίκτουσαν λίποι
τοῖς οἷσιν αὐτοῦ δύστεκνον παιδουργίαν·
γοᾶτο δ' εὐνάς, ἔνθα δύστηνος διπλῇ
ἐξ ἀνδρὸς ἄνδρα καὶ τέκν' ἐκ τέκνων τέκοι.   1250
χὤπως μὲν ἐκ τῶνδ' οὐκέτ' οἶδ' ἀπόλλυται·
βοῶν γὰρ εἰσέπαισεν Οἰδίπους, ὑφ' οὗ
οὐκ ἦν τὸ κείνης ἐκθεάσασθαι κακόν,
ἀλλ' εἰς ἐκεῖνον περιπολοῦντ' ἐλεύσσομεν·
φοιτᾷ γὰρ ἡμᾶς ἔγχος ἐξαιτῶν πορεῖν,   1255
γυναῖκά τ' οὐ γυναῖκα, μητρῴαν δ' ὅπου
κίχοι διπλῆν ἄρουραν οὗ τε καὶ τέκνων.
λυσσῶντι δ' αὐτῷ δαιμόνων δείκνυσί τις·
οὐδεὶς γὰρ ἀνδρῶν, οἳ παρῆμεν ἐγγύθεν.
δεινὸν δ' ἀύσας, ὡς ὑφ' ἡγητοῦ τινος   1260
πύλαις διπλαῖς ἐνήλατ', ἐκ δὲ πυθμένων
ἔκλινε κοῖλα κλῇθρα κἀμπίπτει στέγῃ.
οὗ δὴ κρεμαστὴν τὴν γυναῖκ' ἐσείδομεν,
πλεκταῖσιν αἰωραῖσιν ἐμπεπλεγμένην·
ὁ δ' ὡς ὁρᾷ νιν, δεινὰ βρυχηθεὶς τάλας,   1265
χαλᾷ κρεμαστὴν ἀρτάνην· ἐπεὶ δὲ γῇ
ἔκειτο τλήμων, δεινά γ' ἦν τἀνθένδ' ὁρᾶν.
ἀποσπάσας γὰρ εἱμάτων χρυσηλάτους
περόνας ἀπ' αὐτῆς, αἷσιν ἐξεστέλλετο,
ἄρας ἔπαισεν ἄρθρα τῶν αὑτοῦ κύκλων,   1270
αὐδῶν τοιαῦθ', ὁθούνεκ' οὐκ ὄψοιντό νιν
οὔθ' οἷ' ἔπασχεν οὔθ' ὁποῖ' ἔδρα κακά,
ἀλλ' ἐν σκότῳ τὸ λοιπὸν οὓς μὲν οὐκ ἔδει
ὀψοίαθ', οὓς δ' ἔχρῃζεν οὐ γνωσοίατο.
τοιαῦτ' ἐφυμνῶν πολλάκις τε κοὐχ ἅπαξ   1275
ἤρασσ' ἐπαίρων βλέφαρα· φοίνιαι δ' ὁμοῦ

ΟΙΔΙΠΟΥΣ ΤΥΡΑΝΝΟΣ 51

γλῆναι γένει· ἔτεγγον, οὐδ' ἀνίεσαν
[φόνου μυδώσας σταγόνας, ἀλλ' ὁμοῦ μέλας
ὄμβρος χαλάζης αἱματοῦς ἐτέγγετο.]
τάδ' ἐκ δυοῖν ἔρρωγεν †οὐ μόνου κακά,† 1280
ἀλλ' ἀνδρὶ καὶ γυναικὶ συμμιγῆ κακά.
ὁ πρὶν παλαιὸς δ' ὄλβος ἦν πάροιθε μὲν
ὄλβος δικαίως· νῦν δὲ τῇδε θἠμέρᾳ
στεναγμός, ἄτη, θάνατος, αἰσχύνη, κακῶν
ὅσ' ἐστὶ πάντων ὀνόματ', οὐδέν ἐστ' ἀπόν. 1285
ΧΟ. νῦν δ' ἔσθ' ὁ τλήμων ἔν τινι σχολῇ κακοῦ;
ΕΞ. βοᾷ διοίγειν κλῇθρα καὶ δηλοῦν τινα
τοῖς πᾶσι Καδμείοισι τὸν πατροκτόνον,
τὸν μητρὸς—αὐδῶν ἀνόσι' οὐδὲ ῥητά μοι,
ὡς ἐκ χθονὸς ῥίψων ἑαυτόν, οὐδ' ἔτι 1290
μενῶν δόμοις ἀραῖος ὡς ἠράσατο.
ῥώμης γε μέντοι καὶ προηγητοῦ τινος
δεῖται· τὸ γὰρ νόσημα μεῖζον ἢ φέρειν.
δείξει δὲ καὶ σοί· κλῇθρα γὰρ πυλῶν τάδε
διοίγεται· θέαμα δ' εἰσόψει τάχα 1295
τοιοῦτον οἷον καὶ στυγοῦντ' ἐποικτίσαι.

[Enter O from the palace.]

ΧΟ. ὢ δεινὸν ἰδεῖν πάθος ἀνθρώποις,
ὢ δεινότατον πάντων ὅσ' ἐγὼ
προσέκυρσ' ἤδη· τίς σ', ὢ τλῆμον,
προσέβη μανία; τίς ὁ πηδήσας 1300
μείζονα δαίμων τῶν μακίστων
πρὸς σῇ δυσδαίμονι μοίρᾳ;
φεῦ φεῦ, δύστην·,' ἀλλ' οὐδ' ἐσιδεῖν
δύναμαί σ', ἐθέλων πόλλ' ἀνερέσθαι,
πολλὰ πυθέσθαι, πολλὰ δ' ἀθρῆσαι· 1305
τοίαν φρίκην παρέχεις μοι.

ΟΙ. αἰαῖ, αἰαῖ, δύστανος ἐγώ,
ποῖ γᾶς φέρομαι τλάμων; πᾶ μοι

ΣΟΦΟΚΛΕΟΥΣ

φθογγὰ διαπωτᾶται φοράδαν; 1310
ἰὼ δαῖμον, ἵν' ἐξήλου.
ΧΟ. ἐς δεινόν, οὐδ' ἀκουστόν, οὐδ' ἐπόψιμον.

ΟΙ. ἰὼ σκότου   στρ. α
νέφος ἐμὸν ἀπότροπον, ἐπιπλόμενον ἄφατον,
ἀδάματόν τε καὶ δυσούριστόν ⟨ὄν⟩. 1315
οἴμοι,
οἴμοι μάλ' αὖθις· οἷον εἰσέδυ μ' ἅμα
κέντρων τε τῶνδ' οἴστρημα καὶ μνήμη κακῶν.
ΧΟ. καὶ θαῦμά γ' οὐδὲν ἐν τοσοῖσδε πήμασιν
διπλᾶ σε πενθεῖν καὶ διπλᾶ θροεῖν κακά. 1320

ΟΙ. ἰὼ φίλος,   ἀντ. α
σὺ μὲν ἐμὸς ἐπίπολος ἔτι μόνιμος· ἔτι γὰρ
ὑπομένεις με τὸν τυφλὸν κηδεύων.
φεῦ φεῦ,
οὐ γάρ με λήθεις, ἀλλὰ γιγνώσκω σαφῶς, 1325
καίπερ σκοτεινός, τήν γε σὴν αὐδὴν ὅμως.
ΧΟ. ὦ δεινὰ δράσας, πῶς ἔτλης τοιαῦτα σὰς
ὄψεις μαρᾶναι; τίς σ' ἐπῆρε δαιμόνων;

ΟΙ. Ἀπόλλων τάδ' ἦν, Ἀπόλλων, φίλοι, στρ. β
ὁ κακὰ κακὰ τελῶν ἐμὰ τάδ' ἐμὰ πάθεα. 1330
ἔπαισε δ' αὐτόχειρ νιν οὔ-
τις ἀλλ' ἐγὼ τλάμων.
τί γὰρ ἔδει μ' ὁρᾶν,
ὅτῳ γ' ὁρῶντι μηδὲν ἦν ἰδεῖν γλυκύ; 1335
ΧΟ. ἦν τᾷδ' ὅπωσπερ καὶ σὺ φῄς.
ΟΙ. τί δῆτ' ἐμοὶ βλεπτὸν ἢ
στερκτὸν ἢ προσήγορον
ἔτ' ἔστ' ἀκούειν ἡδονᾷ, φίλοι;
ἀπάγετ' ἐκτόπιον ὅτι τάχιστά με, 1340
ἀπάγετ', ὦ φίλοι, τὸν μέγ' ὀλέθριον,
τὸν καταρατότατον, ἔτι δὲ καὶ θεοῖς 1345
ἐχθρότατον βροτῶν.

ΟΙΔΙΠΟΥΣ ΤΥΡΑΝΝΟΣ 53

ΧΟ. δείλαιε τοῦ νοῦ τῆς τε συμφορᾶς ἴσον,
ὥς σ' ἠθέλησα μηδαμὰ γνῶναί ποτ' ἄν.

ΟΙ. ὄλοιθ' ὅστις ἦν ὃς ἀγρίας πέδας   ἀντ. β
νομὰς ἐπιποδίας μ'ἔλαβε ἀπό τε φόνου ⟨μ'⟩   1350
ἔρυτο κἀνέσωσεν, οὐ-
δὲν εἰς χάριν πράσσων.
τότε γὰρ ἂν θανὼν
οὐκ ἦ φίλοισιν οὐδ' ἐμοὶ τοσόνδ' ἄχος.   1355
ΧΟ. θέλοντι κἀμοὶ τοῦτ' ἂν ἦν.
ΟΙ. οὔκουν πατρός γ' ἂν φονεὺς
ἦλθον, οὐδὲ νυμφίος
βροτοῖς ἐκλήθην ὧν ἔφυν ἄπο.
νῦν δ' ἄθεος μέν εἰμ', ἀνοσίων δὲ παῖς,   1360
ὁμογενὴς δ' ἀφ' ὧν αὐτὸς ἔφυν τάλας.
εἰ δέ τι πρεσβύτερον ἔτι κακοῦ κακόν,   1365
τοῦτ' ἔλαχ' Οἰδίπους.
ΧΟ. οὐκ οἶδ' ὅπως σε φῶ βεβουλεῦσθαι καλῶς.
κρείσσων γὰρ ἦσθα μηκέτ' ὢν ἢ ζῶν τυφλός.

ΟΙ. ὡς μὲν τάδ' οὐχ ὧδ' ἔστ' ἄριστ' εἰργασμένα,
μή μ' ἐκδίδασκε, μηδὲ συμβούλευ' ἔτι.   1370
ἐγὼ γὰρ οὐκ οἶδ' ὄμμασιν ποίοις βλέπων
πατέρα ποτ' ἂν προσεῖδον εἰς Ἅιδου μολών,
οὐδ' αὖ τάλαιναν μητέρ', οἷν ἐμοὶ δυοῖν
ἔργ' ἐστὶ κρείσσον' ἀγχόνης εἰργασμένα.
ἀλλ' ἡ τέκνων δῆτ' ὄψις ἦν ἐφίμερος,   1375
βλαστοῦσ' ὅπως ἔβλαστε, προσλεύσσειν ἐμοί;
οὐ δῆτα τοῖς γ' ἐμοῖσιν ὀφθαλμοῖς ποτε·
οὐδ' ἄστυ γ', οὐδὲ πύργος, οὐδὲ δαιμόνων
ἀγάλμαθ' ἱερά θ' ὧν ὁ παντλήμων ἐγὼ
κάλλιστ' ἀνὴρ εἷς ἕν γε ταῖς Θήβαις τραφεὶς   1380
ἀπεστέρησ' ἐμαυτόν, αὐτὸς ἐννέπων
ὠθεῖν ἅπαντας τὸν ἀσεβῆ, τὸν ἐκ θεῶν
φανέντ' ἄναγνον καὶ γένους τοῦ Λαΐου.
τοιάνδ' ἐγὼ κηλῖδα μηνύσας ἐμὴν

54 ΣΟΦΟΚΛΕΟΥΣ

ὀρθοῖς ἔμελλον ὄμμασιν τούτους ὁρᾶν; 1385
ἥκιστά γ'· ἀλλ' εἰ τῆς ἀκουούσης ἔτ' ἦν
πηγῆς δι' ὤτων φραγμός, οὐκ ἂν ἐσχόμην
τὸ μὴ ἀποκλῆσαι τοὐμὸν ἄθλιον δέμας,
ἵν' ἦ τυφλός τε καὶ κλύων μηδέν· τὸ γὰρ
τὴν φροντίδ' ἔξω τῶν κακῶν οἰκεῖν γλυκύ. 1390
ἰὼ Κιθαιρών, τί μ' ἐδέχου; τί μ' οὐ λαβὼν
ἔκτεινας εὐθύς, ὡς ἔδειξα μήποτε
ἐμαυτὸν ἀνθρώποισιν ἔνθεν ἦ γεγώς;
ὢ Πόλυβε καὶ Κόρινθε καὶ τὰ πάτρια
λόγῳ παλαιὰ δώμαθ', οἷον ἆρά με 1395
κάλλος κακῶν ὕπουλον ἐξεθρέψατε·
νῦν γὰρ κακός τ' ὢν κἀκ κακῶν εὑρίσκομαι.
ὢ τρεῖς κέλευθοι καὶ κεκρυμμένη νάπη,
δρυμός τε καὶ στενωπὸς ἐν τριπλαῖς ὁδοῖς,
αἳ τοὐμὸν αἷμα τῶν ἐμῶν χειρῶν ἄπο 1400
ἐπίετε πατρός, ἆρά μου μέμνησθ' ἔτι
οἷ' ἔργα δράσας ὑμὶν εἶτα δεῦρ' ἰὼν
ὁποῖ' ἔπρασσον αὖθις; ὢ γάμοι, γάμοι,
ἐφύσαθ' ἡμᾶς, καὶ φυτεύσαντες πάλιν
ἀνεῖτε ταὐτὸν σπέρμα, κἀπεδείξατε 1405
πατέρας ἀδελφούς, παῖδας αἷμ' ἐμφύλιον,
νύμφας γυναῖκας μητέρας τε, χὠπόσα
αἴσχιστ' ἐν ἀνθρώποισιν ἔργα γίγνεται.
ἀλλ', οὐ γὰρ αὐδᾶν ἔσθ' ἃ μηδὲ δρᾶν καλόν,
ὅπως τάχιστα, πρὸς θεῶν, ἔξω μέ που 1410
καλύψατ', ἢ φονεύσατ', ἢ θαλάσσιον
ἐκρίψατ', ἔνθα μήποτ' εἰσόψεσθ' ἔτι.
ἴτ', ἀξιώσατ' ἀνδρὸς ἀθλίου θιγεῖν·
πίθεσθε, μὴ δείσητε· τἀμὰ γὰρ κακὰ
οὐδεὶς οἷός τε πλὴν ἐμοῦ φέρειν βροτῶν. 1415
ΧΟ. ἀλλ' ὧν ἐπαιτεῖς ἐς δέον πάρεσθ' ὅδε
Κρέων τὸ πράσσειν καὶ τὸ βουλεύειν, ἐπεὶ
χώρας λέλειπται μοῦνος ἀντὶ σοῦ φύλαξ.
ΟΙ. οἴμοι, τί δῆτα λέξομεν πρὸς τόνδ' ἔπος;
τίς μοι φανεῖται πίστις ἔνδικος; τὰ γὰρ 1420

ΟΙΔΙΠΟΥΣ ΤΥΡΑΝΝΟΣ 55

πάρος πρὸς αὐτὸν πάντ' ἐφεύρημαι κακός.
[Enter Kreon from the city.]
ΚΡ. οὔθ' ὡς γελαστής, Οἰδίπους, ἐλήλυθα,
οὔθ' ὡς ὀνειδιῶν τι τῶν πάρος κακῶν.
ἀλλ' εἰ τὰ θνητῶν μὴ καταισχύνεσθ' ἔτι
γένεθλα, τὴν γοῦν πάντα βόσκουσαν φλόγα   1425
αἰδεῖσθ' ἄνακτος Ἡλίου τοιόνδ' ἄγος
ἀκάλυπτον οὕτω δεικνύναι, τὸ μήτε γῆ
μήτ' ὄμβρος ἱερὸς μήτε φῶς προσδέξεται.
ἀλλ' ὡς τάχιστ' ἐς οἶκον ἐσκομίζετε·
τοῖς ἐν γένει γὰρ τἀγγενῆ μόνοις θ' ὁρᾶν   1430
μόνοις τ' ἀκούειν εὐσεβῶς ἔχει κακά.
ΟΙ. πρὸς θεῶν, ἐπείπερ ἐλπίδος μ' ἀπέσπασας,
ἄριστος ἐλθὼν πρὸς κάκιστον ἄνδρ' ἐμέ,
πιθοῦ τί μοι· πρὸς σοῦ γάρ, οὐδ' ἐμοῦ, φράσω.
ΚΡ. καὶ τοῦ με χρείας ὧδε λιπαρεῖς τυχεῖν;   1435
ΟΙ. ῥῖψόν με γῆς ἐκ τῆσδ' ὅσον τάχισθ', ὅπου
θνητῶν φανοῦμαι μηδενὸς προσήγορος.
ΚΡ. ἔδρασ' ἄν, εὖ τοῦτ' ἴσθ', ἄν, εἰ μὴ τοῦ θεοῦ
πρώτιστ' ἔχρῃζον ἐκμαθεῖν τί πρακτέον.
ΟΙ. ἀλλ' ἥ γ' ἐκείνου πᾶσ' ἐδηλώθη φάτις,   1440
τὸν πατροφόντην, τὸν ἀσεβῆ μ' ἀπολλύναι.
ΚΡ. οὕτως ἐλέχθη ταῦθ'· ὅμως δ', ἵν' ἕσταμεν
χρείας, ἄμεινον ἐκμαθεῖν τί δραστέον.
ΟΙ. οὕτως ἄρ' ἀνδρὸς ἀθλίου πεύσεσθ' ὕπερ;
ΚΡ. καὶ γὰρ σὺ νῦν γ' ἂν τῷ θεῷ πίστιν φέροις.   1445
ΟΙ. καὶ σοί γ' ἐπισκήπτω τε καὶ προτρέψομαι·
τῆς μὲν κατ' οἴκους αὐτὸς ὃν θέλεις τάφον
θοῦ· καὶ γὰρ ὀρθῶς τῶν γε σῶν τελεῖς ὕπερ·
ἐμοῦ δὲ μήποτ' ἀξιωθήτω τόδε
πατρῷον ἄστυ ζῶντος οἰκητοῦ τυχεῖν·   1450
ἀλλ' ἔα με ναίειν ὄρεσιν, ἔνθα κλῄζεται
οὑμὸς Κιθαιρὼν οὗτος, ὃν μήτηρ τέ μοι
πατήρ τ' ἐθέσθην ζῶντε κύριον τάφον,
ἵν' ἐξ ἐκείνων οἵ μ' ἀπωλλύτην, θάνω.
καίτοι τοσοῦτόν γ' οἶδα, μήτε μ' ἂν νόσον   1455

μήτ' ἄλλο πέρσαι μηδέν· οὐ γὰρ ἄν ποτε
θνῄσκων ἐσώθην, μὴ 'πί τῳ δεινῷ κακῷ.
ἀλλ' ἡ μὲν ἡμῶν μοῖρ' ὅποιπερ εἶσ' ἴτω·
παίδων δὲ τῶν μὲν ἀρσένων μή μοι, Κρέων,
προσθῇ μέριμναν· ἄνδρες εἰσίν, ὥστε μὴ 1460
σπάνιν ποτὲ σχεῖν, ἔνθ' ἄν ὦσι, τοῦ βίου·
ταῖν δ' ἀθλίαιν οἰκτραῖν τε παρθένοιν ἐμαῖν,
αἷν οὔποθ' ἡμὴ χωρὶς ἐστάθη βορᾶς
τράπεζ' ἄνευ τοῦδ' ἀνδρός, ἀλλ' ὅσων ἐγὼ
ψαύοιμι, πάντων τῶδ' ἀεὶ μετειχέτην· 1465
αἷν μοι μέλεσθαι· καὶ μάλιστα μὲν χεροῖν
ψαῦσαί μ' ἔασον κἀποκλαύσασθαι κακά.
ἴθ', ὦναξ,
ἴθ', ὦ γονῇ γενναῖε· χερσί τἄν θιγὼν
δοκοῖμ' ἔχειν σφᾶς, ὥσπερ ἡνίκ' ἔβλεπον. 1470
[Enter attendant, bringing Antigone and Ismene.]
τί φημι;
οὐ δὴ κλύω που, πρὸς θεῶν, τοῖν μοι φίλοιν
δακρυρροούντοιν, καί μ' ἐποικτίρας Κρέων
ἔπεμψέ μοι τὰ φίλτατ' ἐγγόνοιν ἐμοῖν;
λέγω τι; 1475
ΚΡ. λέγεις· ἐγὼ γάρ εἰμ' ὁ πορσύνας τάδε,
γνοὺς τὴν παροῦσαν τέρψιν ἥ σ' εἶχεν πάλαι.
ΟΙ. ἀλλ' εὐτυχοίης, καί σε τῆσδε τῆς ὁδοῦ
δαίμων ἄμεινον ἢ 'μὲ φρουρήσας τύχοι.
ὦ τέκνα, ποῦ ποτ' ἐστέ; δεῦρ' ἴτ', ἔλθετε 1480
ὡς τὰς ἀδελφὰς τάσδε τὰς ἐμὰς χέρας,
αἳ τοῦ φυτουργοῦ πατρὸς ὑμὶν ὧδ' ὁρᾶν
τὰ πρόσθε λαμπρὰ προύξένησαν ὄμματα·
ὃς ὑμίν, ὦ τέκν', οὔθ' ὁρῶν οὔθ' ἱστορῶν,
πατὴρ ἐφάνθην ἔνθεν αὐτὸς ἠρόθην. 1485
καὶ σφὼ δακρύω, προσβλέπειν γὰρ οὐ σθένω,
νοούμενος τὰ πικρὰ τοῦ λοιποῦ βίου,
οἷον βιῶναι σφὼ πρὸς ἀνθρώπων χρεών.
ποίας γὰρ ἀστῶν ἥξετ' εἰς ὁμιλίας,
ποίας δ' ἑορτάς, ἔνθεν οὐ κεκλαυμέναι 1490

ΟΙΔΙΠΟΥΣ ΤΥΡΑΝΝΟΣ

πρὸς οἶκον ἵξεσθ' ἀντὶ τῆς θεωρίας;
ἀλλ' ἡνίκ' ἂν δὴ πρὸς γάμων ἥκητ' ἀκμάς,
τίς οὗτος ἔσται; τίς παραρρίψει, τέκνα,
τοιαῦτ' ὀνείδη λαμβάνων ἃ †τοῖς ἐμοῖς†
γονεῦσιν ἔσται σφῷν θ' ὁμοῦ δηλήματα; 1495
τί γὰρ κακῶν ἄπεστι; τὸν πατέρα πατὴρ
ὑμῶν ἔπεφνεν· τὴν τεκοῦσαν ἤροσεν,
ὅθεν περ αὐτὸς ἐσπάρη, κἀκ τῶν ἴσων
ἐκτήσαθ' ὑμᾶς, ὧνπερ αὐτὸς ἐξέφυ.
τοιαῦτ' ὀνειδιεῖσθε. κᾆτα τίς γαμεῖ; 1500
οὐκ ἔστιν οὐδείς, ὦ τέκν', ἀλλὰ δηλαδὴ
χέρσους φθαρῆναι κἀγάμους ὑμᾶς χρεών.
ὦ παῖ Μενοικέως, ἀλλ' ἐπεὶ μόνος πατὴρ
ταύταιν λέλειψαι (νὼ γάρ, ὣ 'φυτεύσαμεν,
ὀλώλαμεν δύ' ὄντε) μή σφε περιίδῃς 1505
πτωχὰς ἀνάνδρους ἐγγενεῖς ἀλωμένας,
μηδ' ἐξισώσῃς τάσδε τοῖς ἐμοῖς κακοῖς.
ἀλλ' οἴκτισόν σφας, ὧδε τηλικάσδ' ὁρῶν
πάντων ἐρήμους, πλὴν ὅσον τὸ σὸν μέρος.
ξύννευσον, ὦ γενναῖε, σῇ ψαύσας χερί. 1510
   σφῷν δ', ὦ τέκν', εἰ μὲν εἰχέτην ἤδη φρένας,
πόλλ' ἂν παρῄνουν· νῦν δὲ τοῦτ' εὔχεσθέ μοι,
οὗ καιρὸς ἐᾷ ζῆν, τοῦ βίου δὲ λῴονος
ὑμᾶς κυρῆσαι τοῦ φυτεύσαντος πατρός.
ΚΡ. ἅλις ἵν' ἐξήκεις δακρύων· ἀλλ' ἴθι στέγης ἔσω. 1515
ΟΙ. πειστέον, κεἰ μηδὲν ἡδύ.
ΚΡ.   πάντα γὰρ καιρῷ καλά.
ΟΙ. οἶσθ' ἐφ' οἷς οὖν εἶμι;
ΚΡ.   λέξεις, καὶ τότ' εἴσομαι
κλύων.
ΟΙ. γῆς μ' ὅπως πέμψεις ἄποικον.
ΚΡ.   τοῦ θεοῦ μ' αἰτεῖς δόσιν.
ΟΙ. ἀλλὰ θεοῖς γ' ἔχθιστος ἥκω.
ΚΡ.   τοιγαροῦν τεύξῃ τάχα.
ΟΙ. φῂς τάδ' οὖν; 1520
ΚΡ.   ἃ μὴ φρονῶ γὰρ οὐ φιλῶ λέγειν μάτην.

ΟΙ. ἄπαγέ νύν μ' ἐντεῦθεν ἤδη.
ΚΡ. στεῖχέ νυν, τέκνων δ' ἀφοῦ.
ΟΙ. μηδαμῶς ταύτας γ' ἕλῃ μου.
ΚΡ. πάντα μὴ βούλου κρατεῖν·
καὶ γὰρ ἀκράτησας οὔ σοι τῷ βίῳ ξυνέσπετο.
[Exeunt attendant leading O into the palace; Kreon, the messenger and the rest to the city.]

ΧΟ. ὦ πάτρας Θήβης ἔνοικοι, λεύσσετ', Οἰδίπους ὅδε,
ὃς τὰ κλείν' αἰνίγματ' ᾔδει καὶ κράτιστος ἦν ἀνήρ, 1525
οὗ τίς οὐ ζήλῳ πολιτῶν ταῖς τύχαις ἐπέβλεπεν·
εἰς ὅσον κλύδωνα δεινῆς συμφορᾶς ἐλήλυθεν,
ὥστε θνητὸν ὄντ' ἐκείνην τὴν τελευταίαν ἔδει
ἡμέραν ἐπισκοποῦντα μηδέν' ὀλβίζειν, πρὶν ἂν
τέρμα τοῦ βίου περάσῃ μηδὲν ἀλγεινὸν παθών.

OIDIPOUS TYRANNOS
COMMENTARY

NOTE: The Preface, List of Abbreviations and Introduction are all to be found in the first volume (Text).

1-150: Prologue. *A group of children, youths and old men have assembled in a position of supplication (seated, and carrying olive or laurel boughs tied with strips of wool) outside O's palace. When questioned by the king, an old priest of Zeus explains that they seek his aid against the plague. O replies that he has already sent Kreon to Delphi to seek advice, and at this moment Kreon returns and reports the oracle's command that the murderers of Laios be discovered and exiled. O begins to ask questions about the case, ending with a vow to find and punish the killer.*

Meter: iambic trimeter (see Introduction pp. 3-4)

1   Κάδμου τοῦ πάλαι νέα τροφή: "the young offspring of ancient Kadmos," the mythical founder of Thebes.
2   ποθ' = ποτε (*elision*), intensifying the question.
     μοι: with a question, command or statement often indicates an interested party ("dative of feeling," S 1486) and may be left untranslated.
     θοάζετε: "sit" (in this meaning only here, but cf. θῶκος); ἕδρας is cognate accusative (S 1567), "what ever seats here (τάσδε) are you sitting?" = "*why* are you sitting here...?"
3   κλάδοισιν: -οισι and -αισι are poetic forms of the regular Attic dat. plural.
     ἐξεστεμμένοι: perf. pass. partic. < ἐκστέφω. "Garlanded with suppliant branches" must be condensed for "carrying in your hands garlanded branches of supplication." For the olive or laurel boughs, tied with strips of wool, which suppliants usually carried, see J. Gould, "Hiketeia," *Journal of Hellenic Studies* 93 (1973) 74-103.
4   πόλις: as often in poetry, noun without article (S 1104).
4-5 ὁμοῦ μὲν...ὁμοῦ δέ: *Anaphora* (emphatic repetition of the first word in the clause) marks a series of parallel expressions, so that μέν/δέ = "not only...but also" (S 2906, cf. 219 below).

	θυμιαμάτων... παιάνων... στεναγμάτων: with γέμει as a "verb of filling" (S 1369). "Paeans" here are not hymns of celebration, but invocations of any sort to Παιάν, a healing god associated with Apollo.
6	**ἀγώ** = ἃ ἐγώ (*crasis*).
	δικαιῶν: pres. partic. masc. nom. sg. < δικαιόω.
6-7	**μὴ παρ' ἀγγέλων...ἄλλων**: "not from others, i.e., messengers" (S 1272).
7	**ὧδ'** = δεῦρο, "hither" (LSJ ὧδε II.1).
	ἐλήλυθα < ἔρχομαι.
8	**πᾶσι**: with κλεινός, "famed among all," rather than καλούμενος (dat. of agent with passives other than the perfect is rare, S 1490).
9	**ἀλλ', ὦ γεραιέ, φράζ'**: ἀλλά prepares for the opening of an address, "well" (*GP* 18).
	ἔφυς: intransitive 2 aor. < φύω ("you were born as" here = "you *are by nature*").
10	**τῶνδε**: used often in this scene (32, 78, 91, 93) to denote the suppliants on stage.
	τίνι τρόπῳ...δείσαντες ἢ στέρξαντες: dat. of manner, explained by the participles : "in what frame of mind are you here—fear or entreaty?" For στέργω = "entreat" see LSJ στέργω IV. See further "Textual Notes" in Vol. 1.
	καθέστατε: intransitive perfect of καθίστημι, "be established," "be in a state of ...," "*be in someone's presence*" (LSJ καθίστημι B.1.b).
11-2	**ὡς θέλοντος ἂν ἐμοῦ**: ὡς with participle (S 2086a) expresses a belief on which the subject acts (here with φράζ', line 9); ἄν in a genitive absolute stands for a potential optative (S 1846b): "(speak up,) *in the assurance that* I would be willing to provide every assistance."
13	**μὴ οὐ κατοικτίρων**: conditional participle, with μὴ οὐ following a negatived expression (cf. 22 below and S 2750; here the δυσ- in δυσάλγητος is virtually a negative): "for I would be unfeeling, if I should not..."
14	**ἀλλ', ὦ...**: See on 9.
15-20	**ὁρᾷς μὲν ἡμᾶς...τὸ δ' ἄλλο φῦλον...θακεῖ**: "(Here) you see us...while the rest of the nation sit (elsewhere)..." This is the basic contrast of the sentence, but it contains other substructures within it: in the first limb ἡλίκοι introduces an enumeration (with μέν/δέ/δέ) of the three age-groups now

COMMENTARY

seen by O (in the second of these the speaker mentions himself); the second limb lists three different places (the agora, the temple of Athena, and of Apollo Ismenios) where other suppliants sit. A diagram can clarify the nested structures:

ὁρᾷς μὲν...ἡλίκοι προσήμεθα
  -οἱ μὲν οὐδέπω μακρὰν πτέσθαι σθένοντες
  -οἱ δὲ σὺν γήρᾳ βαρεῖς
    (ἱερεὺς ἐγὼ μὲν Ζηνός)
  -οἱ δ' ἔτ' ἠθέων λεκτοί·
τὸ δ' ἄλλο φῦλον...θακεῖ
  -ἀγοραῖσι
  -πρός τε Παλλάδος διπλοῖς ναοῖς
  -ἐπ' Ἰσμηνοῦ τε μαντείᾳ σποδῷ.

Despite the presence of three age-groups, both the priest and O consistently call them children (παῖδες 32, 58, 142, 147; τέκνα 1, 6).

15   **ὁρᾷς μὲν ἡμᾶς ἡλίκοι προσήμεθα**: indirect question with relative (S 2668), "you see *how old we are who* sit..." The subject of the indirect question is often placed first, as the object of the main verb (S 2182).

16   **μακράν**: "far" (an adverb as in 220, S 1029).

17   **πτέσθαι**: 2 aor. infin. < πέτομαι.
    σὺν γήρᾳ: with βαρεῖς = simple dative (S 1511).

18   **ἐγὼ μέν**: "I, *at any rate*..." A parenthetical remark, without answering δέ; see *GP* 381.

18-19   **οἱ δ' ἔτ' ἠθέων λεκτοί** "These are selected from those *still* young men" (contrast οὐδέπω...σθένοντες 16-17 above, and see "Textual Notes" in Vol. 1).

19   **ἐξεστεμμένον**: See on 3 above.

20-1   **ἀγοραῖσι...πρός τε...διπλοῖς ναοῖς, ἐπ'...τε...σποδῷ**: Note the variation, with three different ways (dative alone, πρός and ἐπί with dat., cf. on 477-8) to indicate location: "at the agorai (Thebes had two), the twin temples of Pallas (called Athena *Onka* in Thebes) and the prophetic ash of Ismenos (an oracle of Apollo *Ismenios*)." See further "Textual Notes" in Vol. 1.

23   **κἀνακουφίσαι** = καὶ ἀνακουφίσαι, dependent on οἵα τε, "and is no longer able to raise her bow (lit. "head")..."

24   **βυθῶν**: poetic genitive of separation (S 1395), "above the troughs of the blood-red wave."

25-6   **φθίνουσα μέν...φθίνουσα δ'**: See on 4-5.

κάλυξιν... ἀγέλαις... τόκοισι: datives of respect with φθίνουσα.

27 ἐν δ': adverbial, "and along with this..." Plague is the "fire-bearing god" because he brings fever (πυρετός).

29 μέλας: applied to Hades because he is often assumed to be invisible (ἀ-ιδεῖν); πλουτίζεται also recalls his other name, Πλούτων.

31 νυν: enclitic, not temporal but inferential: "now it was not..."

31-4 θεοῖσι... οὐκ ἰσούμενόν σ'... ἀνδρῶν δὲ πρῶτον...κρίνοντες: The contrasting causal participles are in different cases and voices (cf. S 2147h, and on lines 42-43 below): "not because you are thought equal to the gods, but because we judge you first among men..."

31-2 σ'... ἑζόμεσθ' ἐφέστιοι: "we supplicate (lit. "sit," but cf. line 2 ἕδρας, line 15 προσήμεθα) you at your hearth." The ending -μεσθα is a poetic alternative for -μεθα (1 pers. pl.).

34 δαιμόνων ξυναλλαγαῖς: "dealings with gods," objective genitive (S 1332), explained by the following relative clause. (ξυν- is old Attic for συν-; Sophocles uses both forms, often for metrical reasons.)

35 ὅς γ': i.e., "since you..." (GP 141-2).
ἐξέλυσας: "you resolved" = "you ended."
ἄστυ Καδμεῖον: accusative of motion toward without preposition (S 1588), with μολών (2 aor. partic. < βλώσκω).

36 σκληρᾶς ἀοιδοῦ δασμόν: "the tribute for the relentless songstress," i.e., the Sphinx. Sophocles never specifies the riddle that O answered to drive her away, and its contents are first given by Asklepiades of Tragilos (4th cent. B.C.), in his compilation of myths from tragedy: "There is something on earth with one voice which has two feet, four feet and three feet, and it alone, of all that moves crawling on earth or in sky or sea, changes its shape. But whenever it walks leaning on the most feet, then its limbs' swiftness is weakest." The answer is "man," who first crawls on all fours, then walks upright, and finally uses a cane. See in general Lowell Edmunds, *The Sphinx in the Oedipus Legend* (Beiträge zur klassischen Philologie vol. 127, Königstein 1981).

37 καὶ ταῦθ': adverbial, "and at that," emphasizing the concessive participle οὐδὲν ἐξειδώς (S 2083).

38 προσθήκῃ θεοῦ: causal, "with the aid (lit. "supplementary contribution") of a god."

COMMENTARY 63

39 **λέγῃ νομίζῃ θ'**: 2 sg. pass. (θ' is elided from τε), "you are said and considered to have..."
ἡμίν: a metrically convenient Sophoclean alternative for ἡμῖν.
40 **Οἰδίπου κάρα**: "head" with genitive is a frequent affectionate periphrasis for a person in tragedy (S 1293).
42 **του**: without accent = indefinite τινός.
42-3 **εἶτε...ἀκούσας εἶτ'...οἶσθα**: The verbs in the two clauses are not strictly parallel (see on 31-3, and *GP* 506).
43 **που**: "perhaps."
44-5 **ὡς...ὁρῶ**: "since I see" (ὡς is causal also in 47, 54, 56 below).
τοῖσιν ἐμπείροισι καὶ τὰς ξυμφορὰς ζώσας...μάλιστα τῶν βουλευμάτων: "(that) for the experienced, *the results of their plans* (see Jebb's appendix) are also most effective" (lit. "most alive," cf. 482). But LJ-W compare A. *Pers.* 527-8, and suggest that τὰς ξυμφορὰς...τῶν βουλευμάτων might mean rather "the bringing-together of plans [from gods and men]."
46 **ἀνόρθωσον**: aor. imperat. 2 sg. < ἀνορθόω.
46-7 **ἴθ'...ἴθ'**: "come now" (= ἴθι, imperat. 2 sg. < εἶμι), introducing the imperative. For the *anaphora* see on 4-5.
47 **εὐλαβήθηθ'**: (aor. pass. imperat. < εὐλαβέομαι) appeals to O's self-interest: his intervention will *safeguard* his past reputation (47-8) and the continued popularity of his administration (49-50).
47-9 **νῦν μὲν...ἀρχῆς δέ**: The real contrast is not between these two words, but between νῦν and the implied time (future) of μηδαμῶς μεμνήμεθα.
48 **τῆς πάρος προθυμίας**: causal genitive.
49 **ἀρχῆς δὲ τῆς σῆς**: The genitive does not depend directly on anything in the sentence, but introduces the whole topic (S 1381): "may we by no means remember *about your reign* that..."
50 **στάντες τ'...καὶ πεσόντες**: μεμνήμεθα (perf. opt. < μιμνήσκω) governs the participle as a verb of perception; it is nominative because it refers to the subject of the sentence (S 2106): "that we stood upright (i.e., prospered [at first]), but met disaster later." On τε...καί of *adversatives* see *GP* 515.
ἐς ὀρθόν: ἐς is old Attic (and a metrically convenient alternative) for εἰς.

64 OIDIPOUS TYRANNOS

51 ἀλλ': "but instead..." (contrasting with μηδαμῶς μεμνήμεθα). See also "Textual Notes" in Vol. 1.
ἀσφαλείᾳ: adverbial, "in a state of security."

52 ὄρνιθι...αἰσίῳ: modal dat., "with favorable *omen* (i.e., divine approval)."

53 τὰ νῦν: adverbial accusative (S 1611) = νῦν.
γενοῦ: aor. imperat. 2 sg., < γίγνομαι.

54 εἴπερ ἄρξεις...ὥσπερ κρατεῖς: The meanings of the two verbs are the same; the contrast is in their *tenses*.

55 ξὺν ἀνδράσιν...κενῆς: both are attributive (sc. γῆς, S 1027b): "populated...barren."

56 οὐδέν: predicative, "neither a fortress nor a ship is anything..."

57 ἀνδρῶν μὴ ξυνοικούντων ἔσω: not genitive absolute, but dependent on ἔρημος, the negation being superfluous (K-G II.214 n.1): "empty of men dwelling together in it."

60 καί: here in a contrast, "and yet..." (*GP* 292).
νοσοῦντες: concessive participle; plural according to sense, despite the following shift to οὐδείς (S 2148).

61 ἐξ ἴσου = adverb, "equally" (with ὡς ἐγώ).

62-3 εἰς ἕν' ἔρχεται μόνον καθ' αὐτόν: "affects (lit. "goes to") only one man by himself." ἕν(α) is accus. sg. < εἷς.

64 κἀμέ = καὶ ἐμέ.

65 ὕπνῳ γ' εὕδοντα· a (superfluous) dative of accompanying circumstance; cf. θεῖν δρόμῳ (S 1527b).

66-7 πολλὰ μὲν...πολλὰς δ' ὁδούς: *anaphora*; the first accusative is adverbial, "often" (S 1611), the second a cognate object (see on 2).

66 δακρύσαντα δή: The particle emphasizes the strong emotional force of the verb (*GP* 214).

68-9 ἣν...ἴασιν...ταύτην: The antecedent ἴασιν is incorporated into the relative clause (S 2536-8): "The only cure which I could find, this I carried out."

69 γάρ: explains the nature of the cure (*GP* 58), and is not to be translated.

70 γαμβρόν: "brother-in-law" (O had married Kreon's sister, Iokaste).

70-1 τὰ Πυθικά...δώμαθ': i.e., the oracle in the temple of Pythian Apollo at Delphi.

71-2 ὅ τι δρῶν ἢ τί φωνῶν: Forms of both ὅστις and τίς can introduce an indirect question (here with πύθοιθ' =

COMMENTARY 65

πύθοιτο < πυνθάνομαι): "so that he could learn *by doing or saying what* I could save..."
ῥυσαίμην: The optative stands for an original deliberative subjunctive.

73-4 μ' ἦμαρ ἤδη ξυμμετρούμενον χρόνῳ λυπεῖ: "the day, when measured with the time, already makes me uneasy" = "when I count up the days he has been gone so far, I am worried..."

74 τί πράσσει: πράττω here = "experience a certain fortune," "fare" (LSJ πράττω II). The indirect question depends on λυπεῖ (S 2669, K-G 2.517): "troubles me, *about* how he is faring."
τοῦ...εἰκότος πέρα: "beyond what is reasonable."

75 πλείω: accus. sg., with χρόνον. (For the pleonasm see K-G II.586.)

77 μὴ δρῶν: conditional, hence μή rather than οὐ.
δηλοῖ: 3 sg. *subjunctive* (ὅσ' ἄν = "whatever").

78 εἰς καλόν: applies to the coincidence of the two clauses in τε...τε, *GP* 515: "fortunately, just as you spoke, these (children) were telling me that..."
εἶπας = 2 aor.< εἶπες.

80-1 O makes a wish based on Kreon's apparently happy expression (cf. *Oid. Col.* 319-320): "may he come as bright in respect of (LSJ ἐν I.7) some saving fortune (cf. Aesch. *Ag.* 664) as he does in his face" (with ὄμματι sc. again ἐν).

82 ἀλλ' εἰκάσαι μέν: The infinitive is used absolutely to limit a statement (S 2012d): "well (see on 9), to form a guess..."
μέν = "at least," *GP* 382.
ἡδύς: i.e., with welcome news (LSJ ἡδύς II.1).

82-3 οὐ γὰρ ἄν...ὧδ' εἷρπε: contrary to fact (εἷρπε is imperf. < ἕρπω), "for (otherwise) he would not be walking this way..." On ὧδε see on 7.
κάρα πολυστεφής...δάφνης: accusative of respect and genitive of material with the adjective: "garlanded *on* his head *with* laurel." Donning a garland indicated celebration.

84 εἰσόμεσθα: fut.< οἶδα.
ξύμμετρος...ὡς κλύειν: result (ὡς = ὥστε), "at the right distance to hear us."

85 κήδευμα: "kinsman." For abstract nouns describing persons in Sophocles, see A. A. Long, *Language and Thought in Sophocles* (London 1968) 114-25.

87-8 **λέγω...εἰ τύχοι...ἂν εὐτυχεῖν**: a future less vivid condition in indirect statement (the infinitive with ἄν stands for the optative).
88 **κατ' ὀρθὸν ἐξιόντα**: "turn out straight," supplementary partic. (< ἐξέρχομαι) with τύχοι.
89 **τοὔπος** = τὸ ἔπος, referring to the oracle's answer.
90 **οὔτε...οὔτ' οὖν**: The addition of οὖν stresses the second clause (*GP* 420): "nor *for that matter*..." (For the *periphrasis* in προδείσας εἰμί see S 1961.)
91 **τῶνδε**: See on 10.
92 **ἕτοιμος**: sc. εἰμί.
 εἴτε καὶ στείχειν ἔσω: sc. ἕτοιμός εἰμι, εἰ χρῄζεις.
93 **τῶνδε**: objective genitive (S 1331) with τὸ πένθος, "grief *for* them."
93-4 **πλέον...ἢ καί**: "more than even..."
94 **πέρι**: The accent on the first syllable indicates that the preposition refers backward (*anastrophe,* S 175; cf. θεοῦ πάρα in the next line).
95 **λέγοιμ' ἄν**: The potential optative may be a weaker, less willful form of the future.
 οἵ = οἷα.
96 **ἐμφανῶς**: with ἄνωγεν, cf. on σαφῶς 106 below.
97 **μίασμα χώρας**: genitive of separation with ἐλαύνειν.
 μίασμα is the collective impurity of a whole group owing to an individual's crime: purification could be obtained in many ways (often by a religious ritual), so that O does not at first take ἐλαύνειν literally. See in general Robert Parker, *Miasma* (Oxford 1983).
 ὡς τεθραμμένον χθονί explains Apollo's grounds for the command ἐλαύνειν (see on 12-13, and ὡς...χειμάζον in 101): "inasmuch as a pollution has been nourished in this land..."
98 **ἀνήκεστον τρέφειν**: "nourish it (to be) past healing," the predicate indicates the result (*proleptic,* S 1579).
99 **τῆς ξυμφορᾶς**: "the occurrence," a euphemism for the crime which led to pollution.
100 **ἀνδρηλατοῦντας**: with ἡμᾶς 96, answering O's first question, "by driving a man into exile."
 φόνῳ φόνον: *polyptoton* (repetition of the same word in different cases, S 3028d).
101 **ὡς τόδ' αἷμα χειμάζον πόλιν**: accusative absolute (which usually needs an *impersonal* verb, but cf. S 2078); effectively answers O's second question.

COMMENTARY 67

τόδ': referring back to the notion of murder first introduced in φόνον (100).
102 μηνύει: sc. Apollo, as with ἐπιστέλλει 106) and ἔφασκε (110).
104 ἀπευθύνειν: "govern."
105 οὔ...πω: "not at all," as in 594, 1130 (rather than "not yet," see D).
106 σαφῶς: here not "clearly," but "truthfully," used especially of oracles (cf. 390, 1011, *Oid. Col.* 623, Aristoph. *Lys.* 777). In fact, the reference to *several* murderers here is neither clear nor true.
107 τοὺς αὐτοέντας...τινας: "some group of murderers." The article shows that a specific group is meant, but the indefinite pronoun adds that their identity is uncertain (K-G 1.662-3).
χειρί: "by hand" = "physically" (with τιμωρεῖν = "kill," as in 140).
108 οἱ δ': The article may have the force of a demonstrative before certain particles (S 1107).
ποῦ γῆς: partitive (S 1439a), "where *on* earth...?"
108-9 τόδ'...ἴχνος παλαιᾶς...αἰτίας: "this track of long-ago guilt" = "the track of *this* long-ago guilt" (*enallage*, a poetic figure; cf. 480 below).
109 δυστέκμαρτον: "difficult to interpret."
110-11 τὸ δὲ ζητούμενον...τἀμελούμενον: The article with participle is generic (S 1124): "whatever is looked for...whatever is neglected."
112 πότερα: like πότερον, introduces an alternative ("either/or," S 2656) question, and is best left untranslated.
'ν ἀγροῖς = ἐν ἀγροῖς (*prodelision*, occurring only in poetry, S 76).
113 συμπίπτει: present for past, as often in narrative (historical present).
114 ὡς ἔφασκεν: The subject is Laios. As LJ-W note, the verb does not necessarily imply he was not to be believed.
115 οὐκέθ' ἴκεθ', ὡς ἀπεστάλη (aor. pass. < ἀποστέλλω): "he no longer returned as he set out," i.e., "the homecoming we expected did not follow his departure." On the idiom see D.
117 ὅτου = οὗτινος (< ὅστις, here as relative pronoun), with ἐκμαθών: "from whom, if someone had learned, he could have made use (of the knowledge)." The relative pronoun is

not connected with the main verb of the clause, but governed only by the participle (S 2543, cf. 285 below).
118 **θνήσκουσι**: historical present.
γάρ: *"yes,* for..." (*GP* 73-74).
119 **ὧν εἶδε**: partitive with οὐδέν, short for τούτων ἃ εἶδε, "none of what he saw."
εἶχ': ἔχω with infin. = "be able."
120 **ἕν...μαθεῖν**: "one fact could find out how to learn many of them."
123 **κτανεῖν**: 2 aor. infin. < κτείνω.
νιν: poetic 3 pers. pronoun, accus. sg. = "him."
124 **ὁ λῃστής**: It is curious that, despite Kreon's insistence on the plural, O almost always (139, 225, 230, 236) speaks as if he is hunting for a *single* adversary. (See D, introduction p. 9.)
124-5 **εἴ τι μὴ...ἐπράσσετ' ἐνθένδ'**: The verb is passive, "unless some financial transaction were being carried out from this end," i.e., O suspects Laios' assassin was hired in Thebes.
125 **ἐς τόδ'...τόλμης**: "to such a point of daring" (S 1325).
126 **δοκοῦντα ταῦτ' ἦν**: "these things (that it was a hired assassin) were what was thought."
130 **τὸ πρὸς ποσί**: "what was at our feet" = "what was right in front of us."
131 **μεθέντας...τἀφανῆ**: aor. partic. < μεθίημι, "disregarding what was mysterious."
134 **τήνδ' ἔθεσθ' ἐπιστροφήν**: (aor. < τίθημι) "you applied this concern, *paid this attention.*"
135 **ὄψεσθε**: fut. < ὁράω.
138 **αὐτὸς αὐτοῦ**: also with ὑπέρ, "for my very own sake," a strong reflexive (S 1235; for reflexive αὑτοῦ with smooth breathing see Fraenkel on Aeschylus, *Agamemnon* 836, K-G 1.564-5).
μύσος = μίασμα (97).
139 **τάχ' ἄν**: with or without potential optative (here with repeated ἄν) = "perhaps."
142 **βάθρων**: "*from* the steps" (see on 24).
143 **ἄραντες** < αἴρω (contraction of ἀείρω).
144 **ὧδ'**: See on 7. "The people of Cadmus" will be the chorus, which will enter at 151.
145 **ὡς πᾶν ἐμοῦ δράσοντος**: See on 11-12.
147 **χάριν**: with preceding genit. = "for the sake of..."
148 **καί**: "binds the demonstrative (τῶνδε) more closely to the following words" (*GP* 307) and is not to be translated.

COMMENTARY 69

ὧν: attracted from the accusative to the genitive after τῶνδε (S 2522a), "we came for the sake of these things *which* this man now proclaims."
150 σωτήρ...παυστήριος: predicative, "*as* our savior, and destroyer of the plague."

151-215 Parodos. (See Introduction p. 2) The citizens of Thebes assemble (but without the customary anapaests as they march in, see Introd. p. 5).
What has the oracle said? We call upon Athena, Apollo and Artemis (str.-antistr. A).
The plague is horrible (str.-antistr. B).
We pray that Ares depart (str. Γ), Apollo and Artemis turn kind, and that Dionysus come to save his own city (antistr. Γ).

Note on dialect: The choral lyrics of tragedy adopt by convention Doric α for η; note in the first strophe and antistrophe ἁδυεπές (151), τᾶς, ἔβας (152) Δάλιε (154), Φήμα (158), ᾿Αθάνα (159), ἅ (= ἥ, rel. pron., 161), ἑκαβόλον (163), and ἅτας...ὑπερορνυμένας (164-5). The vocabulary and syntax are often highly stylized also, with frequent omission of articles, accumulations of adjectives, hyperbaton (dislocated word order) and apostrophe (direct address to gods or even abstract concepts).

This particular section shows in addition frequent epic forms, because its lyric meter is predominantly dactylic. It is analyzed by Dale, *Metrical Analyses* fasc. 3, pp. 270-1.

151-3 ὦ Διὸς ἁδυεπὲς φάτι...: "sweet-voiced message of Zeus, *who* (i.e., in what form) have you come *from* (see on 24) Pytho rich in gold *to* (see on 35) glorious Thebes?" Even though Apollo controls the oracle, Zeus has overall charge of human events (see Easterling on Soph. *Trachiniai* 1278), and they work in concert: cf. 499, 738, 904.
153   ἐκτέταμαι < ἐκτείνω.
       φοβερὰν φρένα: accusative of respect.
154   ἰήιε: vocative, "invoked with the cry ἰή" (cf. on 211).
       Παιάν: See on 4-5.
155-6 ἢ νέον ἢ περιτελλομέναις ὥραις πάλιν: "either new (attributive with χρέος), or again as the seasons roll around" (for the unusual dat. of time cf. Aristophanes, *Birds* 696,

Orphica fr. 127.3 Kern). I.e., "is this a repetition of Thebes' troubles (after the Sphinx and Laios' death), or a new and unrelated event?"

157 **χρέος**: here evidently = χρῆμα, with τί.
158 **κεκλόμενος**: formed as if present = κέλομαι, "calling upon." The expected main verb never materializes, since the construction changes to a command below (163-7 προφάνητε...ἔλθετε). See also "Textual Notes" in Vol. 1.
161-2 **κυκλόεντ' ἀγορᾶς θρόνον εὐκλέα**: "the glorious circular throne in the agora."
163 **προφάνητε**: aor. pass. imperative < προφαίνω, "be revealed," "*appear.*"
164-5 **προτέρας ἄτας ὑπερορνυμένας πόλει**: genit. absolute, "when an earlier doom was rushing over the city."
166 **ἐκτοπίαν**: predicative with ἠνύσατε, lit. "made the fire of disaster displaced" (i.e., banished it).
170 **στόλος**: "expedition, troop, *band*" (here of citizens).
ἔνι = ἔνεστι, "is present."
171 **ἔκγονα**: neut. pl. as substantive, "offspring."
172-3 **τόκοισιν...καμάτων ἀνέχουσι**: perhaps "women do not emerge *from* labor *with* children" (D).
173 **ἰηίων** < ἰήιος, "full of cries for healing" (see on 154 above).
175 **ἄλλον...ἄλλῳ**: "one...after another." The addition of the dative suggests *frequency* (K-G I.444); for the repetition of forms of ἄλλος cf. 184 below.
175 **ἅπερ**: adverbial = ὥσπερ.
εὔπτερον ὄρνιν: attracted into the accusative to match ἄλλον, with which it is compared (S 2465).
176 **κρεῖσσον...πυρός**: evidently "more strongly" here = "faster." Fire has many associations in poetry, including speed and death (C. H. Whitman, *Homer and the Heroic Tradition* [Cambridge, Mass. 1958] 129-145) but it may also refer to the funeral pyres, which during the plague of Athens could not burn fast enough to consume the dying (Thucydides 2.52.4).
ἀμαιμακέτου: a Homeric epithet for fire, perhaps = "irresistible."
ὄρμενον: "speeding," 2 aor. partic. < ὄρνυμι (an epic form).
177 **ἀκτὰν πρός**: *anastrophe* (see on 93-94).

COMMENTARY

ἑσπέρου θεοῦ: Hades. For the realm of the dead as located in the west see *Odyssey* 12.81, E. Vermeule *Aspects of Death in Early Greek Art and Poetry* (Berkeley 1979) 169.

179 ὧν...ἀνάριθμος: genitive with α-privative adjective (S 1428): "with an unlimited number of which (the dead)."

180 νηλέα: passive, "unpitied."

183 ἐν δ'...τ' ἔπι: both adverbial (see on 27), "and among them...and besides..."

184 ἀκτὰν παρὰ βώμιον: "beside the edge of the altar (at which the wives and mothers are suppliants)."
ἄλλοθεν ἄλλαι: "different women from different places," i.e., "everywhere" (S 1274).

185 λυγρῶν πόνων: causal genit., common with verbs of emotion (S 1405).

186 παιών: See on 4-5.
λάμπει: For the metaphor of a song "shining" see D.

187 τῶν ὕπερ: article = relative pronoun as in epic (S 1105).

188 εὐῶπα: accus. sg. < εὐώψ, "fair-faced" = "welcome to see."

190-3 Ἀρεά τε...παλίσσυτον δράμημα νωτίσαι πάτρας: The accusative and infinitive represents a wish (S 2014): "and would that Ares would retreat (lit. "turn his back") in a backward-rushing run from my homeland." δράμημα is internal accusative object of a normally intransitive verb (S 1573) usually best translated as an adverb, e.g. 264-5 τάδ'...ὑπερμαχοῦμαι "I engage in this fight," 661 ὅ τι πύματον...ὀλοίμαν "may I die in the most extreme way," 883 ὑπέροπτα...πορεύεται "behaves arrogantly."

191 ἄχαλκος ἀσπίδων: "without the bronze of shields," i.e., he kills even without war (for the genitive see on 179).

192 περιβόητος ἀντιάζων: "attacking surrounded by cries" (from his victims).

194 ἔπουρον εἶτ' ἐς: with δράμημα, "carried on the wind, either toward..."

195 Ἀμφιτρίτας: sea-nymph, wife of Poseidon (her bedchamber must be the Atlantic Ocean).

196 ἀπόξενον ὅρμων: "inhospitable to anchoring" (genitive as in 179). The Black Sea is meant, where the coastal natives were unfriendly, but whose local name *Aksaena* (="dark") was understood by Greeks as ἄξενος (sometimes euphemized to εὔξενος).

198-9 "For if the night neglects (ἀφῇ, 3 sg. aor. subj. ἀφίημι, here as if with ἐάν, S 2327a and cf. 873 below) to finish anything, the day undertakes (ἐπ'...ἔρχεται = ἐπέρχεται, *tmesis* S 1650) this." There is no obvious sign of textual corruption, but the connection of this sentence with the rest of the strophe (on Ares) has never been satisfactorily explained (D). For "day and night" as a polar expression for constant disease cf. Hesiod, *Theogony* 102-104.

200 τόν = ὅν (Ares). The article often stands for the relative pronoun in tragedy to avoid hiatus.

200-1 ⟨τᾶν⟩...ἀστραπᾶν is Doric for τῶν ἀστραπῶν.

201 κράτη: neut. pl. accus. < κράτος. Poetic plural for singular, as in 237.

202 φθίσον: aor. imperative < φθίνω.

203 Λύκει' ἄναξ: Lykeios (either "wolf-god" or "Lycian") is a cult-title of Apollo at Argos and in poetry generally.

203-4 χρυσοστρόφων...ἀγκυλᾶν: "bow-strings woven with gold."

205 θέλοιμ' ἄν: See on 95.

205-6 βέλεα...ἐνδατεῖσθαι ἀρωγὰ προσταθέντα: accus. with infin. with θέλοιμ' ἄν, the adjective being predicative: "that your arrows be distributed (apportioned) as helpers, stationed in front of us (προσταθέντα < προΐστημι, to ward off the plague)." Usually Apollo's arrows *bring* plague (*Iliad* 1.45-52).

206-7 τάς τε...αἴγλας: "the gleams," i.e., her torches (sc. again ἐνδατεῖσθαι).

208 Λύκι' ὄρεα: "the mountains of Lycia" (an uncontracted poetic form of ὄρη); usually *Apollo* is called Lycian, but for Artemis in this region see Walter Burkert, *Greek Religion* (Cambridge, Mass. 1985) 407 n.4 (LJ-W).

210 τᾶσδ' ἐπώνυμον γᾶς: "name-giver of our land." (Thebes is sometimes described as "Bacchic.")

211 εὔιον: "invoked with shouts" (< εὐοῖ, cf. on 154).

212 Μαινάδων ὁμόστολον: "amidst a *band* (see on 170) of Maenads" (lit. "madwomen," the divinely-possessed female worshippers of Dionysus).

215 'πί = ἐπί (*prodelision*, see on 112): "*against* the god dishonored among gods," i.e., Ares.

216-462 First Episode. (See Introduction p. 2) *O proclaims an investigation into Laios' death, and decrees punishment if anyone hides the* *murderer. He questions the chorus, and then the seer Teiresias, who at first refuses to speak; an angry O accuses him of complicity in the murder, which finally goads Teiresias into saying that O himself is the killer. O now suspects Kreon and Teiresias of plotting to overthrow him.*

Meter: iambic trimeter.

216-75 Oidipous' Proclamation. Several features of Athenian legal procedure in a homicide investigation can be paralleled here: the requirement of kinship and citizenship to be a litigant (cf. O's words at 258-268); a proclamation cursing the murderer, even if his identity cannot be discovered (see on 235); but especially close to the opening request for information (224-232) is the process of ζήτησις ("public investigation") known from the events of 415 in Athens (see especially Lewis).

216-23 Preface to the proclamation: I need your help.
224-32 Let one of you come forward as informer; this will be best for both murderer and informant.
233-43 If I receive no information (and am thus unable to name the killer), then I will proclaim that he—whoever he is— be exiled, denied all human contact and participation in religion.
[244-51 are assumed to be interpolated; see "Textual Notes" in Vol. 1]
252-8 You must obey me and the god, and should have investigated the murder of your king in any case;
258-68 I have personal ties with the dead man also, which prompt me to pursue his killer.
269-75 May the gods punish those who disobey, and reward those of you who do.

216 **ἃ δ' αἰτεῖς**: left without a construction in what follows: "as to what you request..." Note that the chorus may be addressed either in the plural or (when only the leader is meant) the singular.

τἀμ' = τὰ ἐμά (with ἔπη, looking forward to his proclamation in 224ff.)

217 "receive my words and serve the disease" = "obey my decree and help *against* the plague" (cf. 164-165, 313 ῥῦσαι...μίασμα, 496 ἐπίκουρος ἀδήλων θανάτων).

218 **λάβοις ἄν**: equivalent to a future (see on 95), so that the condition with ἐὰν θέλῃς is actually future more vivid.
219-22 O's demand for information (226) is prefaced with several parenthetical justifications: he is unacquainted with the story of the crime; unable to investigate it without help; and a recent arrival in the city.
219 **ἀγώ** = ἃ ἐγώ (the antecedent is ἔπη in 216).
219-20 **ξένος μὲν τοῦ λόγου τοῦδ'... ξένος δὲ τοῦ πραχθέντος**: (for the anaphora see on 4-5) "even though I am unacquainted with this story, and unacquainted with what happened" (i.e., the story of what happened; contrasts between *word* and *deed* in Greek are sometimes artificial).
220-1 **οὐ γὰρ ἄν...ἴχνευον**: "for I would not be going far on the track myself, if I did not have some link" (binding me to you; for this meaning of σύμβολον see LJ-W 84-5).
μακράν: See on 16.
220 **αὐτός**: "myself" here = "without help from others."
221 **μὴ οὐκ ἔχων**: conditional (for the negatives see on 13).
222-3 **νῦν δ' (ὕστερος γάρ...τελῶ) προφωνῶ**: "but as it is (contrasting with the preceding contrafactual, *GP* 182)—because I have been enrolled among the citizens as a citizen too late (to have first-hand knowledge of Laios' murder)."
222 **εἰς ἀστοὺς τελῶ**: lit. "pay taxes for..." (LSJ τελέω II.3) = "be enrolled among..."
224-5 **Λάϊον... ἀνδρὸς ἐκ τίνος διώλετο**: "by what man *Laios* was killed" (see on 15).
224 **τὸν Λαβδάκου**: "son of L."
227-8 **κεἰ μὲν φοβεῖται, τοὐπίκλημ' †ὑπεξελών†**: difficult to interpret for several reasons: 1) φοβεῖται needs a more clearly expressed subject (it must be the murderer himself); 2) the construction of the participle is unclear; and 3) there is no imperative to match μὴ σιωπάτω in 231 and introduce γάρ in 228. *OCT* follows Groeneboom and D in suggesting a verse is missing after 227 (perhaps it also began with αὐτός, which would account for its being skipped by a copyist). The sense might have been something like "on the one hand, even if he is afraid, ⟨let the murderer himself leave the country⟩ after removing (i.e., clearing up by confessing) the indictment against himself; for he will suffer nothing intolerable..."
228 **αὐτὸς κατ' αὐτοῦ**: See on 137-138.
πείσεται < πάσχω.
229 **ἄπεισιν**: acts as future of ἀπέρχομαι.

COMMENTARY 75

232 τελῶ: future, "I will pay."
χή (= καὶ ἡ) χάρις προσκείσεται: "and there will be my gratitude besides."

233-4 ἢ φίλου...ἀπώσει τοὔπος ἢ χαὑτοῦ τόδε "will thrust away (< ἀπωθέω) this edict, either from a relative or even himself..."

235 ἃκ τῶνδε = ἃ ἐκ τῶνδε, with the deictic pronoun referring to what precedes (S 1247), "*in this case...*" (lit. "after this happens").
δράσω: Note the tense; despite the present ἀπαυδῶ (236), O is describing a possible *future* outcome (*pace* Lewis, "Procedural Basis," 44): even if he does not learn the murderer's identity, O will nevertheless proclaim (anonymously) the curse customary in such cases. An exact parallel is Plato, *Laws* 9.874a-b: "If a man is discovered dead, but his killer is unknown and is not found even after a vigorous inquiry, let the same proclamations be made as in other cases, but let him proclaim them 'against whoever did the murder;' and after concluding the case, let him proclaim in the agora to 'whoever has killed so-and-so and is guilty of murder' not to enter shrines, nor even any part of the country of the victim, since if he is found and recognized, he will be killed and cast out of the victim's country without burial."

236 τὸν ἄνδρ'...τοῦτον: i.e., the murderer.

236-8 γῆς τῆσδ'...μήτ'...τινα: "that no one of this land..." (accus. subject of the infinitives).

237 κράτη τε καὶ θρόνους: a phrase frequent in Sophocles, with poetic plural for singular.

240 χέρνιβος νέμειν: partitive, "give him a share in lustral water."

241 ὠθεῖν δ'...: "but instead (I command) that all thrust him out..."

241-2 ὡς μιάσματος τοῦδ'...ὄντος: "since this man is a pollution for us," expressing the grounds for O's curse (see on 11-12); genitive absolute, even though the reference is the same as accus. τὸν ἄνδρ'...τοῦτον above (S 2073b).

243 ἐξέφηνεν: aor. < ἐκφαίνω.

244 ἐγὼ μὲν οὖν: κατεύχομαι δέ in 246 and ἐπεύχομαι δ' in 249 simply repeat the same idea; the contrast lies in ὑμῖν δέ 252.

244-5 τοιόσδε...σύμμαχος: "this sort of ally."

246-51 On the deletion of these lines (redundant after 236-43) see "Textual Notes" in Vol. 1.

255-6 οὐδ' εἰ γὰρ ἦν τὸ πρᾶγμα μὴ θεήλατον... εἰκὸς ἦν: contrary to fact, "even if the matter were not driven on by a god, it would not be proper to..." (on the omission of ἄν in the apodosis with a phrase of obligation like εἰκός see S 2313).

258 ff ἐπεὶ κυρῶ τ' ἐγώ: τε here (not "irregularly placed," *pace* J and D) corresponds to τε in 261 to divide the clause into two main parts, which are subdivided in turn:
κυρῶ <u>τ</u>' ἐγὼ
 ἔχων <u>μὲν</u>
 ἔχων <u>δὲ</u>
κοινῶν <u>τε</u> παίδων κοίν' ἄν...ἦν ἄν ἐκπεφυκότα
 νῦν <u>δ</u>'...ἐνήλαθ' ἡ τύχη
Eventually the clause begun with ἐπεί rambles so far that Oedipus has to break it off and start over in 264 (ἀνθ' ὤν...).

258-9 κυρῶ...ἔχων: κυρέω is used with a supplementary participle like τυγχάνω in poetry (S 2096).

259-60 ἔχων μέν...ἔχων δέ: See on 4-5.

259 πρίν: adverb, "previously."

261 κοινῶν...παίδων κοίν': lit. "shared things of shared children" = "children closely shared." For the intensifying genitive see K-G I.21 (and cf. 465 ἄρρητ' ἀρρήτων); for the periphrasis with the neuter see M 14-15.
γένος...'δυστύχησεν: "if his race had not been unfortunate" = "if he had not died childless."

262 ἦν ἄν ἐκπεφυκότα: Pluperfect (for aorist) in a contrary-to-fact condition stresses the completion of the act (S 2306a, cf. 690 and 984 below): "would have been born (and now be alive)." For repeated ἄν see S 1765a.

263 νῦν δ': "but as it is..."
ἐνήλαθ': "leapt upon," < ἐνάλλομαι.

264-5 τάδ'...ὑπερμαχοῦμαι: internal accusative (see on 190-4), "I shall engage in this fight on his behalf."

265 κἀπὶ πάντ' ἀφίξομαι: lit. "I shall go to all things" = "I shall do everything I can" (cf. Eur. *Hippolytus* 284).

267 τῷ Λαβδακείῳ παιδί: "the son of Labdakos" (i.e., Laios). The following genitives add the father of each preceding father, as O repeats the entire lineage which he thinks has now become extinct.

COMMENTARY 77

269 **ταῦτα τοῖς μὴ δρῶσιν**: "upon whoever does not do these things..." (μή for οὐ because generic, S 2734, cf. on 110 and 569). Decrees are regularly concluded with an imprecation on those who may disobey.
270 **ἀνιέναι** < ἀνίημι.
271 **μήτ' οὖν**: See on 90.
271-2 **τῷ πότμῳ τῷ νῦν**: i.e., with the plague.
272 **φθερεῖσθαι** < φθείρω, not future middle, but passive (K-G I.117). Normally εὔχομαι governs the aorist infin. for a single action, but here "the reference to the future [is] especially prominent" (*MT* 113).
273 **ὑμῖν δέ**: O politely assumes that the chorus will all be among the obedient.
274 **τάδ'**: The deictic pronoun refers to the whole preceding speech (see on 235).
275 **χοἰ πάντες** = καὶ οἱ πάντες (for the position of the article see S 1174).
276 **ὥσπερ...ὧδ'**: i.e., my information will be as honest as your curse is serious.
277 **γάρ**: follows a sentence "denoting the giving ...of information" (*GP* 59) and is not to be translated.
278-9 **τοῦ πέμψαντος ἦν Φοίβου τόδ' εἰπεῖν**: predicative genitive (S 1304), "it was the job of Apollo, who sent us the investigation, to tell us this, namely who..."
281 **ἄν**= ἃ ἄν, the relative being the object of "to do," understood with ἀναγκάσαι.
οὐδ' ⟨ἂν⟩ εἷς = οὐδεὶς ἄν.
283 **παρῇς**: aor. subj. < παρίημι.
τὸ μὴ οὐ φράσαι: article with double negative after a negative verb of prevention, "so as not to tell" (S 2744.10).
284 **ἄνακτ' ἄνακτι**: *polyptoton* (see on 100) with the two nouns in the next line. The dative is governed by ταὔθ' = τὰ αὐτά, "(sees) *the same things as*...".
285-6 **παρ' οὗ...ἐκμάθοι**: See on 117. σκοπῶν is conditional.
287 **ἐν ἀργοῖς**: adverbial (cf. ἐν τάχει, M 106), "sluggishly."
289 **πάλαι δὲ μὴ παρὼν θαυμάζεται**: conditional participle (for θαυμάζω with conditions see S 2247), lit. "if he hasn't arrived a long time ago, he is surprising." I.e., "I am surprised that..."
290 **καὶ μήν**: "indeed" (expressing general agreement with O's actions, *GP* 354).

τά γ'...ἔπη: "The rest of the information is insubstantial and out of date."
292 πρός: with genitive of agent (instead of ὑπό) as often in tragedy.
293 τὸν δὲ δρῶντ': i.e., the perpetrator.
294 ἀλλ'...μὲν δή: "yet, at any rate..." (GP 394).
297 ἀλλ' οὑξελέγξων...: "But here is the man who can find him out." For the article with the future participle see S 2044.
298 ὧδ' = δεῦρο (see on 7).
298-9 ᾧ τἀληθὲς ἐμπέφυκεν: "in whom truth is innate," the neuter adjective being used as an abstract substantive (S 2051).
302 πόλιν μέν...φρονεῖς δ' ὅμως: Despite the initial placement, the true contrast is between βλέπεις and φρονεῖς (GP 180-181)—πόλιν is placed first for other reasons (see next note).
302-3 πόλιν...φρονεῖς...οἵᾳ νόσῳ σύνεστιν = φρονεῖς οἵᾳ νόσῳ ἡ πόλις σύνεστιν (see on 15).
304 μοῦνον: μοῦνος is a metrically convenient Ionic by-form for μόνος.
305 εἰ καὶ μὴ κλύεις: "in case you haven't heard" (GP 303).
306 ἀντέπεμψεν: introduces an indirect statement, "sent us back the reply that..."
308 τοὺς κτανόντας: Either O quotes the oracle's plural (cf. on 124) or uses a vaguely allusive plural (see on 1246).
312 ῥῦσαι: aor. mid. imperat., ῥύομαι, "protect" (for the *anaphora* see on 4-5). "Protect the pollution" = "be a protector *against* the pollution" (see on 217).
314 ἐν σοί: "in your power."
ἄνδρα δ' ὠφελεῖν: in apposition to κάλλιστος πόνων (S 1987), "it is the fairest of tasks that a man should aid..."
314-5 ἀφ' ὧν ἔχοι τε καὶ δύναιτο: "from whatever he has and can" = "with all his possessions and capabilities." The subjunctive with ἄν would have been expected, but for the optative in a present generalization cf. 979 below and Soph. *Antig.* 666 ἀλλ' ὃν πόλις στήσειε, τοῦδε χρὴ κλύειν, and S 2573.
316 φρονεῖν ὡς δεινὸν ἔνθα: exclamatory, "how horrible it is to be wise (in a case) *where...*"
316-7 τέλη λύῃ = λυσιτελῇ, impersonal. ἄν is sometimes omitted in poetry in generalizing relative clauses with subjunctive (cf. 1231 below, and *MT* 540, S 2567b).

φρονοῦντι: dat. of advantage.
317 γάρ: here and in the next line, explains the tone of his exclamation (φεῦ φεῦ) rather than its contents (*GP* 61) and is not to be translated.
318 διώλεσ': here = "I forgot."
γάρ: "for otherwise..."
320 ἄφες < ἀφίημι, aor. imperat.
323 τήνδ' ἀποστερῶν φάτιν: "when you deprive us of (i.e., refuse to reveal) this prophecy."
324-5 οὐδὲ σοὶ τὸ σὸν φώνημ' ἰὸν πρὸς καιρόν: "that what you have said is not turning out well (lit. "going toward opportunity") either." ἰόν = pres. partic. neut. < ἔρχομαι.
325 Teiresias intends to say "therefore, so that I don't suffer the same thing as well (I won't speak now)," but suppresses his conclusion.
326 φρονῶν γ': conditional participle with γε (*GP* 143).
ἀποστραφῇς: aor. pass. subj. < ἀποστρέφω, "turn away."
328-9 οὐ μή...ἐκφήνω < ἐκφαίνω. οὐ μή with aor. subj. = strong future denial (S 1804, 2755a).
329 τἄμ': sc. κακά. "my evils" here = "what grieves me."
ὡς ἂν εἴπω μὴ τὰ σ': sc. κακά, "so that I not speak of *yours*." (For ἂν in purpose clauses see S 2201.)
333 ἄλλως: "in vain."
335 ὀργάνειας: aor. opt. ὀργαίνω = ὀργίζω, "enrage."
336 φανῇ: fut. mid. indic., 2 sg. < φαίνομαι.
337 ἐμέμψω: aor. mid. indic., 2 sg. < μέμφομαι.
339-40 ἔπη...ἃ...ἀτιμάζεις πόλιν: double accusative with the equivalent of a verb of saying (S 1622): "words of dishonor which you are saying about the city."
341 ἥξει γὰρ αὐτά: "they will come *without prompting*" (see on 221); the subject shifts from ἔπη to one left intentionally vague.
κἂν = καὶ ἐάν (στέγω is subjunctive).
343 οὐκ ἂν πέρα φράσαιμι: See on 95.
343-4 πρὸς τάδ'...θυμοῦ: defiant imperative (< θυμέομαι), "in response to this (see D on 426) go ahead and rage..."
344 δι' ὀργῆς: adverbial, strengthened by ἥτις ἀγριωτάτη (K-G II.499), "with as wild an anger as possible."
345 καὶ μήν...γ': "all right, then..." (*GP* 355).
345-6 παρήσω γ' οὐδέν...ἄπερ ξυνίημ': "I won't omit (< παρίημι) any (of the things) which I know."

ὡς ὀργῆς ἔχω: "in accordance with my anger" (lit. "as I hold in rage," see S 1441).
346 ἴσθι...δοκῶν: indirect statement with participle after a verb of perception, "know that you seem to me..."
γάρ: See on 277.
347-8 ὅσον μή: lit. "to the extent that not," i.e., "except for..." (S 2765).
350 ἄληθες: indignant adverb (note the accent): "really?"
ἐννέπω: here "command."
350-1 τῷ κηρύγματι ᾧπερ προεῖπας ἐμμένειν: attraction of the relative from accusative to dative (see on 148), "to abide by the proclamation which you decreed (in line 238)."
352 προσαυδᾶν: "address, speak to" (cf. 238).
353 ὡς ὄντι: referring to O, now in dative (despite σε in line 350) to avoid ambiguity with ἐμέ in the preceding line (K-G II.113, S 2148a).
355 ῥῆμα: i.e., μιάστωρ.
ποῦ τοῦτο φεύξεσθαι δοκεῖς; "where do you think you will escape from *this* (rash remark)?"
356 ἰσχῦον: participle.
τρέφω: Sophocles uses τρέφω in such a wide variety of phrases that it often merely = "have" (see LSJ τρέφω II.6).
357 πρὸς τοῦ: "by whom?" (see on 292; τοῦ is the interrogative pronoun).
358 προὐτρέψω: 2 sg. aor. mid. < προτρέπω.
360 'κπειρᾷ: *Prodelision* (see on 112), 2 sg. pres. mid. of ἐκπειράομαι, "test."
361 οὐχ ὥστε γ' εἰπεῖν γνωστόν: answers the first of the questions in the last line: "no (I did *not* understand), so as to say it is known (what you mean)."
362 φονέα...τἀνδρὸς οὗ ζητεῖς: abbreviated for "the murderer of the man whose (murderer) you seek."
κυρεῖν: sc. ὄντα (see on 258), "(I say) that you happen to be..."
363 οὔ τι χαίρων: i.e., not at all without suffering (Bruhn 247.21).
πημονάς: "injuries," i.e., slanders.
364 εἴπω: deliberative subjunctive.
τι...κἄλλ' = καὶ ἄλλο τι, "another thing as well."
ὀργίζῃ πλέον: "become more angry" (2 sg. pres. mid. subj. < ὀργίζομαι).

COMMENTARY 81

366 λεληθέναι < λανθάνω, with supplementary participle ὁμιλοῦντ', "that without knowing it you are living ..."

367 αἴσχισθ': superlative adverb, "most shamefully."

ἵν': "where." For the partitive genitive κακοῦ see on 108.

368 ἢ καί...δοκεῖς: "do you actually think..." (*GP* 285).

371 τά τ' ὦτα τόν τε νοῦν τά τ' ὄμματ': accusatives of respect (see on 82-3) with τυφλός (ὦτα < οὖς). For the alliteration cf. 425, and Bruhn 241.

373 οὐδεὶς ὃς οὐχὶ τῶνδ': lit. "there is no one of these who will not..." = "everyone of these people here."

374 μιᾶς: i.e., *continuous* blindness. For πρός see on 292.

τρέφῃ: 2 sg. pass., "you are controlled by..." (see on 356).

375 βλάψαι ποτ' ἄν: sc. σε as subject; the infinitive with ἄν stands for potential optative.

376 οὐ...μοῖρα: with accus. and infin., "it is not fate that..."

377 ἱκανὸς Ἀπόλλων: i.e., to destroy O.

380-1 τέχνη τέχνης ὑπερφέρουσα: "skill surpassing skill." (O is referring to his own great achievements.)

381 τῷ πολυζήλῳ βίῳ: "in the competitive life."

382 ὅσος...φυλάσσεται: exclamatory, "how much envy is stored up with you," i.e., "how much those who possess you (tyranny, wealth and skill) are prone to being envied."

383 οὕνεχ': οὕνεκα = ἕνεκα.

384 δωρητόν...αἰτητόν: fem. with ἥν in 383 (two-ending adjectives).

385 ταύτης: with μ'...ἐκβαλεῖν, "to expel me from this rule."

οὐξ = ὁ ἐξ.

387 ὑφείς: aor. partic. < ὑφίημι, "plant, suborn."

388 ἐν τοῖς κέρδεσιν: "when profit is involved (i.e., when he's paid)."

389 δέδορκε: perfect (with present meaning) < δέρκομαι.

ἔφυ: See on 9.

390 ποῦ: i.e., "on what occasion?"

σαφής: See on 106.

391 ὅθ' = ὅτε. (ὅτι, like τι itself, never elides.)

ῥαψῳδός...κύων: i.e., the Sphinx (see on 36).

392 ηὔδας < αὐδάω.

393 τοὐπιόντος = τοῦ ἐπιόντος (< ἐπέρχομαι), the genitive being predicative (see on 278-9) and the participle generic (see on 110): "it was not the work of whoever arrived to describe the riddle."

394 μαντείας: genit. with ἔδει "there was a need for..."

395 **προύφάνης**: aor. pass. < προφαίνω, with ἔχων (S 2143): "you *clearly* did not possess..."
396 **του**: "some" (see on 42).
397 **ὁ μηδὲν εἰδὼς Οἰδίπους**: an ironic joke about the presumed derivation of his name (he will later learn it is different, see on 1033). μή for οὐ with generic participle; see on 269.
398 **γνώμῃ κυρήσας**: "succeeding (LSJ κυρέω II.2) by intelligence." γνώμη is applied to the mind in general and has a wide range of meaning, including "attitude," "intellect," or "plan."
399 **ὃν δή**: expressing indignation (*GP* 219), "whom you actually..."
401-2 **κλαίων δοκεῖς μοι...ἀγηλατήσειν**: lit. "you seem to me to be going to drive (me) out...with weeping," i.e., "I think that you will be sorry you ever tried to drive out..."
402 **'δόκεις** = ἐδόκεις (in a mixed past-present contrary to fact condition), "if you did not look so old..."
403 **ἔγνως** < γιγνώσκω, 2 aor.
404 **ἡμῖν μὲν εἰκάζουσι**: both dative with δοκεῖ: "to us, when we think about it..."
405 **ὀργῇ**: dat. of manner.
λελέχθαι: perf. pass. infin. < λέγω.
406 **δεῖ δ' οὐ τοιούτων**: See on 394.
406-7 **ὅπως...λύσομεν**: explaining τόδε (S 2211), "how we can best resolve..."
408 **εἰ καί**: "even though" (*GP* 300).
ἐξισωτέον: verbal adjective, "it must be granted equally (lit. "equalized") at least to give an equal reply."
411 **οὐ...γεγράψομαι**: future perfect, with predicative genitive, "I won't stand enrolled as belonging to Kreon (as) protector."
413-4 **καὶ δέδορκας κοὐ βλέπεις ἵν'...οὐδ' ἔνθα...οὐδ' ὅτων...μέτα**: You have sight, but you don't see where...or where...or with whom..." For καί...καί in contrasts see *GP* 324. Note that each new sentence in this speech is introduced merely with καί (413, 415, 417).
414 **ὅτων**: genit. pl. < ὅστις, with μέτα (see on 93).
416 **τοῖς σοῖσιν αὐτοῦ**: "your very own." The genitive agrees with the pronoun implied in the possessive adj., cf. 1248 and S 1199.1.c.
νέρθε κἀπὶ γῆς ἄνω: i.e., both living and dead.
418 **ἐλᾷ** < ἐλαύνω.

COMMENTARY 83

419 **νῦν μὲν ὀρθ', ἔπειτα δὲ σκότον**: Both adjective (= ὀρθά) and noun are internal accusatives (see on 190-4) with βλέποντα: "who now see straight, but then (will see) dark (i.e., not at all)."

420 **βοῆς...ποῖος οὐκ ἔσται λιμήν**: "what sort of harbor will there not soon be for your screaming?" i.e., "where will it not be heard?"

421 **ποῖος Κιθαιρών**: same form as the last question (*anaphora*), even though there is only one Mt. Kithairon, where O will turn out to have been exposed (1026).

422 **καταίσθῃ** < καταισθάνομαι.

422-3 **τὸν ὑμέναιον...ἄνορμον**: "the marriage (lit. "wedding-song") that was no harbor (see on 1207-12)." An α-privative adjective can negate a cognate noun (e.g., 1214 below τὸν ἄγαμον γάμον, S 3035), but here it negates the metaphor in εἰσέπλευσας: "the disastrous harbor of a marriage in the house, into which you sailed."

423 **εὐπλοίας τυχών**: concessive, "although you had attained a smooth voyage."

425 **ἅ σ' ἐξισώσει κτλ**: Note the alliteration (cf. 371).

426 **πρὸς ταῦτα**: See on 343.

428 **κάκιον**: comparative adverb.

430 **οὐκ εἰς ὄλεθρον; οὐχὶ θᾶσσον**: sc. ἄπει (future 2 sg., ἀπέρχομαι) The question "will you not..." often = a command (S 1918), here virtually "go to hell."
θᾶσσον: "quickly" (the comparative adverb here with positive force, LSJ ταχύς C.I.2).

431 **ἀποστραφείς**: aor. pass. partic. < ἀποστρέφω (see on 326).

433 **ᾔδη** < οἶδα, followed by participle in indirect statement.
ἐπεί: "since *otherwise...*"

434 **σχολῇ**: "slowly," i.e., "hardly."
οἴκους τοὺς ἐμούς: accusative of motion toward without preposition (see on 35).

437 **ποίοισι**: with γονεῦσι.
μεῖνον: aor. imperat. < μένω.
ἐκφύει: historical present.

439 **ὡς**: exclamatory, with αἰνικτὰ κἀσαφῆ, "how..."

440 **εὑρίσκειν**: with ἄριστος, "best at finding out."

441 **οἷς**: antecedent τοιαῦτα, with μέγαν, "*in which* (you will find me) great."

442 αὕτη...ἡ τύχη: i.e., your luck in solving the riddle of the Sphinx.
443 οὔ μοι μέλει: i.e., "I don't care (if I *am* destroyed)."
446 συθείς: aor. pass. < σεύω, conditional participle, "if you hurry away."
O does not speak again in the scene, and it is scarcely credible that he would have let Teiresias' final speech pass without an answer—especially since 457-60 are quite plain, and correspond to the prophecy O later says he received (790-793). Rather than label the scene dramatically defective (D 11-12) or suggest that O is too confused to answer (Oliver Taplin, *Greek Tragedy in Action* [Berkeley 1978] 44), we may guess that Teiresias speaks the words as O departs, and that ἰὼν εἴσω (460) is the blind man's reaction to the noise of the house-door finally closing. Similarly plain but unheard threats are yelled after departing characters in other plays. See B. M. Knox, "Sophocles, *O. T.* 446: Exit Oedipus?," *Greek, Roman and Byzantine Studies* 21 (1980) 321-332.
447 εἰπὼν ἄπειμ': "I will leave *after saying,...*" i.e., "I won't leave until I say..."
448 οὐ...ἔσθ' ὅπου: "there is no place where..." = "it is impossible that..."
449-51 τὸν ἄνδρα τοῦτον, ὅν...ζητεῖς: The original nominative (picked up later in οὗτος) is attracted into the accusative before ὅν (S 2533).
450-51 κἀνακηρύσσων φόνον τὸν Λαΐειον: "and proclaiming Laios' murder" = "and proclaiming an investigation into..."
452-3 ξένος λόγῳ...εἶτα δ'...φανήσεται· "as a foreign resident—by reputation ...but then he will be revealed as..."
453 ἡσθήσεται < ἥδομαι.
454 τῇ ξυμφορᾷ: See on 99.
455 ξένην ἔπι: sc. γῆν (see on 55).
456 σκήπτρῳ προδεικνὺς γαῖαν: "pointing to the earth (i.e., feeling his way) with a staff."
458 αὐτός (= ὁ αὐτός) καί: "and at the same time..." (lit. "the same person also," emphatic like Latin *idem*).
460 ὁμόσπορος: "fellow-sower," i.e., impregnator of the same woman.
461 λογίζου: mid. imperat. < λογίζομαι, "think that over as you go inside."
κἄν = καὶ ἐάν.

COMMENTARY 85

λάβῃς: here "catch," sc. με.
ἐψευσμένον: perf. partic. < ψεύδομαι (sc. με).
462 **φάσκειν:** infinitive for imperative (S 2013), hence μηδέν for οὐδέν.
ἤδη: in the apodosis of a condition = "accordingly" (LSJ I.4.a).

463-512 First Stasimon. *Whom has Delphi denounced? He ought to flee the angry gods, and the men who will hunt him everywhere (str.-antistr. A). I do not understand Teiresias' frightening prophecies, nor O's anger; I have no reason to suspect him. (str. B). Gods are infallible, but mortal prophets are not. Some may be better than others, but until I have proof I will not blame O, whose patriotism and wisdom were proven against the Sphinx. (antistr. B).*

Meter: aeolo-choriambic, analyzed by Dale, *Metrical Analyses* fasc. 2, pp. 36-7.

463 **τίς ὅντιν':** "who is it whom...?"
464-6 **εἶπε...τελέσαντα:** The verb of saying governs the participle instead of infinitive (see "Textual Notes" in Vol. 1).
465 **ἄρρητ' ἀρρήτων:** "the most unspeakable acts" (for the intensification see on 261-2).
467 **ὥρα:** sc. ἐστίν, "it is time that..."
468 **φυγᾷ:** dat. of manner.
470 **πυρὶ καὶ στεροπαῖς:** "with fire and lightning = "with fiery lightning" (the expression of a noun-adjective as two coordinate nouns is called *hendiadys*, S 3025).
γενέτας: "son," i.e., Apollo.
473-5 **ἔλαμψε...φήμα:** "there shone forth (see on 186) the word that..." (with accus. and infin.).
473-5 **τοῦ νιφόεντος...Παρνασοῦ:** Ambiguous genitives are characteristic of lyric style; this one might be genit. of separation with ἔλαμψε or φανεῖσα, or possessive with φήμα.
475-6 **τὸν ἄδηλον ἄνδρα πάντ':** The first noun is accus. object of the infin. ἰχνεύειν, the second subject: "that everyone must hunt down..."
477-8 **ὑπ' ἀγρίαν ὕλαν ἀνά τ' ἄντρα καὶ πετραῖος:** three ways of indicating place (cf. on 20-1), "in the wild forest, in caves and rocks."

86   OIDIPOUS TYRANNOS

478   ὁ ταῦρος: "(wanders) *like* a bull" (who proverbially abandoned the herd during breeding time; see "Textual Notes" in Vol. 1).
479   μέλεος μελέῳ: *polyptoton* (see on 100).
480-1 μεσόμφαλα γᾶς...μαντεῖα: i.e., "prophecies from the navel in the midst of the earth." ὀμφαλὸς γῆς is a title of Delphi (for possible meanings see Walter Burkert, *Homo Necans* [Berkeley 1983] 126-7), here expressed through *enallage* (see on 108-9).
      ἀπονοσφίζων: "trying to keep...at a distance."
481   τὰ δ': "But they (the oracles)..."
481-2 αἰεί...περιποτᾶται: "always hover about (him)."
482   ζῶντα: See on 44-5.
484   δεινά...δεινά: anaphora with adverbial accusative (see on 419), "troubles me terribly."
485   οὔτε δοκοῦντ': evidently = "approving."
      ὅ τι λέξω δ' ἀπορῶ: "but I am at a loss what to say." (λέξω is deliberative aor. subj.)
487   πέτομαι δ' ἐλπίσιν: "I am excited (lit. "flying") with expectations." (ἐλπίς here may be either "hope" or "anxiety.")
487-8 οὔτ' ἐνθάδ' ὁρῶν οὔτ' ὀπίσω: "seeing neither here nor backward" = "since I understand neither the present nor the future." (For ὀπίσω in this sense see LSJ, ὀπίσω II.)
489-91 ἢ Λαβδακίδαις ἢ τῷ Πολύβου...νεῖκος: The chorus view the hostility as emanating from one side or the other, and so phrase the question as "what hostility existed, either for the Labdakids (against O) or for Polybos' son (against the Labdakids)?"
493-4 πρὸς ὅτου...βασάνῳ: indirect question (after ἔμαθον): "at the touchstone of what..." i.e., "on the basis of what proof..." (But the translation is uncertain, since the meter of the corresponding antistrophe shows a word is missing after βασάνῳ.)
495-6 ἐπὶ τὰν ἐπίδαμον φάτιν εἶμ': "I will go against (attack) O's public reputation," i.e., believe him to be evil rather than good.
496   Οἰδιπόδα: Doric genit. of the by-form Οἰδιπόδης.
      Λαβδακίδαις: dat. of advantage, with ἐπίκουρος.
497   ἐπίκουρος: with genit., "as a helper *of* (i.e., *against*, see on 217)..."

COMMENTARY

ἀδήλων θανάτων: poetic plural (see on 237). The adjective is emphatic; it is too late to do anything about Laios' *death*, but its *mystery* can at least be cleared up.

498 **μέν**: balanced by ἀνδρῶν δ'.

499 **ἀνδρῶν**: "among mortals," partitive with μάντις and ἐγώ.

500 **πλέον...φέρεται**: "gets more" = "is superior."

501 **κρίσις οὐκ ἔστιν ἀληθής**: i.e., "there is no infallible means of deciding..." (with ὅτι).

503-4 **σοφίᾳ δ' ἂν σοφίαν παραμείψειεν**: "might surpass (another's) wisdom with (greater) wisdom."

505 **πρὶν ἴδοιμ' ὀρθὸν ἔπος**: "until I see (Teiresias') word justified." Optative (not subjunctive) with πρίν by assimilation, S 2450.

505-6 **μεμφομένων**: genitive absolute with subject omitted (S2072b), "when people blame (him)."

506 **καταφαίην** < κατάφημι, "assent" (for repeated ἂν see on 262).

507 **φανερά**: predicative, "visibly" (emphatic like ὤφθη: of his *past* services there is *proof.*)

509 **ὤφθη** < ὁράω.

510 **τῶν**: relative pronoun (see on 200), causal genitive (S 1405): "for which deeds..." See also "Textual Notes" in Vol. 1.

511 **ὀφλήσει**: fut. < ὀφλισκάνω. ("Owe" with accus. = "be guilty of...")

513-813 Second Episode. First part: O and Kreon (518-648); second part: *kommos* (shared lyrics) with O, Kreon and Iokaste (649-696); third part, dialogue with O and Iokaste (697-862).

Meter: iambic trimeter.

Second episode, first part (518-648). *O makes an accusation of treason against Kreon, who defends himself. Iokaste enters and tries to calm them down. Finally, Kreon swears an oath to his innocence.*

513 **δείν' ἔπη**: internal accusative with κατηγορεῖν, "that O makes terrible words of accusation against me."

515 **ἀτλητῶν**: partic., "refusing to endure it" (the word is known only here).

516 **πρός γ' ἐμοῦ**: of agent (see on 292).

517 **λόγοισιν εἴτ' ἔργοισιν**: sc. εἴτε with λόγοισιν also (cf. *GP* 507-8).

εἰς βλάβην φέρον: "(anything) tending toward harm (i.e., harmful, Bruhn 247.26)," with πεπονθέναι. For the omission of the article with the generic participle see K-G 1.609.

519 φέροντι: conditional, "if I must bear..."
519-21 οὐ γὰρ εἰς ἁπλοῦν...φέρει, ἀλλ' ἐς μέγιστον: "does not *relate to* a simple matter, but to the most important one."
522 κεκλήσομαι: future perfect passive, καλέω.
523 ἀλλ'...μὲν δή: See on 294.
τάχ' ἄν: See on 139.
524 ὀργῇ βιασθὲν μᾶλλον ἢ γνώμῃ φρενῶν: The datives are not really parallel, the first being instrumental, the second modal: "constrained by anger rather than (said) with good sense." (For γνώμῃ see on 398.)
525 τοὔπος (= τὸ ἔπος): amplified by ὅτι: "Did the statement appear (i.e., was it said) that..."
ταῖς ἐμαῖς γνώμαις: with πεισθείς, but placed in front of ὅτι for emphasis. γνώμη here = "plot."
526 λέγοι: optative in indirect statement after a past main verb.
527 γνώμῃ τίνι: "(I do not know) *with what attitude*..."
528 ἐξ ὀμμάτων...ὀρθῶν: adverbial (LSJ ἐκ III.8), "with straight (i.e., not rolling in madness) eyes."
κἀπ' could be either καὶ ἀπό ("as a result of," so LJ-W) or καὶ ἐπί ("dependent on," LSJ ἐπί A.I.2.b).
529 κατηγορεῖτο: passive.
531 This line is missing from a papyrus of the play; it was probably inserted later to make O's entrance obvious.
532 οὗτος σύ: "you there" (S 1288a).
532-3 τοσόνδ'...τόλμης πρόσωπον: "so great a face of boldness" = "so bold (unashamed) a face."
533-4 τὰς ἐμὰς στέγας ἵκου (2 pers. sg. aor. < ἱκνέομαι): See on 35.
534 τοῦδε τἀνδρός: i.e., himself (as in 815, 829, 1018, 1464).
537 ἰδών: causal participle.
ἐβουλεύσω: 2 sg. aor. mid. < βουλεύω.
ποεῖν = ποιεῖν (S 43).
538 ἤ...ὡς οὐ γνωριοῖμι: indirect statement (with future optative, see on 526), for which an introductory verb like "believing..." must be understood from ἰδών above.
538-9 τοὔργον...τόδε...προσέρπον: accus. with participle in indirect statement after γνωρίζω, "that this activity was sneaking up on me..." (τοὔργον is placed early for emphasis).

COMMENTARY

539 **κοὐκ**: "*or else* would not..." (for καί linking alternatives see *GP* 292).
     μαθών: conditional.
542 **ὅ**: "a thing which" (the antecedent is τυραννίδα, S 2502d).
543 **οἶσθ' ὡς ποήσον** = "do you know how you should act?" (the aorist imperative is substituted for the future, S 1842a).
544 **κᾆτα** = καὶ εἶτα.
545-6 **μανθάνειν δ' ἐγὼ κακὸς σοῦ**: The infinitive limits the adjective: "but I am bad at learning—from *you*."
546 **βαρύν**: here "harmful."
547 **τοῦτ' αὐτό**: object of ὡς ἐρῶ, "how I will explain (rebut) this very thing."
548 **ὅπως**: relative adverb, "how" (S 2668c), explaining τοῦτ' αὐτό.
549-50 **κτῆμα...τι**· i.e., a valuable quality.
550 **τοῦ νοῦ χωρίς**: "without good sense."
551-2 **ἄνδρα συγγενῆ κακῶς δρῶν**: "if you do wrong to a kinsman."
553 **σοι**: not only with ξύμφημι, but also dat. of agent with εἰρῆσθαι.
     ἐνδίκ': predicative (S 1043), "that these things have been said *with justice.*"
555 **χρείη**: optative < χρή, in indirect statement.
555-6 **μ' ἐπί...πέμψασθαί τινα**· "that I send someone for (i.e., to fetch)..."
557 **αὐτός** = ὁ αὐτός, with dat. of respect.
558 **πόσον τιν'...χρόνον**: accusative of duration; Kreon interrupts to demand that he complete the question.
560 **ἔρρει** < ἔρρω, present expressing an enduring result (S 1887), "*has been* dead."
561 **μακροὶ παλαιοί τ' ἂν μετρηθεῖεν χρόνοι**: "long and old times would be measured" = "it would turn out to be far in the past (if we were to count it exactly)."
562 **ἦν ἐν τῇ τέχνῃ**: "was practicing his craft."
563 **σοφός γ'**: γε suggests an affirmative answer (*GP* 130).
     κἀξ ἴσου: See on 61.
565 **ἐμοῦ γ' ἑστῶτος οὐδαμοῦ πέλας**: genitive absolute, "at least (γε) when I was standing anywhere near."
566 **ἔρευναν τοῦ κανόντος** (< καίνω, "kill"): "a search for the murderer."
567 **παρέσχομεν**: sc. ἔρευναν. After simple ἔσχετε above, the compound may imply the search was not concluded.

OIDIPOUS TYRANNOS

κοὐκ ἠκούσαμεν: adversative καί, "and yet we did not hear…" (Kreon is interrupted before he can finish).

569 **ἐφ' οἷς** = ἐπὶ τούτοις ἅ, "(to keep silent) *about* things *which* I don't understand" (the relative clause generalizes, hence μή, S 2506, and cf. on 269 above).
φιλῶ: here "am accustomed."

570 **λέγοις ἄν:** See on 95.
εὖ φρονῶν: conditional.

572 **ὁθούνεκ'** = ὅτι.
εἰ μὴ σοὶ ξυνῆλθε: contrary to fact, "if he (Teiresias) had not joined (conspired) with you…"

572-3 **τὰς ἐμὰς…διαφθοράς:** "*my* murder of Laios" (as if I had done it).

575 **μαθεῖν…ταῦθ' ἅπερ:** i.e., to question you *just as* you have me.
ἅπερ κἀμοῦ σύ: Logically, καί should have been placed in the first clause (*GP* 295), i.e., "I *too* desire…what you…"

576 **ἁλώσομαι:** fut. < ἁλίσκομαι, here "be discovered to be…"

577 **τί δῆτ':** introduces the topic: "what about this, then?" (*GP* 270).
γήμας ἔχεις: aor. partic. in a periphrasis for the perfect (S 1963).

579 **ἄρχεις δ' ἐκείνῃ ταὐτὰ γῆς ἴσον νέμων:** rearranged word-order for "do you rule the land equally, wielding the same powers as she?" (I.e., did you not take over the throne after you married into my family?)

580 **ἄν** (= ἅ ἄν) **ᾗ θέλουσα:** "whatever she is wanting" (periphrasis for ἐθέλῃ, see on 90).

581 **σφῷν:** 2 pers. dat. dual.

583 **διδοίης…σαυτῷ λόγον:** "give an account to yourself" = "reflect."

584 **σκέψαι:** aor. imperat. < σκέπτομαι.

584-5 **τιν' ἄν…ἑλέσθαι** (< αἱρέω): represents a potential optative in indirect statement ("that anyone would choose…").

586 **ἄτρεστον εὕδοντ':** with τιν' in 584 (parallel to ξὺν φόβοισι).

587 **μὲν οὖν:** "corrective" (*GP* 478-479), answering the question just posed, "*in fact* neither I myself nor…"

588 **τύραννα:** object of δρᾶν, "(do) what a tyrant does."

591 **ἔδρων:** imperf. 1 sg. < δράω.

592 **ἡδίων ἔχειν:** "more pleasant *to have* than…" (with genitive).

COMMENTARY 91

594 οὔπω: See on 105.
ἠπατημένος κυρῶ: See on 258 (the participle is from ἀπατάω).
596-7 νῦν...νῦν...νῦν: *anaphora*.
596 πᾶσι χαίρω: i.e., everyone says χαῖρε (an imperative = "hello") to me.
597 ἐκκαλοῦσί με: i.e., seek me out, pay me court.
598 τὸ γὰρ τυχεῖν αὐτοῖσι πᾶν ἐνταῦθ' ἔνι (= ἔνεστι): "since all succeeding for them is present here," i.e., "since all their success depends on me."
599 κεῖν' = the life of O; τάδε = Kreon's current life.
600 "If it has good sense, no mind would become wicked." An irrelevant generalization which must have been written in the margin as a parallel and wrongly inserted into the text by a copyist.
603 τῶνδ' ἔλεγχον: "as proof of these things...," accusative in apposition to the sentence (S 991b).
603-5 τοῦτο μέν...τοῦτ' ἀλλ': "on the one hand...on the other." The neuter pronouns emphasize the contrast and need not be translated (for the absence of δέ see *GP* 377).
604 πεύθου: pres. imperat. < πεύθομαι (an older form of πυνθάνομαι).
607 διπλῇ δέ: "*but* with a double (vote)."
608 γνώμῃ...ἀδήλῳ = "with an unproven conjecture." For γνώμη see on 398.
χωρίς: "separately" here = "without checking my story with others first."
αἰτιῶ: pres. imperat. < αἰτιάομαι.
611-2 ἴσον...καί: "is the same thing *as*" (*GP* 292).
616 εὐλαβουμένῳ πεσεῖν: dat. of reference, "for a man who is guarding against a fall."
617 φρονεῖν...ταχεῖς: "hasty in thinking."
618 ταχύς τις: predicative, "rather swiftly" (for the force of τις see S 1268).
620-1 τὰ τοῦδε μὲν πεπραγμέν' ἔσται, τἀμὰ δ' ἡμαρτημένα: The contrast lies in the two perfect participles: "his plans will have been put in action, and my mistakes will have been made."
624 ὅταν προδείξῃς οἷόν: "when (i.e., since) you exemplify what a terrible thing envy is." The line makes little sense in its current context; LJ-W suppose it is the remnant of a

longer speech which has fallen out of the manuscripts, and mark lines before and after it as missing.

625 ὡς οὐχ ὑπείξων: "with no intention of yielding" (for ὡς see on 12-13).

626 τὸ γοῦν ἐμόν: sc. φρονῶ εὖ.

628 ἀρκτέον: "I must rule,"< ἄρχω.

629 οὗτοι κακῶς γ' ἄρχοντος: genitive absolute with subject omitted (see on 505), "not if one rules badly."
ὦ : exclamatory (note the accent).

631 καιρίαν: predicative, "opportunely."

633 εὖ θέσθαι: "put in good order, settle."
χρεών= χρή.

635 ἐπήρασθ': 2 pl. aor. mid. < ἐπαίρω.

637-8 οὐκ εἶ (< εἶμι)...καὶ μὴ...οἴσετε: Lit. "will you not go...and *not* bring...?" = "go, and do not bring..." (see on 430).

638 τὸ μηδὲν ἄλγος εἰς μέγ' οἴσετε = οἴσετε τὸ μηδὲν εἰς ἄλγος μέγα ("turn what is nothing into a great grief"). ἄλγος is placed before its preposition for emphasis (cf., κἀκ' εἰς μέγιστ' 1180); for τὸ μηδέν cf. 1019, 1187, and see Bruhn 247.19.

639-40 δεινά μ'...δρᾶσαι: "do terrible things to me" (for double accusatives with δρᾶν and ποιεῖν see S 1622).

640 †δυοῖν ἀποκρίνας κακοῖν†: probably corrupt; "having set aside (one) of two punishments" makes doubtful sense, and δυοῖν would have to be scanned as a monosyllable.

643 τοὐμὸν σῶμα: object of δρῶντα κακῶς, "doing harm to my person."

644ff. "Creon, very probably in accord with Attic procedure, swears an oath to his own innocence. That confronts O with a dilemma. If he takes an oath himself in the opposite sense, the case must go to trial, and with nothing better than conjecture to back his case he must lose. On the other hand, in yielding to the persuasion and advice of Iocasta and the chorus to accept Creon's oath and swearing none to the contrary himself, he thereby allows the charge against Creon to lapse...the consequence is that in withdrawing his own allegations he has failed to nullify those of the seer, and therefore they must remain 'on the file,' as it were." (Lewis, "Procedural Basis" 59).

644 μὴ...ὀναίμην: aor. opt. < ὀνίνημι ("may I not be blest").

COMMENTARY 93

645 ὧν: partitive with τι in 644 (for the attraction to genitive see on 148).
  ἐπαιτιᾷ: 2 sg. < ἐπαιτιάομαι.
647 ὅρκον...θεῶν: "oath *by* the gods."
  αἰδεσθείς: aor. pass. partic., αἰδέομαι.

Kommos (649-96). (See Introduction p. 2.) *O dismisses Kreon, but remains angry. Iokaste asks the cause of their quarrel.*

Meter: lyric iambic and dochmiac, analyzed by Dale, *Metrical Analyses* fasc. 3, p. 213.

651 τί...θέλεις...εἰκάθω: internal accusative, "what do you wish me to yield?" Deliberative subjunctive (here of εἴκαθον, aor. < εἴκω) for infinitive after a verb of wishing, S 1806.
652-3 οὔτε πρίν...νῦν τ': οὔτε and τε are parallel (*GP* 508): "the man (Kreon) who was no fool before, and now is formidable because of his oath."
653 καταίδεσαι: aor. imperat., < καταιδέομαι.
656 ἐναγῆ: "under oath."
656-7 μήποτε σ'...βαλεῖν: "(I ask) that you not cast him out."
657 λόγων ἄτιμον: "dishonored of words." i.e., "considered not worth addressing."
658 ἐπίστω (pres. imperat. < ἐπίσταμαι): with ζητῶν (for the construction see on 50), "know that you are seeking..."
659 ὄλεθρον ἢ φυγεῖν: both with ζητῶν, "seeking either my death, or that I be exiled."
660 οὐ τὸν...θεόν: "no, *by* the god..." (For the omission of μά after the negative see S 1596b and line 1088 below.)
661 ὅ τι πύματον: internal accusative with ὀλοίμαν, "may I suffer whatever death is most extreme."
667 προσάψει: evidently intransitive, with subject τάδ'...τὰ πρὸς σφῷν: "if these (quarrels) from you two will join..."
669 ὁ δ' οὖν ἴτω: "Well then, let him (Kreon) go."
670 ἀπωσθῆναι: aor. pass. infin. < ἀπωθέω.
673 στυγνὸς μὲν εἴκων δῆλος εἶ: "you obviously yield sullenly (i.e., with a bad grace)."
673-4 ὅταν θυμοῦ περάσῃς: aor. subj. περάω, the genitive being partitive (J): "whenever you go beyond the bounds *in* your anger" (lose your temper).
676 "Won't you leave me and go away?" (see on 637); κἀκτός = καὶ ἐκτός.

677 ἐν δὲ τοῖσδε σῶς: "but saved by their (the chorus') help" (LSJ ἐν III).
678 μέλλεις: "delay."
679 τόνδ': i.e., Oidipous.
680 μαθοῦσά γ': affirming (GP 135), "(I will take him) when I've learned..."
ἥτις ἡ τύχη: i.e., what has happened.
681 δόκησις...λόγων: "a verbal suspicion" (i.e., a spoken accusation).
δὲ καί: καί = "in turn," see GP 305.
τὸ μὴ 'νδικον: "injustice," the neuter adjective being used as an abstract substantive (S 2051).
683 ἀμφοῖν ἀπ' αὐτοῖν: "on both their parts?" Iokaste wishes to know if *both* of the chorus' vague statements apply to *both* O and Kreon, and is told that they do: the "ignorant suspicion" was spoken both against O (he killed Laios) and Kreon (he is plotting against the king), while those whom this "injustice" (i.e., a false accusation) wounds" are both Kreon and O.
685 γᾶς προνοουμένῳ: with ἐμοί, "as I take thought for our land."
686 ἔνθ' ἔληξεν, αὐτοῦ μένειν: "that it (the λόγος of 684) remain *there, where* it left off (and proceed no further)."
687-8 ὁρᾷς ἵν' ἥκεις...παριεὶς καὶ καταμβλύνων: "Do you see *where* you have come, as you try to relax (pres. partic. < παρίημι) and dull my temper?" I.e., if I obey you and do nothing, my rule is in danger. The chorus respond by asserting their continued devotion.
689-90 εἶπον μέν...ἴσθι δέ: The manner of expression changes slightly, so that the parallelism is lost: "I have said it not just once...but be assured that..."
690-1 παραφρόνιμον...πεφάνθαι μ' ἄν: The perf. infin. (< φαίνομαι) stands for pluperfect indicative with ἄν (*pace* Pearson as quoted by LJ-W) in a contrary-to-fact condition (see on 262): "that I would have been revealed as a madman, helpless in sensible things, if I were deserting you."
694 ὅς γ': "*since* you..." (see on 35).
695 κατ' ὀρθὸν οὐρίσας (aor. 2 sg. indic. < οὐρίζω): lit. "you 'breezed' it straightly" = "you helped it sail on a straight course."
696 τὰ νῦν δ' εὔπομπος αὖ γένοιο: "may you now be a good guide once again" (continuing the metaphor of travel in 695).

COMMENTARY   95

Second Episode, third part (697-862). *To prove that oracles are not always right, Iokaste cites a prediction on the death of Laios; a detail in her story (the fork in the road) leads O to think Laios may be the man whom he fought and killed after leaving Delphi (where he had received an oracle that he would kill his father and marry his mother). The servant of Laios who witnessed the event is summoned for questioning.*

698-9 ὅτου...πράγματος: causal genitive.

699   στήσας ἔχεις: "you have set up..." For the periphrasis (again in 702 below) see on 577.

700   τῶνδ' ἐς πλέον (= μᾶλλον): "(I honor you) *more* than (I do) *them* (the chorus)."

701   Κρέοντος: genitive because it answers the indirect question ὅτου...μῆνιν...πράγματος in 698-9.

   οἷά...ἔχει: The exclamation "what sorts of things he has plotted" = "*because* he has plotted *such things*" (S 2687).

702   τὸ νεῖκος ἐγκαλῶν: internal accusative, lit. "when you accuse the quarrel" = "in fixing blame for the quarrel."

703   καθεστάναι: perf. infin. καθίστημι, virtually = εἶναι (see on 10).

705   μὲν οὖν: without following δέ, introduces a disagreement (see on 587): "no, it was rather..."

   μάντιν...κακοῦργον εἰσπέμψας: "by foisting on me a corrupt prophet..."

706   τό γ' εἰς ἑαυτόν: accus. of respect (see on 82-83), lit. "as far as the matter in regard to himself."

   πᾶν ἐλευθεροῖ στόμα: "he keeps his mouth entirely free (of accusations)."

707   ἀφείς...πέρι: aor. partic., ἀφίημι, "letting yourself loose from what you are talking about" = "putting your mind at rest about..."

708   σοι: dat. of feeling (see on 2).

709   βρότειον οὐδέν: "no mortal," abstract neuter for persons (see on 85, and cf. βροτῶν οὐδέν, 1194-5).

   μαντικῆς ἔχον τέχνης: partitive genit., with participle in indirect statement, "has any share of the art of prophecy."

711   γάρ: See on 277.

713-4 ἥξοι μοῖρα πρὸς παιδὸς θανεῖν ὅστις γένοιτ': The optatives stand for the future indicative and aorist subjunctive

(with ἄν) of the direct statement (S 2607, 2619b): "that a fate would come that he be killed by whatever child was born..."
715 καί: "and yet" (*GP* 292).
716 φονεύουσ': historical present (see on 113).
ἐν τριπλαῖς ἁμαξιτοῖς: "at three highways."
717-8 "Three days did not separate (from us) the birth of the child, and..." = "three days had not elapsed *when*..." (*GP* 293).
718 ἄρθρα...ποδοῖν: accusative of respect, "the limbs of his feet" = "the parts *consisting of* his feet" (genitive of definition; see D, and cf. Euripides *Cyclops* 625).
719 ἄλλων χερσίν: i.e., not personally, but through another's agency.
720 κἀνταῦθ': "and *here*" = "and *in this case*."
οὔτ'...ἤνυσεν < ἀνύω, with accus. with infin., "did not bring it about that..."
722 τὸ δεινόν: accus. in apposition to the sentence (see on 603).
οὐφοβεῖτο = ὃ ἐφοβεῖτο.
723 τοιαῦτα: scornful, "that's the sort of thing that..."
724 ἐντρέπου: imperat. < ἐντρέπομαι, "pay attention to" (with genit.).
μηδέν: "in no way."
724-5 ὧν...ἂν...χρείαν ἐρευνᾷ: "whatever he seeks the need of" = "whatever he needs."
726 οἷον: exclamatory, "what distraction...and disturbance..."
728 ποίας μερίμνης...ὑποστραφείς: aor. pass. partic. < ὑποστρέφω, with causal genitive: "startled (lit. "turned around") at what anxiety...?"
729 ἔδοξ': 1 sg., "I thought."
730 κατασφαγείη < κατασφάζω.
731 οὐδέ πω λήξαντ' ἔχει: "nor has it stopped yet (being said)."
732 'σθ' = ἐστι.
οὗ: "where."
734 κἀπό: with *both* genitives, "leads from Delphi and Daulia to the same place."
735 οὐξεληλυθώς = ὁ ἐξεληλυθώς, "elapsed," perf. partic. < ἐξέρχομαι (with dat. of reference = "since these events").
736 σχεδόν τι πρόσθεν ἤ: "just before (the time when) you..."
740 τὸν δὲ Λάϊον: actually the subject of εἶρπε (see on 15).

COMMENTARY

740-1 φύσιν τίν' εἴρπε...τίνα δ' ἀκμὴν...ἔχων: "with what physical appearance, and what peak of his youth (wishful thinking, as D points out) did he set out?"

742 μέγας, χνοάζων ἄρτι λευκανθὲς κάρα: "tall, and just beginning to grow a down" (< χνόος, "film, light covering," here of grey hair) on a head that blossomed with white."

743 ἀπεστάτει < ἀποστατέω, "be far from."

744-5 ἔοικ'...προβάλλων...οὐκ εἰδέναι: lit. "I seem not to have known that I was exposing myself to..."

749 ἃ δ' ἂν ἔρῃ: "whatever you ask" (2 sg. subj. < ἔρομαι), object of ἐρῶ (fut. < λέγω).
μαθοῦσ': "once I've learned (what your question is)."

750 πότερον: See on 112.
βαιός: "slight" here = "without fanfare."
ἔχων: i.e., "*with* ..." (S 2068a).

751 οἷ' ἀνὴρ ἀρχηγέτης: οἷα introduces an explanatory appositive, "since he was..." (Cf. Thuc. 2.65.11, Hdt. 3.43.2, 1.66.1)

754 ἤδη: not temporal but inferential (see on 462), "this, *then*, is clear."

758 ἀφ' οὗ...ἦλθε: "*after* he had come..."

759 ἔχοντα...ὀλωλότα (< ὄλλυμι): lit., "he saw that you held power and that Laios was dead" = "he saw (then) that you had become king, just as (before) he had seen Laios dead." For τε...τε connecting a present and preceding event cf. Eur. *Hecuba* 519-520, *GP* 515. But even so, this statement badly misrepresents the sequence of events: Laios must have been killed first (and the servant "saw" it), next the servant returned to Thebes (with the news that the king was dead), then O became the new king.

760 θιγών < θιγγάνω (governs the genit.).

761 σφε: tragic 3 pers. pronoun accus. sg. = "him."
κἀπί = καὶ ἐπί, with <u>both</u> ἀγρούς and νομάς.

762 πλεῖστον: with ἄποπτος, "farthest out of sight."

763-4 οἷ' ἀνὴρ δοῦλος: limiting, "for a slave" (S 2993).

764 τῆσδε καὶ μείζω: "even greater than this."

766 πάρεστιν is ambiguous; it usually means "he is present," but here turns out to be impersonal = "it is possible" (LSJ πάρειμι III).
πρὸς τί: "to what end?"
ἐφίεσαι < ἐφίεμαι (middle of ἐφίημι), "desire."

767-8 δέδοικ' ἐμαυτόν...μὴ πόλλ' ἄγαν εἰρημέν' ᾖ μοι: The accusative is placed first as if "lest I have said too much" will follow (see on 15), but the construction changes to passive.

769-70 ἀλλ' ἵξεται μέν· ἀξία δέ...κἀγώ: "well (GP 20), he *will* come; but surely (GP 491) I too deserve to find out..."

770 τά γ' ἐν σοὶ δυσφόρως ἔχοντ': "what is unfortunate in your judgment" (for ἐν in this sense see Barrett on Euripides, *Hippolytus* 1320).

771 κοὺ μὴ στερηθῇς γ': See on 328-9.

772 βεβῶτος < βαίνω.

772-3 τῷ...καὶ κρείσσονι...ἢ σοί: "and to whom better than you...?" On κρείσσονι see LJ-W; for καί in explanatory rhetorical questions see *GP* 314.

775 ἡγόμην: "I was considered" (< ἄγω).

776-7 τύχη τοιάδ': "the following chance event."

778 σπουδῆς γε μέντοι...οὐκ ἀξία: "but not worth my attention (the trouble I took over it)." O seems to mean that the slur on his parentage turned out to be false, and was replaced by a more important problem (787-797 below).

779-80 μ'...καλεῖ...ὡς εἴην: See on 15.

779 ὑπερπλησθεὶς μέθης: aor. pass. partic., ὑπερπίμπλημι with genit. (see on 4-5), "crammed full of..."

780 πλαστός "pretended," i.e., illegitimate (placed before ὡς for emphasis).

781-2 τὴν μὲν οὖσαν ἡμέραν...θατέρᾳ (= τῇ ἑτέρᾳ) δ': "*for* that day I just barely held back, but *on* the next one..."

783 ἤλεγχον: imperf. < ἐλέγχω, "questioned them."

784 τῷ μεθέντι τὸν λόγον: dat. of reference: "against the man who had launched (aor. partic. < μεθίημι) the story."

785 τὰ μέν: The article is adverbial, adding emphasis to μέν, and not to be translated (S 1111).
κείνοιν ἐτερπόμην: dual dat., "I was pleased by them," i.e. satisfied with their response.

786 ὑφεῖρπε...πολύ: "it crept about (was talked of) widely" (see J, and Bruhn 247.24), rather than "it got under my skin in full force" (D).

788-9 ὧν μὲν ἱκόμην ἄτιμον: short for ἄτιμον τούτων ἅ ἱκόμην, "dishonored of the things *for* which (cf. 1005) I came." For the genitive cf. 697.

789 ἀθλίῳ: sc. μοι.

790 προὐφάνη λέγων: "was manifest saying," i.e., "clearly declared" (cf. Euripides, *Helen* 516 χρῄζουσ' ἐφάνη).

COMMENTARY 99

791 μιχθῆναι: aor. pass. < μείγνυμι, a euphemism for sexual intercourse.
792 ὁρᾶν: limiting infin. with ἄτλητον, "unbearable...to see."
794 'πακούσας = ἐπακούσας.
795-6 ἄστροις τὸ λοιπὸν τεκμαρούμενος: future partic., "intending forevermore to estimate (its position) by the stars," i.e., give it a wide berth.
796 ἔφευγον, ἔνθα μήποτ' ὀψοίμην: "I fled the land of Corinth, (to a place) where I would never see..." The normal future indicative (μή in a generic relative clause) is replaced by future optative, perhaps because an indirect statement is implied; see *MT* 574, S 2554a.
798 στείχων: "as I traveled..."
799 ὄλλυσθαι: pres. infin. standing for imperf., "that he was being killed."
801 ἦ: 1 pers. sg. imperf. < εἰμί (with πέλας).
802-3 κἀπὶ πωλικῆς...ἀπήνης ἐμβεβώς: "mounted (< ἐμβαίνω) on a horse-drawn wagon."
804 ξυνηντίαζον: In O's account of the killing one would expect mostly the aorist tense, but he often uses the narrative imperfect (S 1899) and historical present (see on 113).
805 ἠλαυνέτην: imperf. dual < ἐλαύνω.
806 τὸν ἐκτρέποντα, τὸν τροχηλάτην: "the man who was pushing me aside, the driver." As D notes, O mentions only three people: the herald (also called ἡγεμών), Laios (the old man mounted on the wagon), and the driver; but his list is not exhaustive (cf. 752).
807 δι' ὀργῆς: "in a rage," cf. 344.
808 ὄχους παραστείχοντα τηρήσας: "keeping an eye on me as I walked beside the wagon" (ὄχους is poetic plural).
808-9 μέσον κάρα...μου καθίκετο: "came down (< καθικνέομαι) right on (lit. "in the middle of") my head."
810 ἴσην: "equally" (see on 16).
συντόμως: "immediately."
811 τυπείς: aor. pass. partic. < τύπτω.
811-2 ὕπτιος...εὐθὺς ἐκκυλίνδεται: "he was rolled straight out onto his back."
813-4 εἰ δὲ...τι συγγενές: euphemistically vague, "If some kinship to Laios is related to this foreigner."
815 τοῦδέ γ' ἀνδρός: O means himself (cf. 534, 829).
817 ᾧ: dat. of reference, "*in whose case ...*"
817-8 μηδ'...δέχεσθαι, μηδὲ προσφωνεῖν τινα: cf. 238.

819	ὠθεῖν δ': "but instead (they must all) cast me out (cf. 241)." Still governed by ἔξεστι, although the verb no longer suits it (*zeugma.*)
819-20	τάδ'...τάσδ' ἀράς: O restates the object more precisely: "and all this—no one but I have put these curses on myself."
821	ἐν χεροῖν ἐμαῖν: "*with* my hands."
822	ἆρ': Even without the negative (cf. ἆρ' οὐχί 823) the question expects the answer "yes" (*GP* 46).
823	πᾶς: "totally." φυγεῖν: i.e., be banished from Thebes.
824	μήστι: = μή ἔστι. τοὺς ἐμούς: i.e., his presumed mother and father in Corinth.
825	ἤ...δεῖ: "or else (if I *do* flee back to my mother and father) I must..."
826	ζυγῆναι: aor. pass. infin. < ζεύγνυμι.
829	ἐπ' ἀνδρὶ τῷδ' ἂν ὀρθοίη λόγον: "would have the right story in this man's (i.e., *my own*, cf. 815) case." For the repetition of ἂν see on 262.
834	δ'...οὖν: marking an especially important contrast (*GP* 460).
835	πρὸς τοῦ παρόντος: "from the man who was there," (the eyewitness); for the imperfect force of the participle see D.
838	πεφασμένου: perf. pass. partic. < φαίνομαι, in a genitive absolute with subject omitted (see on 505), "and when he *has* appeared, what is your desire?"
840	ἂν ἐκπεφευγοίην: "I would have escaped..."
841	περισσόν: "special, noteworthy."
842-3	ἔφασκες αὐτόν...ἐννέπειν ὡς: "you said that *he* (the shepherd) said that..." λῃστάς...ἄνδρας...ὡς...κατακτείνειαν: The subject of the indirect statement is anticipated in the accusative (see on 15).
846	οἰόζωνον: "single-girded" = "traveling alone." Travelers wore a belt (ζώνη) holding up their clothing to speed their walking.
846-7	σαφῶς...ἐστίν...εἰς ἐμὲ ῥέπον: The metaphor is from a balance-scale (*Iliad* 22.209-13): it is the *loser* whose side of the scale dips lower.
847	ἤδη: See on 754.
848	ὡς φανέν γε τοὔπος ὧδ': "that the tale appeared *thus* (with several killers)." Normally verbs of perception govern

accus. with partic., but often with imperatives of *knowing*, ὡς is added (S 2120, K-G 2.94-5).
849 **ἔστιν** = ἔξεστιν.
ἐκβαλεῖν πάλιν: i.e., "repudiate."
851-3 **εἰ δ' οὖν...οὗτοι ποτ'...φανεῖ**: "But even if he were to deviate somewhat...he will never (at any rate) show ..." The condition becomes more vivid as it proceeds (see S 2361a).
853 **δικαίως ὀρθόν**:"truly correct" (i.e., according to the prophecy).
ὅν γε: See on 35.
857 **μαντείας**: with οὕνεκ', "as far as prophecy goes."
857-8 **οὔτε τῇδ'...οὔτε τῇδ'**: "I would look neither this way nor that from now on." The phrase is perhaps drawn from observing the flight of birds for omens (J).
860 **στελοῦντα**: fut. partic. (< στέλλω) expressing purpose.
ἀφῇς: aor. subj. < ἀφίημι ("neglect").
862 **ὧν οὔ σοι φίλον** = τούτων ἃ οὔ σοι φίλον ἐστὶ πρᾶξαι.

863-910 Second Stasimon. *I pray for holiness in word and deed, whose laws alone are divine and eternal (str. A).*

Hybris leads to one-man rule, and after too much success it stumbles, and plunges to disaster. Let our political rivalries be regulated by god (antistr. A).

May the scorner of Justice and the Gods be damned; if such a man is unpunished, all is lost. (str. B).

I will no longer visit the gods' shrines, if this is unfulfilled. Zeus, do not overlook this; the disregard of Apollo's oracle means the end of belief in the gods. (antistr. B)

In many ways this is one of the most puzzling choral odes of Sophocles. (For bibliography, see "Topics for Discussion" in Vol. 1, section III.1.) If it is a response to the previous episode (O's anger, his quarrel with Kreon and Iokaste's belittling of the oracle) it seems too harsh a condemnation of O by a chorus which has hitherto supported him; yet if it only expresses general fears for the political stability of Thebes while the murderer is at large, it makes the chorus seem oddly detached from what has just occurred.

Yet the Sophoclean chorus is a somewhat unusual participant in the play: it does not have "the same consistency or coherence of character as we would expect from an individual...different and sometimes conflicting reactions being presented in the same play or the same ode..." (R. Burton, *The Chorus in Sophocles* [Oxford 1980]

3); and when its judgments seem one-sided or irrelevant in their immediate context, they may have wider unintended reference, either to the play's as yet unforeseen outcome (O will in fact plunge to his doom, and the oracle will be strikingly confirmed), or even beyond the play entirely to the political and social concerns of an Athenian audience in wartime. Comparable is the "Ode on Man" in the first stasimon of *Antigone*, 332-375.

Meter: aeolo-choriambic, analyzed by Dale, *Metrical Analyses* fasc. 2, pp. 38-9.

863-4 εἴ... ξυνείη φέροντι... ἀγνείαν: εἰ = εἴθε (S 1815), "may *moira* keep me company when I win piety" evidently = "may I win for my lot in life to behave piously" (contrasted with κακὰ μοῖρα, 887 below).

864-5 λόγων ἔργων τε πάντων: "*in* all words and deeds."

865-6 ὧν νόμοι πρόκεινται ὑψίποδες: "(words and deeds) *for which* laws are displayed standing on high." Athenian laws were written on inscriptions; here the chorus imagines a similar set of laws in heaven—contrast the "unwritten laws," ἄγραφοι νόμοι, in *Antigone* 454-5 and W. K. C. Guthrie, *The Sophists* (Cambridge 1971) 117-131.

868 **νιν**: i.e., τοὺς νόμους. νιν is usually singular (see on 123), but may be plural, see S 325e.

869 **θνατά** = θνητή.
ἀνέρων: epic form for ἀνδρῶν.
ἔτικτεν: The imperfect (aorist ἔτεκεν would have been expected) seems to mean "was their parent" (J).

869-70 οὐδὲ μήποτε... κατακοιμάσῃ: "will absolutely never (see on 771) make them sleep (become ineffectual). "

871 μέγας ἐν τούτοις θεός: The sentence in asyndeton (without a connecting particle) summarizes the preceding strophe (S 2167a). "God is great in them," i.e., "by these laws divinity shows its power."

872-3 ὕβρις φυτεύει τύραννον· ὕβρις, εἰ... ὑπερπλησθῇ: asyndeton with anaphora (S 2167c), as in 881 θεὸν αἰτοῦμαι· θεὸν οὐ λήξω. Asyndeton here denotes a strong *contrast* (S 2167d) with the metaphors of divine generation above (τεκνωθέντες, πατήρ, ἔτικτεν): "but arrogance begets one-man rule."

COMMENTARY

It is difficult to apply this strophe directly to the previous scene: Oidipous last referred to his wealth, tyranny and skill in somewhat arrogant terms only in 380ff, and τύραννος (on which see "Topics for Discussion" in Vol. 1, section II.4) is not otherwise a word of reproach in the play. But the word is never used *positively* (Ahl, *Evidence and Self-Conviction* [see "Topics for Discussion" in Vol. 1, section III.3] translates it as "dictator") and its contemporary associations were so unhealthy that they must have been easy to recall.

873 **ὑπερπλησθῇ**: See on 779; subjunctive as if with ἐάν, see on 198-9.
875 **ἃ μή**: μή because generic (see on 569).
876 **γεῖσ'**: accus. pl. < γεῖσον, "cornice" (the overhang of a roof), accus. of motion without a preposition (see on 35).
ἀναβᾶσ' < ἀναβαίνω.
877 **ὤρουσεν** < ὀρούω, gnomic aorist equivalent to a generalizing present (S 1931): "rushes to a precipitous necessity," i.e., a steep and unavoidable fall.
879-80 **τὸ καλῶς δ' ἔχον πόλει πάλαισμα**: "the competition which is beneficial for the city," i.e., healthy political rivalry.
883-4 **ὑπέροπτα...πορεύεται**: internal accus., lit. "traverses disdainful things," i.e., "behaves arrogantly."
χεροῖν ἢ λόγῳ: i.e., in deed or word (see on 219).
885 **Δίκας ἀφόβητος**: See on 179.
887 **ἕλοιτο** < αἱρέω, in a wish.
888 **δυσπότμου χάριν χλιδᾶς**: "because of his ill-fated arrogance." For the meaning of χλιδή (lit. "luxury") see Griffith on *Prometheus Bound* 436-7.
889-91 **εἰ μή κτλ.**: another conditional clause, even though the sentence already began with one (883-6). μή goes with both κερδανεῖ and ἕρξεται, but not with ἕξεται.
889 **τὸ κέρδος κερδανεῖ**: fut. indic., with cognate accus.
890 **ἔρξεται** < εἴργω, "keep himself away from."
891 **ἕξεται**: "cling to" with genit.
ματάζων: participle derived from μάτην, "being a fool."
892 **ἐν τοῖσδ'**: neuter, "under these circumstances" (i.e., if he does what is condemned in 889-891).
894 **†ἔρξεται†** makes no sense; it seems to have been copied from 890, replacing an original verb which completed the phrase "who amidst such things...to ward off the arrows of anger from his soul?"

896 τί δεῖ με χορεύειν: "why should I dance?" "Dance" might be stretched to mean "worship the god," and this chorus later promises to celebrate Kithairon by *dancing* (1092-5). Yet the old men of Thebes are not dancing as dramatic characters in the play, only as performers, so that here the despairing chorus might be asking "if such unholiness is not punished, why should we perform in this play?" Other Sophoclean choruses refer (with more dramatic justification) to their own role as dancers in a play at *Ajax* 701 and *Trachiniae* 216-7. (I owe these references to an unpublished essay by Albert Henrichs.)

897 εἶμι: fut. indic. < ἔρχομαι.

898 γᾶς ἐπ' ὀμφαλόν: See on 480.

900 'Αβαῖσι: "at Abai," a town on the border between Phokis and Boiotia which also had an oracle of Apollo (Herodotus I.46, VIII.33).

901 τὰν 'Ολυμπίαν: sc. γῆν. For families of prophets at Olympia see H. W. Parke, *The Oracles of Zeus* (Oxford 1967) 164-193.

903 ὀρθ' ἀκούεις: internal accusative (see on 190-4).

904 μὴ λάθοι: The subject (something like "the current disbelief in your oracles") is left unexpressed.

906-7 φθίνοντα... Λαΐου θέσφατ': "the waning oracles *about* Laios (see on 49)." But the text is missing four syllables (it must correspond with the strophe at 892—although that too may be corrupt, see on 894).

908 ἐξαιροῦσιν: "(people) are removing (i.e., disregarding)..." For the omission of the subject see S 931d.

909 τιμαῖς ἐμφανής: "bright in honors."

910 ἔρρει: See on 560.

911--1085 Third Episode. *Iokaste comes out to beg Apollo for help in relieving Oidipous' troubled mind. An old man appears offering news in hopes for a reward: O is to be named king of Corinth now that Polybos has died. When O is still worried about returning to his mother because of the oracle, the old man tells him further that he is not her son—he was given to him by a shepherd from the house of Laios, the same servant whom they are already seeking as the eyewitness to Laios' murder. Over Iokaste's desperate objections, Oidipous resolves to learn his origin, no matter how humble it may be.*

COMMENTARY

The messenger from Corinth is an incongruously ridiculous character: his first three verses contain a laughable rhyme, he addresses O too familiarly, and freely admits his only motive is a reward. (See Bernd Seidensticker, *Palintonos Harmonia: Studien zu komischen Elementen in der griechischen Tragödie* (Hypomnemata vol. 72, Göttingen 1982) 85-88.) O calls him "a nothing" and "a common laborer," and seems disgusted at the thought that this man has anything to do with his childhood.

Perhaps this preoccupation explains why O fails in this scene to see the truth: he learns that Polybos is not his real father, of his exposure, that his feet had been pierced (like the baby already mentioned by Iokaste), and even that Laios' household was the source from which he came. Yet he still does not put things together.

But there is a third character present also, and she realizes everything; her panic results in a harsh argument, so that at this stage the couple which has hitherto worked together becomes estranged; they no longer share their thoughts, and begin to view each other with suspicion.

Meter: iambic trimeter

911 παρεστάθη: aor. pass. παρίστημι, "the thought has occurred to me to..."
912 ναούς: accus. of motion.
913 στέφη < στέφος, τό.
λαβούσῃ: with μοι, line 911.
κἀπιθυμιάματα: "and offerings of incense."
914 ὑψοῦ...αἴρει θυμόν: "raises high his spirit" = "becomes excited."
915-6 ὁποῖ' ἀνήρ ἔννους: ὁποῖα adverbial, "*like* a sensible man."
916 τὰ καινὰ τοῖς πάλαι τεκμαίρεται: "interpret the new by the old." Iokaste thinks O should ignore the more recent prediction of his crimes against his parents, because the old oracle to Laios was not fulfilled.
917 ἐστι τοῦ λέγοντος: predicative genit. (see on 278), "he is in the power of whoever is talking."
918 ὅτ' = ὅτε (ὅτι is never elided), but here causal (S 2240) rather than temporal.
παραινοῦσ': modal, "by offering advice."

οὐδὲν ἐς πλέον ποιῶ: The standard phrase is οὐδὲν πλέον ποιεῖν, "accomplish nothing helpful," but here "nothing (tending) toward what is helpful."

919 ἄγχιστος: "closest." "Most Greek houses would have a cult stone or altar of Apollo Agyieus ("of the street") before the door, and there is clear evidence that this stone was represented on the tragic (and comic) stage" (Oliver Taplin, *The Stagecraft of Aeschylus* [Oxford 1977] 319).

920 ἀφῖγμαι: perf. < ἀφικνέομαι.

920-1 τοῖσδε σὺν κατεύγμασιν, ὅπως: The noun introduces the following object clause with subjunct. (S 2218): "with the following prayers, (namely) that you provide..."

921 πόρῃς < ἔπορον, a poetic verb which occurs only in the aorist (see LSJ *πόρω).

922 ἐκπεπληγμένον: "struck senseless,"< ἐκπλήσσω.

923 ὡς κυβερνήτην νεώς: "just as (we would fear seeing disabled) the pilot of a ship."

926 μάλιστα: "better yet..." (see Bruhn 247.17).
αὐτὸν εἶπατ'...ὅπου: sc. ἐστίν (the subject is anticipated).
κάτισθ' = κάτιστε < κατ-οῖδα.

929-30 ἀλλ' ὀλβία...γένοιτ': ἀλλά introduces a wish (*GP* 15).

930 γ' οὖσα: conditional (see on 326).

931 αὕτως: "in the same way, likewise."
καὶ σύ γ': sc. ὄλβιος γένοιο.

932-3 ὅτου...χώ τι (= καὶ ὅ τι): indirect questions with φράζ'.
ἀφῖξαι: perf. 2 sg. < ἀφικνέομαι.

935 παρὰ τίνος: i.e., who sent you?

936 οὐξερῶ = ὁ ἐξερῶ.

937 ἴσως: "perhaps."

939-40 τύραννον...στήσουσιν: "will make him tyrant" (αὐτόν = Oidipous).

940 ηὐδᾶτ': imperf. pass. < αὐδάω (the old man is reporting a rumor).

941 τί δ': "what?" (expressing surprise, *GP* 175).
ἐγκρατής: "in control."

945 ὦ πρόσπολ': addressed to a (non-speaking) servant standing by.

945-6 οὐχὶ...λέξεις; see on 430.
ὡς τάχος = ὡς τάχιστα, "as quickly as possible."

947 ἵν' ἐστέ: exclamatory, "just look where you are" (i.e., nowhere).

COMMENTARY 107

948 **ἔφευγε**: "was in exile."
949 **πρὸς τῆς τύχης**: See on 292.
951 **ἐξεπέμψω**: aor. mid. 2 sg. < ἐκπέμπω.
953 **ἵν'**: indirect question with σκόπει.
955 **ἀγγελῶν**: fut. partic. of purpose.
956 **ὡς οὐκέτ' ὄντα...ἀλλ' ὀλωλότα**: For the superfluous ὡς see on 848.
957 **σημήνας γενοῦ**: "indicate it" (for the periphrasis see on 90).
960 **πότερα**: See on 112.
   νόσου ξυναλλαγῇ: "contact with disease."
961 **σμικρά**: fem., with ῥοπή.
962 **ἔφθιτο**: "died" (intransitive 2 aor. mid. < φθίω).
963 **τῷ μακρῷ γε συμμετρούμενος χρόνῳ**: lit. "measured together with his long time" = *suitably* for his advanced age.
965 **τὴν Πυθόμαντιν ἑστίαν**: "the Pythian-prophetic hearth" on which laurel leaves were burned in the temple of Apollo at Delphi before the Pythian priestess gave her prophecies (Walter Burkert, *Greek Religion* [Cambridge, Mass. 1985] 116).
966 **ὄρνις**: accus. pl.
967 **κτανεῖν**: The aorist infin. with μέλλω is rare, but for examples see K-G I.179.
   ὁ δέ: "*but* he (my father)..."
969 **ἄψαυστος ἔγχους**: See on 179.
   εἴ τι μή: τι is adverbial, "unless in any way..."
   τὠμῷ πόθῳ: "because of longing for me," the possessive adjective being equivalent to an objective genitive (S 1197).
970 **κατέφθιθ'** = κατέφθιτο.
   ἂν θανὼν εἴη: potential optative in a deduction (*MT* 238).
971 **τὰ δ' οὖν παρόντα κτλ.**: "At any rate, having gathered up (and taken with him) the *current* prophecies (even if not all prophecies in general), which are worthless, Polybos lies in Hades."
974 **παρηγόμην**: "I was being led astray."
977 **ἄνθρωπος, ᾧ κτλ.**: "a man *for whom* luck is in the ascendant, and there is accurate prior knowledge of nothing." (The second clause applies generally, not only to Oidipous.)
979 **εἰκῇ**: "at random" = "without specific goals."
   ὅπως δύναιτο: "however one can." For the optative (instead of subjunctive with ἄν) see S 2477d, and on 314-5.

981 **κἂν ὀνείρασιν**: "In dreams *too* (as well as in oracles)." Dreams too, she implies, are an uncertain indication of the future. For incestuous dreams see Herodotus 6.107, Artemidorus, *Oneirokritika* 1.79, Georges Devereux, *Dreams in Greek Tragedy* (Berkeley 1976) xxii, John J. Winkler, *The Constraints of Desire: The Anthropology of Sex and Gender in Ancient Greece* (New York, 1990) 37-8.

983 **παρ' οὐδέν**: predicative, "of no importance."
ῥᾷστα: adverbial neut. pl. accus. of superlative < ῥᾴδιος.

984 **ἂν ἐξείρητο**: For pluperf. in a contrary-to fact condition see on 262; σοι is dat. of agent.

985 **'κύρει** = ἐκύρει, in a contrary-to-fact-condition: "if she did not happen to be alive" (see on 258).

987 **μέγας ⟨γ'⟩ ὀφθαλμός**: "a great advantage" (LSJ ὀφθαλμός IV). The fact that they can speak so of Polybos' death (and consider Merope's being still alive an annoyance) shows how much more concerned they are about O's part in the deeds than the deeds themselves.

990 **ᾤκει** < οἰκέω.

991 **τί δ' ἔστ' ἐκείνης**: "what is there *about* her...? For the genitive see on 49.
ἐς φόβον φέρον: See on 517.

993 **θεμιστόν**: sc. ἐστί, with accus. and infin., "lawful that..."

994 **γάρ**: See on 277.

995 **μιγῆναι** < μείγνυμι, aor. pass. (cf. 791-2).

998 **μακρὰν ἀπῳκεῖτ'**: lit. "was lived far-away-from."

999 **ὄμμαθ'**: here "faces."

1000 **ἦ γάρ**: interrogative particles, not to be translated (*GP* 284-5).

1002-3 **τί δῆτ' ἐγὼ οὐχὶ...ἐξελυσάμην**: a rhetorical question addressed to himself, "why haven't I relieved you...?" = "I must immediately relieve you..." (see Barrett on Euripides, *Hippolytus* 1060-1.)

1004 **χάριν...ἀξίαν**: "the thanks you deserve."

1005 **τοῦτ' ἀφικόμην, ὅπως**: "I came *for this reason* (S1610, cf. 788-9) to..."

1006 **εὖ πράξαιμί τι**: "get some advantage," i.e., he wants a reward once O is king in Corinth.

1008 **καλῶς εἶ δῆλος οὐκ εἰδώς**: "You *obviously* (see on 673) do not *really* (LSJ καλός C.II.3) know..."

1009 **πρὸς θεῶν**: πρός with genit. in requests, "in the name of."

COMMENTARY 109

1010 **φεύγεις**: "are avoiding," with μολεῖν.
1011 **ταρβῶν γε**: "yes, *because* I am afraid...," explaining φεύγεις in the preceding line.
  σαφής: See on 106.
1014 **πρὸς δίκης**: "justly," "justifiably."
1016 **ὁθούνεκ'**: "because."
  οὐδὲν ἐν γένει: "not at all related."
1018 **τοῦδε τἀνδρός**: i.e., myself.
  ἴσον: adverbial, "just as much," i.e., not at all.
1019 **ἐξ ἴσου τῷ μηδενί**: "equally with nothing" (see on 638).
1020 **ἐγείνατ'**: 3 sg. 1 aor. mid. < γείνομαι, "begat."
1021 **ἀντὶ τοῦ**: interrogative pronoun, i.e., "why."
1022 **δῶρον...λαβών**: "because he got you as a gift."
1023 **κᾆθ' ὧδ'...ἐστέρξεν μέγα**: εἶτα expresses surprise (S 2653), "you mean to say he loved me so much...?"
1024 **ἡ...πρὶν...ἀπαιδία**: "his previous childlessness."
1025 **ἐμπολήσας, ἢ τυχών**: "after buying me, or (getting me) by chance?"
  δίδως: historical present (as often below).
1026 **ναπαίαις ἐν...πτυχαῖς**: "the wooded folds" = "the winding forest valleys."
1027 **ὡδοιπόρεις** < ὁδοιπορέω.
  πρὸς τί: "for what purpose?"
1028 **ἐπεστάτουν** < ἐπιστατέω, "be in charge of" (with dat.).
1029 **κἀπὶ θητείᾳ πλάνης**: lit. "a wanderer for hire" = "a common laborer."
1030 **σοῦ δ'...σωτήρ γε**: "yes (I *was* a laborer) but to *you* I was a savior" (*GP* 153).
1031 **τί δ' ἄλγος ἴσχοντ'**: The question merely picks up the implications of σωτήρ. O seems to have no memory of his feet having been pierced (see the next note), nor of why he received his name "swollen-foot" (< οἰδέω, "swell"). He is affected by the news (1033 οἴμοι) although he does not notice the repetition of a phrase from 718 (ἄρθρα...ποδοῖν)—but of course Iokaste does.
1033 **τί...κακόν**: could mean either "why do you mention this old wound?" (implying that O has always known the reason for his name) or "what old wound is this that you mention?" (implying that his wounds had long ago healed, so that he only now learns what had happened). Only the latter interpretation makes dramatic sense (see on 367 and 1031, and D.

J. Mastronarde, *Contact and Discontinuity* (Berkeley 1979) 80 n. 10).

1034 ἔχοντα διατόρους ποδοῖν ἀκμάς: lit. "pierced foot-edges."

1035 σπαργάνων ἀνειλόμην: genit. of separation, "I took up from my swaddling-clothes a terrible disgrace." O assumes that his parents were as lowly as this messenger; the verb is ironic, being usually applied to acknowledging a newborn child as one's own (LSJ ἀναιρέω B.I.4). (σπάργανα were tightly-wrapped bands which prevented a newborn child from moving.)

1037 πρὸς μητρὸς ἢ πατρός; of agent. O's question is ambiguous, since it might refer to ὠνομάσθης in 1036 (did I get my name from my parents?) or ἔχοντα διατόρους ποδοῖν ἀκμάς in 1034 (did my parents actually maim me?).

1038 λῷον: comparative adverb, "better."

1042 δήπου...ὠνομάζετο: "I think he was called one of Laios' men."

1046 εἰδεῖτ': optative < οἶδα, "you locals would know that best."

1050 ὁ καιρός: governs accus. with infin., "it's time that these things be found out." (ηὑρῆσθαι perf. pass. infin. < εὑρίσκω).

1052 κἀμάτευες = καὶ ἐμάτευες (< ματεύω, "seek").

1055 ἐφιέμεσθα: imperf. < ἐφίεμαι.

1056 τί δ' ὄντιν' εἶπε: dismissive, "what about the man he mentioned?" I.e., "who cares?"
ἐντραπῇς: 2 aor. subj. pass. < ἐντρέπω, "don't pay any attention)."

1057 ῥηθέντα: aor. pass. partic. < ἐρῶ (future of λέγω).
βούλου μηδὲ μεμνῆσθαι: imperative, "don't even desire to remember."

1058-9 ὅπως...οὐ φανῶ: explaining τοῦτο (see on 406-7).

1060-1 τι...κήδῃ: 2 sg., κήδομαι, "are at all concerned about."

1062-3 τρίτης...μητρός...τρίδουλος: "thrice a slave since my great-grandmother."

1063 φανῶ: aor. pass. subj.

1064 πιθοῦ μοι: aor. mid. imperat. < πείθω < "listen to (lit. "obey") me."

1065 μὴ οὐ...ἐκμαθεῖν: "so as not to find out..." (see on 283).

1067 τὰ λῷστα τοίνυν ταῦτά κτλ.: spoken in annoyance: "well, this 'what's best for me' has been a nuisance for some time now" (for πάλαι used of fairly recent events see Bruhn 247.22).

COMMENTARY 111

1068 εἴθε μήποτε γνοίης: 2 aor. opt. (< γιγνώσκω) in a negative wish.
1070 πλουσίῳ χαίρειν γένει: "rejoice in her golden family." O assumes that her reluctance to learn more comes from shame at his low birth.
1071-2 τοῦτο...μόνον: i.e., δύστηνε.
1073 βέβηκεν: perf. < βαίνω.
1073-4 ὑπ' ἀγρίας...λύπης: "under the influence of uncontrollable grief."
1074 ᾄξασα: "rushing off," aor. < ἀίσσω.
1074-5 ὅπως μὴ...ἀναρρήξει: ὅπως μή with fut. indic. (< ἀναρρήγνυμι, "break out") in a clause of fearing (S 2231).
1076 ὁποῖα χρῄζει ῥηγνύτω: 3 sg. imperat. pres., "let there burst forth whatever things will."
1077 βουλήσομαι: The desire is really present, but the tense is influenced by the futurity of *what* is desired; see Page on Euripides, *Medea* 259, K-G 1.172-3.
1078 φρονεῖ...μέγα: i.e., "has big ideas, is proud."
ὡς γυνή: "since she is a woman" (see on οἷα, 751).
1080-5 In defiance of the imagined shame of his wife, O exults in the indeterminacy of his birth: chance is his mother, and the months are his kin. Fortune and time have defined him rather than any legacy from parents.
1080 νέμων: "considering."
1082 τῆς is a demonstrative, "from *this* mother..."
1083 μικρὸν καὶ μέγαν διώρισαν: "have defined (< διορίζω) me as small or great."
1084 τοιόσδε δ' ἐκφύς: causal partic.
ἐξέλθοιμ': aor. opt. < ἐξέρχομαι, "turn out."

1086-1109 Third Stasimon. *If I am right, we will be thanking Kithairon soon for O's upbringing (str.)*
Your mother must have been a goddess or nymph, but who was your father? Was it Pan? Apollo? Hermes? Dionysus? *(antistr.)*

All three characters have different ideas about O's parentage: Iokaste knows the truth, while O thinks he is low-born; now we learn that the chorus hopes he may be the son of a god.

Meter: dactylo-epitrite, analyzed by Dale, *Metrical Analyses* fasc. 1, pp. 34-5.

1088 οὐ τὸν Ὄλυμπον: See on 660.

1088-90 ἀπείρων...οὐκ ἔσῃ...μὴ οὐ: "you will not be without experience that..." For the double negative see on 283; ἀπείρων in this sense (= ἄπειρος) only here.

1089-91 τὰν αὔριον πανσέληνον... σέ γε τὸν πατριώταν...καὶ τροφὸν καὶ ματέρ' αὔξειν: pres. infin., but with future sense after μὴ οὐ, "that tomorrow's all-night festival will exalt you as homeland, nurse and mother of O."

1092-3 καὶ χορεύεσθαι πρὸς ἡμῶν: The subject changes: "and that *you* will be celebrated by us in dance."

1095 ὡς ἐπίηρα φέροντα: with σε, "on the grounds that you rendered service..."

1098 τίς...τίς: The mother is the subject of the question, but the emphasis is on the identity of the father (Πανός, Λοξίου) and his affinity for mountains.

ἔτικτε: For the tense see on 869.

1100 ὀρεσσιβάτα: For the genitive see on 496.

1101 πελασθεῖσ' < πελάζω, "brought near to" with genit., a euphemism for sexual intercourse.

1101-2 ἤ σέ γ' εὐνάτειρά τις Λοξίου: "or else (was your mother) some bedmate of Apollo?" (σε is repeated a third time for emphasis, and need not be translated).

1102 τῷ is a demonstrative: "to *him* (Apollo)..." (cf. 1082).

πλάκες ἀγρόνομοι: "pastures (< πλάξ) where fields are grazed."

1104 ὁ Κυλλάνας ἀνάσσων: "the ruler of Mt. Kyllene" (in Arcadia) is Hermes.

1106-7 εὕρημα δέξατ': sc. σε, "took you as a foundling." (Note the omission of the augment in tragic lyric and messenger's speeches, S 438.)

του = τινος.

1110-1185 Fourth Episode. *The servant of Laios is a hostile witness, but O forces him to reveal that he is the man who gave him as an infant to the Corinthian, and learns that he is Iokaste's son. He rushes into the palace.*

Meter: iambic trimeter

1110-1 τι...σταθμᾶσθαι: "to make some estimate."

μὴ συναλλάξαντά πω: "although I have not had dealings (see on 34) with him yet." (μή in the protasis with εἰ χρή.)
1112-3 ἕν τε γάρ...σύμμετρος: lit. "he is harmonious with this man (the one you spoke of), equal to him in his advanced age."
1114 ἄλλως τε: "and besides...," answering ἕν τε in 1112.
1116 προὔχοις = προ-έχοις, "surpass."
1118 πιστὸς ὡς νομεύς: limiting (see on 763-4) "reliable, for a shepherd."
1121 δεῦρο: with βλέπων.
1123 ἦ: 1st pers. sg. imperfect < εἰμί (the normal form in tragedy, see Barrett on Eur. *Hippolytus*700).
1124 μεριμνῶν < μεριμνάω.
1125 συνειπόμην < συνέπομαι.
1127 ἦν μὲν Κιθαιρών, ἦν δὲ κτλ.: anaphora, "there was Kithairon, and there was its neighborhood."
1128 οἶσθα τῇδέ που μαθών: "are you aware of knowing anywhere there..."
1129 καὶ λέγεις: καί because the question explains his reluctance (*GP* 315), "and whom do you mean?"
1130 ξυναλλάξας: sc. again οἶσθα.
πω: See on 105.
1134 ἦμος: "when."
1134-5 τὸν Κιθαιρῶνος τόπον ὁ μέν...ἐγὼ δ': The required verb (e.g., ἐναίομεν or εἴχομεν) is missing, so LJ-W assume at least one following line has been lost from the text.
1135 διπλοῖσι ποιμνίοις...ἑνί: perhaps dat. of accompaniment, or perhaps governed by a verb missing after 1135.
1136-7 τρεῖς...χρόνους: "for three whole six-month periods from spring (< ἦρ) to fall" (lit. "to Arktouros," the star that appeared in the fall sky).
1138 χειμῶνι δ' ἤδη: "then, in the winter..."
ἔπαυλ' = ἔπαυλα, "barns."
1140 λέγω τι τούτων: λέγω τι = "I am speaking rightly" (LSJ λέγω III.6), so this seems to mean "am I saying any *of this* correctly?"
1146 οὐκ εἰς ὄλεθρον: See on 430.
1148 δεῖται: with genit., "require a punisher."
1151 ἄλλως: "uselessly."
1152 πρὸς χάριν μὲν οὐκ...κλαίων δ': "if not to please me...then howling (in pain)."

1154 ἀποστρέψει χέρας: i.e., tie his hands behind him as a prelude to torture. For the torture of slaves in homicide investigations see Lewis, "Procedural Basis," 63.
1155 δύστηνος: of himself, "I'm doomed."
1156 ὅν: antecedent is τὸν παῖδα.
1157 ὀλέσθαι δ' ὤφελον: aor. of ὀφείλω with infin. in a unattainable wish, lit. "I ought to have perished..."
1158 εἰς τόδ': i.e., to death.
1160 ἐς τριβὰς ἐλᾷ: "will be insistent on (lit. "will drive to") delays."
1161 πάλαι: See on 1067.
1162 οἰκεῖον: "one of your own household."
1168 γεγώς < γίγνομαι.
1169 πρὸς αὐτῷ γ' εἰμὶ τῷ δεινῷ λέγειν: The infinitive limits the adjective, "I am right next to the very thing that is horrible to say."
1170 κἀγωγ' ἀκούειν: "and I (am next to what is horrible) to hear."
1171 ἐκλῄζεθ': "was called," < κλῄζω.
1174 ἀναλώσαιμι: aor. opt. ἀναλόω, here "kill."
1178-9 ὡς ἄλλην χθόνα δοκῶν ἀποίσειν, αὐτὸς ἔνθεν ἦν: "in the belief that he (the Corinthian) would take (the baby) away to another country—the one from which he himself came."
1181 γεγώς: with ἴσθι, "know that you were born..."
1182 ἂν ἐξήκοι σαφῆ: "turns out to have been true" (see on 970).
1183 τελευταῖον: adverb, "for the last time."
1184 πέφασμαι < φαίνομαι, with the participles: "since I am obviously born...and living...and the killer of..."
1184-5 οὐ χρῆν... οὐ χρῆν... οὐκ ἔδει: φῦναι, ὁμιλεῖν and κτανεῖν should be understood respectively.

1186-1222 Fourth Stasimon. *Oidipous, your fate shows that human aspirations are vain; even the most successful are only doomed to fail in the end. You reached the heights of fortune, routing the Sphinx and becoming our savior and king (str.-antistr. A).*
But now, whose life has changed to greater misery? You shared a wife with your father—how could she do it?—but time found you out. I lament you; you have truly given me both hope and despair (str.-antistr. B).

COMMENTARY   115

Meter: aeolo-choriambic, analyzed by Dale, *Metrical Analyses* fasc. 2, pp. 40-1.

1187 ὡς: exclamatory.
1187-8 ἴσα καὶ τὸ μηδέν: adverbial with ζώσας (for καί see on 611-612, for τὸ μηδέν see on 638). "I consider you living equally as nothing" = "I think your lives are worthless."
1191-2 ἢ τοσοῦτον ὅσον δοκεῖν καὶ δόξαντ' ἀποκλῖναι: with πλέον φέρει, with ὅσον introducing a result clause (S 2497), "than enough (happiness) so that he thinks (he is happy), and then, after having thought so, declines." For the repetition of δοκέω in the aor. partic. see J. D. Denniston, *Greek Prose Style* (Oxford 1952) 95-6.
1193-4 τὸν σόν...τὸν σόν...τὸν σόν: all three with δαίμονα.
1195-6 βροτῶν οὐδέν: See on 709.
1197-8 καθ' ὑπερβολὰν τοξεύσας ἐκράτησας: "by shooting too far, you mastered (with genit.)..."
1198-9 οὐ πάντ' εὐδαίμονος ὄλβου: "a prosperity not happy *in all respects*."
1198-1201 κατὰ μὲν φθίσας...θανάτων δ'...πύργος ἀνέστας: the construction changes, with a participle in the first clause and indicative in the second, a common type of anacoluthon (S 2147c, *GP* 379).
1198 κατά...φθίσας < καταφθίνω (*tmesis*, see on 198-9).
1201 ἀνέστας: "you rose up (< ἀνίστημι) as a bulwark against death."
1202 ἐξ οὗ: "since which time."
καλῇ: pres. 2 sg. pass. < καλέω, equivalent to an English pres. perfect, "you have been called my king."
1203 τὰ μέγιστ': adverbial with ἐτιμάθης (α for η).
1205 τέν πόνοις, τίς ἄταις ἀγρίαις†: The meter does not respond to the antistrophe, and a comparative to match ἀθλιώτερος seems missing.
1206 ἀλλαγᾷ βίου: "through a change (reversal) in his life."
1207-12 μέγας λιμὴν αὐτός...αἱ πατρῷαι...ἄλοκες: "The same great harbor" and "your father's furrows" are metaphors for sexual intercourse with Iokaste (cf. 422-3) and for birth from her also, (for birth from "the harbors of Aphrodite" see Empedocles, fr. 98 Diels-Kranz).
1208-10 ἤρκεσεν παιδὶ καὶ πατρὶ θαλαμηπόλῳ πεσεῖν: "sufficed for the child (to be born from) and the father to fall into as a bridegroom (lit. "bedchamber-attendant")."

1211-3 πῶς ποθ'... φέρειν... ἐδυνάθησαν ἐς τοσόνδε: "how were they able to endure you so long in silence?" The chorus cannot believe that her body itself would not recoil from incest. For a similar attitude to parricide cf. Herodotus 1.137.2: "(The Persians) believe that no one has ever yet killed his own father or mother, but that all such incidents which have happened would, if investigated, necessarily be discovered to be cases of adoption or illegitimacy. For it is just not possible, they say, that a real parent can be killed by his own child."

1213 ἄκονθ': "unwittingly." O did not know that his investigation would lead to this.

1214 δικάζει: "judge, *condemn.*"
τὸν ἄγαμον γάμον: "the marriage that was no marriage"; see on 422-3.

1215 τεκνοῦντα καὶ τεκνούμενον: "both begetting and begotten (by and from the same woman)." The participles would have suited O himself, but are transferred to the marriage. (LJ-W suggest that τεκνούμενον is middle rather than passive, with a sinister connotation ["begetting children—and more besides"] perhaps paralleled at Aeschylus, *Agamemnon* 750.)

1217 εἰδόμαν: aor. indic. mid. (< ὁράω) in a wish that cannot be fulfilled.

1218-9 ὡς...περίαλλ': adverbial exclamation, "how extravagantly I lament."
ἰάν: "voice, cry" (cf. Euripides, *Hippolytus* 585).

1220-1 τὸ δ' ὀρθὸν εἰπεῖν: absolute infin. (S 2012), "to speak the truth." It does not mean that the metaphor which follows is to be taken literally (*pace* D), but that it represents a profound feeling.

1221-2 ἀνέπνευσά τ'...καὶ κατεκοίμησα: lit. "from you I drew breath, and put my eye to sleep." This might mean either "you were everything for me," or (as I prefer) "you gave me renewed life (from the Sphinx) and now cause my death," i.e., "you have given me both hope and despair."

1223-1530 Exodos. First part: Messenger and chorus (1222-1296); second part: *kommos* (shared lyric lament) with O and the chorus (1297-1368); third part, O, chorus and Kreon (1369-1530).

COMMENTARY   117

Meter: 1223-1296, 1369-1514: iambic trimeter; 1515-1530: trochaic tetrameter (see Introduction p. 4-5). For the lyric *kommos* see on 1297-1368.

Exodos, first part (1223-1296). *A messenger comes out of the house to tell of Iokaste's suicide and O's blinding.*

1223 μέγιστα: adverbial, with τιμώμενοι (passive).
1224 οἴ...οἴα...ὅσον: exclamatory.
1225 ἀρεῖσθε: fut. indic. mid. < αἴρω.
1227-8 οὔτ' ἂν Ἴστρον οὔτε Φᾶσιν ἂν νίψαι: "that neither the Istros nor the Phasis (modern Danube and Rioni, great rivers at the ends of the earth) could wash away (< νίζω)..." For repeated ἄν see on 262.
1228 ὅσα κεύθει: "*because* it contains *such things*" (see on 701).
1229 τὰ δ'...κακά: "but *these* evils" (see on 1102).
1230 ἑκόντα κοὐκ ἄκοντα: i.e., self-inflicted.
1231 φανῶσ': aor. pass. 3 pl. subj.; for the omission of ἄν see on 316-317.
1232-3 λείπει μὲν οὐδ' ἃ πρόσθεν ᾔδεμεν τὸ μὴ οὐ βαρύστον' εἶναι: "what we knew (plpf. < οἶδα) before does not fall short of being lamentable either." For the construction see on 283.
1233 πρός: with dat. = "in addition."
1237 αὐτὴ πρὸς αὑτῆς: See on 138.
1238 πάρα = πάρεστιν (see on 766).
1239 ὅσον γε κἀν ἐμοὶ μνήμης ἔνι: "however much of memory is present (see on 170) in me" = "to the extent that I can describe it." For the limiting force of καί here see *GP* 295.
1240 πεύσῃ: fut. 2 sg. indic. < πυνθάνομαι.
1241 ὅπως: temporal, "when" (again in 1244).
ὀργῇ χρωμένη: i.e., "frantic" (J).
1241-2 παρῆλθ' ἔσω θυρῶνος: "passed inside the hallway (and out of sight of those outside)."
1242 ἵετ' εὐθύ: imperf. mid., "she threw herself straight toward..."
1243 σπῶσ': pres. partic. < σπάω, "pull."
ἀμφιδεξίοις ἀκμαῖς: "with the fingers of both hands."
1244 ἐπιρράξασ' < ἐπιρράσσω, "shut" with πύλας (εἰσῆλθε goes with ἔσω).
1245 ἤδη...πάλαι νεκρόν: i.e., "now long-dead."
1246 μνήμην...ἔχουσ': i.e., "recalling."

παλαιῶν σπερμάτων: "the ancient seeds" = "the child begotten long ago (Oidipous)." From this point on the actions of O, Iokaste and Laios are often alluded to vaguely in the plural (S 1007); see in general Diskin Clay, "Unspeakable Words in Greek Tragedy," *American Journal of Philology* 103 (1982) 277-298.

1247 θάνοι...λίποι: opt. in implied indirect statement (S 2622).
1248 τοῖς οἷσιν αὐτοῦ: "for his very own children," 3 pers. reflexive (S 1203b, cf. on 416).
δύστεκνον παιδουργίαν: abstract noun in apposition to τὴν τίκτουσαν, "he left behind the mother (to be) a childbearing of evil birth."
1249 γοᾶτο: augment omitted in a messenger's speech (see on 1106-7).
1251 χὤπως = καὶ ὅπως, in an indir. question with οἶδα.
ἐκ τῶνδ': "after these events."
1252 εἰσέπαισεν: "burst (lit. "smashed") in" (< εἰσπαίω).
1253 οὐκ ἦν ἐκθεάσασθαι: "it was not possible to observe..." (< ἐκθεάομαι).
1255 φοιτᾷ: "rushed all about" (LSJ φοιτάω I.2).
1256 γυναῖκά τ' οὐ γυναῖκα...ὅπου: indirect question after ἐξαιτῶν, but the interrogative is placed late and its emphatic words anticipated (see on 15): "(asking) *where* he could find his wife—who was no wife, but a double maternal furrow for himself and his children."
1257 κίχοι: aor. opt (replacing a deliberative subjunctive) < κιχάνω.
οὗ: 3 pers. pron. genit. sg., here used as reflexive (S 1229).
1260 ἀΰσας: aor. partic. < ἀΰω, "shout."
ὡς ὑφ' ἡγητοῦ τινος: "as if under (conducted by) some guide."
1261 ἐνήλατ': aor. < ἐνάλλομαι, "leap at."
1261-2 ἐκ δὲ πυθμένων ἔκλινε κοῖλα κλῇθρα: lit. "bent the hollowed doors off their foundations," i.e., leaned inward until they were bowed out and came loose from the wall. κλῇθρα must mean "doors" (Barrett on Euripides, *Hippolytus* 577-81), not the customary "bars," since Iokaste had *barred* the doors from the inside.
1263 οὗ: "where."
1265 δεινὰ βρυχηθείς: See on 419.
1267 τλήμων: of Iokaste (two-ending adj.).
τἀνθένδ' = τὰ ἐνθένδε, "what happened next."

COMMENTARY

1268-9 ἀποσπάσας...ἐξεστέλλετο: "After ripping from her body the golden clothing-brooches with which she was dressed (i.e., which fastened her clothing)..."

1270 ἄρας: aor. partic. < αἴρω, "having raised them up..."
ἄρθρα τῶν αὑτοῦ κύκλων: lit. "the joints (moveable parts) of his own circles" = "his eyes" (see on 718).

1271 ὁθούνεκ' = ὅτι, introducing indirect statement with future optatives.
ὄψοιντο: subject οἱ κύκλοι.

1274 ὀψοίαθ'...γνωσοίατο: 3 *plural* optative future (an Ionic alternative form used occasionally in tragedy, S 465f).
οὕς δ' ἔχρῃζεν οὐ γνωσοίατο: "and wouldn't recognize those whom he had wanted (to recognize, i.e., his parents.)"

1276 ἤρασσ': "kept beating," imperf. < ἀράσσω.
ἐπαίρων βλέφαρα: perhaps "raising his eyes" to meet the blow (cf. Seneca, *Oedipus* 962f. [LJ-W]), but better sc. περόνας (cf. 1269-70), taking βλέφαρα only with ἤρασσε.

1277 γλῆναι: "eyeballs."
γένει': "chin."
ἀνίεσαν: imperf. 3 pl. < ἀνίημι, here "stop." The next two lines ("not oozing drops, but a black shower of bloody hail") were probably interpolated by later actors seeking sensationalism.

1280 ἔρρωγεν: intransitive perf. < ῥήγνυμι (subject τάδε). The end of the line seems to have little point, and is considered corrupt.

1282 ὁ πρίν...μέν: not so much in praise of their past as a foil to the coming contrast, "their earlier happiness may have been genuine, but..."

1285 ἀπόν: pres. neut. partic. < ἄπειμι.

1286 ἔν τινι σχολῇ κακοῦ: "in some respite from his misery."

1287 διοίγειν κλῇθρα: "open wide the doors" (not "bars," see on 1261-2).

1290-1 ὡς...ῥίψων...οὐδ'...μενῶν: fut. partic. of purpose.

1291 ἀραῖος ὡς ἠράσατο: i.e., "under the sort of curse that he had placed upon himself" (in 244-251).

1292 γε μέντοι: "however."

1293 μεῖζον ἢ φέρειν: "too great to bear."

1294-5 κλῇθρα...πυλῶν: "doors of the portal."

1296 οἷον καὶ στυγοῦντ' ἐποικτίσαι: of result (see on 1191-2): "such that even one who hates him would feel pity."

Kommos (1297-1368). Shared lyrics with O and the chorus.

Meter: 1297-1306: "marching" anapaests (see West, *Greek Metre* p. 54, 95); 1307-1311: lyric anapaests; 1313-1368: lyric iambic and dochmiac, with iambic trimeters at 1317-20, 1325-28, 1335, 1347-8, 1355, 1367-8. It is analyzed by Dale, *Metrical Analyses* fasc. 3, pp. 34-5.

1299 προσέκυρσ': "met with" (< προσκυρέω, here with accus. for the more common dat.).
1301 μείζονα...τῶν μακίστων: internal accus. with πηδήσας: "who is the divinity that has made leaps greater than the longest ones against your unhappy fate?"
1304 ἐθέλων: concessive.
πόλλ' ἀνερέσθαι: "ask many questions," 2 aor. < ἀνέρομαι, with internal accus.
1309 ποῖ γᾶς: "where on earth?"
1310 φοράδαν: "in a rush," = φοράδην, adverb derived from φέρω.
1311 ἵν' ἐξήλου: "where have you leapt?" (aor. 2 sg. < ἐξάλλομαι, in a rhetorical question).
1312 ἐς δεινὸν κτλ.: sc. ἐξήλατο ὁ δαίμων.
1314 ἀπότροπον, ἐπιπλόμενον ἄφατον: "horrible, attacking me *unspeakable*" (i.e., indescribably).
1315 δυσούριστον: "with an ill wind."
1317 εἰσέδυ: "entered me" = "overcame me," 2 aor. 3 sg. < εἰσδύω.
1327 τοιαῦτα σὰς ὄψεις μαρᾶναι: "to extinguish (< μαραίνω) your sight *in this way*" (cf. on 190-3).
1328 ἐπῆρε: "urged you on," aor. < ἐπαίρω.
1331 αὐτόχειρ: i.e., with his own hand.
νιν: i.e., τὰς ὄψεις from 1328 (see on 868).
1331-2 οὔ τις ἀλλ' ἐγώ: "no one *but* I" (*GP* 4).
1335 ὅτῳ γ' ὁρῶντι: "since to me (see on 35), when I *could* see..."
1336 τᾷδ' = τῇδ' adverbial, "it is *thus*, as you say."
1337-9 τί...βλεπτὸν ἢ στερκτὸν ἢ προσήγορον ἔτ' ἔστ' ἀκούειν ἡδονᾷ: "What can be seen by me, or loved, or what can still speak (for me) to hear with pleasure?" O im-

plies that he ought to lose hearing as well as sight, cf. 1386-9. (On the text, see "Textual Notes" in Vol. 1.)

1347 τοῦ νοῦ τῆς τε συμφορᾶς ἴσον: causal genitives explaining δείλαιε, "*equally* for your state of mind and for your misfortune."

1348 ὡς...ἠθέλησα...ἄν: past potential (S 1784), "how I could have wished..."

1349 ὄλοιθ': intransitive 2 aor. < ὄλλυμι: "may the wanderer die, whoever he was, who ..."

1349-50 πέδας...μ' ἔλαβε: genit. of separation, "took me from the rough bond on my feet."

1351-2 ἔρυτο κἀνέσωσεν: "rescued and saved," aorists from ἐρύω and ἀνασῴζω.

1354 τότε γὰρ ἂν θανών: conditional (ἄν with ἦ, 1 sg. imperf., in a contrary to fact statement), "if I had died then, I would not be..."

1356 θέλοντι κἀμοὶ τοῦτ' ἂν ἦν: "this would have been for me wishing as well," i.e., "I too would have wished this," an extension of the dat. of reference (S 1487).

1359 βροτοῖς: dat. of agent with ἐκλήθην.

1361 ὁμογενὴς δ' ἀφ' ὧν αὐτὸς ἔφυν: "having a common offspring (as those) from whom I myself was born (i.e., Laios; for the plural see on 1246)."

1365 τι πρεσβύτερον...κακοῦ κακόν: "any evil still more advanced (lit. "older") than evil."

1367 φῶ: deliberate subjunctive < φημί, "I do not know how I can say that you have planned well."

1368 κρείσσων: personal construction for impersonal (S 1982a), although ἄν is omitted as if it *had* been impersonal (see LJ-W, and on 255-6 above) = "*it* would have been better *that* you no longer live, than to live blind."

Exodos, third part (1368-1530). *O explains to the chorus his reasons for blinding himself, laments his misery and asks for exile* (1369-1415); *then Kreon arrives to ask O to withdraw from public view* (1416-1431). *O begs Kreon for exile, and for the chance to embrace and lament his daughters* (1432-1467). *Kreon grants the second request but refuses to act on the first one yet, and the closing trochaic tetrameters continue the dispute as O is forced into the palace.* (1468-1523)

On the motives and symbolism of O's blinding, and the curious inconclusiveness of this final scene see the works cited in "Topics for Discussion" in Vol. 1, section IV.1-3.

1369 **μέν**: without answering δέ in opening speeches, GP 383.
1371-2 **ὄμμασιν ποίοις...ποτ' ἂν προσεῖδον**: indirect question, contrary to fact, "gazing with what sort of eyes I could have looked at..."
1373-4 **οἶν...δυοῖν**: dat. of disadvantage with ἐστὶ...εἰργασμένα, "to which two people deeds have been done by me..."
1374 **κρεῖσσον' ἀγχόνης**: "things stronger than hanging" = crimes for which a death like Iokaste's is too mild a punishment.
1375 **ἦν ἐφίμερος**: "was desirable" (*without* ἄν, thus not contrary-to-fact like 1372, but expressing O's thoughts at the time he blinded himself).
1376 **βλαστοῦσ' ὅπως ἔβλαστε**: causal participle, formally in agreement with ὄψις, even though it refers to τέκνων (see on 1215): "since they were born—in the way they were born" (i.e., from incest).
προσλεύσσειν: limiting with ἐφίμερος.
1378-9 **οὐδ' ἄστυ γ', οὐδὲ πύργος, οὐδὲ...ἀγάλμαθ'**: sc. ἦν ἐφίμερα προσλεύσσειν.
1379 **ὧν**: with ἀπεστέρησ'.
1380 **ἀνὴρ εἷς**: emphasizing the superlative adverb κάλλιστ' (S 1088), "even though I was brought up most nobly of any man at Thebes." Yet O was not really 'brought up' in Thebes, but in Corinth (cf. 1396 below), and it has been suggested that the line is an interpolation.
1381 **ἐννέπων**: modal, "by commanding that..."
1383 **φανέντ'...γένους τοῦ Λαΐου**: predicative genit. (see on 278), "revealed *as a member of the family of Laios*." (although this was not part of the initial proclamation, but discovered later).
1386-7 **τῆς ἀκουούσης...πηγῆς δι' ὤτων φραγμός**: "a blockage of the hearing-spring through the ears" = "a way to stop the passage of sound through my ears."
1387-8 **οὐκ ἂν ἐσχόμην τὸ μὴ κτλ**: "I would not have restrained myself (aor. mid. < ἔχω) from..." (For the construction see S 2744.9.)
1388 **ἀποκλῇσαι** < ἀποκλείω, "shut out."
1389 **ἵν' ἦ**: imperf. indic. in a purpose clause that cannot be fulfilled.
1390 **τὴν φροντίδ'...οἰκεῖν**: with γλυκύ, "that the mind should live away from miseries."

COMMENTARY 123

1392 ὡς ἔδειξα μήποτε: impossible purpose again, "so that I would never have shown..."
1393 ἐμαυτὸν...ἔνθεν ἢ γεγώς: "where I was born from;" see on 223.
1395 λόγῳ: with πάτρια, "in name only."
ἆρα: not interrogative, but = ἄρα (S 2800) used in a discovery (S 2795).
1396 κάλλος κακῶν ὔπουλον: "a beauty consisting deep down (lit. "underneath the scar") of evils."
1400 τοὐμόν: ambiguously placed as if solely with αἷμα, but then turns out to belong mostly to πατρός in the next line.
1401 ἐπίετε: aor. < πίνω.
1402 ὑμῖν: dat. of reference, "(what I did) *in your case*," i.e., at the crossroads.
1403 αὖθις: "once again" (with Iokaste, when he arrived in Thebes).
1404-5 φυτεύσαντες...ἀνεῖτε (aor. < ἀνίημι): "after giving birth, you sent forth once again the same seed"; like several statements in this speech, not a very precise formulation.
1405 κἀπεδείξατε < ἐπιδείκνυμι. In the following pairs of words the first is the object, the next is predicate (see Colin Macleod, *Collected Essays* [Oxford 1983] 45-6): "You revealed fathers (to be) brothers, children (to be) kindred bloodshed (i.e., parricides), brides (to be) wives *and* (τε) mothers, and all that is most shameful..."
1410 ἔξω: i.e., out of the city.
1412 ἐκρίψατ' < ἐκρίπτω, with θαλάσσιον (sc. με),"throw me out into the sea."
ἔνθα μήποτ': μή for οὐ in a relative clause expressing purpose (S 2705f).
1413 ἀξιώσατ' ἀνδρὸς ἀθλίου θιγεῖν: "deign to touch (< θιγγάνω) a wretched man," i.e., touch him in the process of expelling or killing him.
1415 οἷός τε...φέρειν: "is *able* (see on 23) to bear." He means that his pollution is too unusual for others to be infected by it.
1416 ὧν ἐπαιτεῖς = τούτων ἃ ἐπαιτεῖς, "*concerning the things* (see on 49) which you ask..."
1417 τὸ πράσσειν καὶ τὸ βουλεύειν: The infinitives (for the addition of the article see S 2034e) limit ἐς δέον πάρεσθ', "is here when he should be, for acting and deliberating."

1420-1 τά...πάρος...πάντ': accus. of respect (see on 1197-8) with κακός, "in all earlier matters" (i.e., about which we disputed before).

1421 ἐφεύρημαι: perf. pass., ἐφευρίσκω.

1423 ὡς ὀνειδιῶν: fut. partic. of purpose.

1424 καταισχύνεσθ': For the rest of this first speech, Kreon ignores O and addresses the chorus or other attendants.

1426 αἰδεῖσθ': αἰδέομαι usually governs *either* accus. *or* complementary infin., here both: "feel shame before...at displaying..."

1427 τό = ὅ.

1427-8 μήτε γῆ...προσδέξεται: i.e., all nature recoils from his presence.

1431 εὐσεβῶς ἔχει: impersonal (see S 1438), "it is most pious for *only* kindred to..."

1432 ἐλπίδος μ' ἀπέσπασας: "you have dragged me away from my expectation," i.e., treated me better than I feared.

1433 ἐλθών: causal, "because you, the best of men, came (to console) me, the worst."

1434 πιθοῦ τί μοι: lit. "obey me in something" (see on 1064), i.e., "do me this favor."

πρὸς σοῦ: "from your point of view," i.e., in your interest."

1435 τοῦ...χρείας: interrogative pronoun, genit. with τυχεῖν, "what request do you ask me to receive?"

1436 ὅσον τάχισθ' = ὡς τάχιστα.

ὅπου: "where," antecedent γῆς ἐκ τῆσδε.

1437 θνητῶν...μηδενὸς προσήγορος: "able to be spoken to *by* no mortal." Genitive for dat. by analogy with α-privative adjectives (see on 179) as if μηδενὸς προσήγορος = ἀπροσήγορος πάντων (K-G 1.402 n.7).

1438-9 ἔδρασ' ἄν...εἰ μή...ἔχρῃζον: mixed present-past contrary-to-fact condition, "I would have done it, if I did not want..."

1440 ἐκείνου: i.e., τοῦ θεοῦ.

πᾶσ' ἐδηλώθη φάτις: with infin., "the whole decree has been made clear, to kill..."

1442-3 ἵν' ἕσταμεν χρείας: causal-exclamatory (see on 701) with partitive genitive of place (S 1448), "because of where of need we stand" = "in such an emergency."

COMMENTARY 125

1444-5 O's argument: "surely I am too miserable now to justify the trouble of a god." Kreon's argument: "surely you are convinced now that the god is to be believed."

1446 καὶ σοί γ': Normally καί...γε introduces an additional idea (*GP* 157), but here the two particles seem to act separately (the first in a *contrast* [as in 60], the second cohering closely with σοί), as O refines his initial request and appeals to Kreon as protector of the city: "*and yet* it is *to you* (as opposed to the god) that I command and enjoin..." A possible parallel is *Philoctetes* 29, τόδ' ἐξύπερθε, καὶ στιβοῦ γ' οὐδεὶς κτύπος "(Philoctetes' cave) is that one up above, *and yet* there is no sound of any *walking*."

προτρέψομαι: For the future imperative with present meaning see on 1077.

1447 τῆς μὲν κατ' οἴκους: Iokaste.

1448 θοῦ: aor. imperat. < τίθημι, "*make* what burial you yourself desire (without having to consult the god)."
τελεῖς: fut. indic., "you will make the final determination."

1449 ἀξιωθήτω: imperat. 3 sg. aor. pass. < ἀξιόω, "let my this city of my father never be thought worthy to obtain me as an inhabitant while I am alive."

1451-2 κλῄζεται οὑμός: "is called mine (because I was exposed there)."

1453 ἐθέσθην: aor. mid. 3 pers. dual < τίθημι.

1454 ἐξ...ἀπωλλύτην: conative imperf. (S 1895), "at the hands of those two who tried to kill me," i.e., in the way they wanted, by exposure on Kithairon.

1455-6 μήτε μ' ἂν νόσον...πέρσαι < πέρθω, infin. with ἄν standing for potential optative; μή for οὐ in a confident assertion (S 2727).

1457 θνῄσκων: "as I was dying (when an infant)."
μὴ 'πὶ τῳ δεινῷ κακῷ: The negative shows the phrase is conditional (sc. σωθείς), "if not (saved) for some terrible misery."

1458 ὅποιπερ εἶσ' ἴτω: He dismisses the topic: "let it go where it will."

1459-60 μὴ...προσθῇ μέριμναν: 2 sg. aor. mid. subj., "do not assume concern for..."

1461 σπάνιν...τοῦ βίου: "want of livelihood."
ἔνθ' ἂν ὦσι: "wherever they are."

1462 ταῖν...ἐμαῖν: fem. genit.-dat. dual (usually the fem. dual is the same as the masc., e.g. τώδε 1465, τοῖν φίλοιν 1472).

1463 αἶν: dat. of advantage.

1463-4 ἡμὴ...βορᾶς τράπεζ': ἡμὴ = ἡ ἐμή. If the text is sound, "for whom my table of food was never set apart" = "who always had dinner with me." O's dinner-table figured in the curse he laid on his sons, according to the epic version; see "Topics for Discussion" in Vol. 1, section I.1.

1464 ἄνευ τοῦδ' ἀνδρός: "without this man," i.e., me, (see on 534); redundant after ἡμή, but such "pleonasm" is not rare (K-G 2.586-7).

1465 ψαύοιμι: optative in a conditional relative clause (past general), "whatever I touched, they always shared it all."
μετειχέτην: imperf. dual.

1466 αἶν μοι μέλεσθαι: infin. as imperative (see on 462), "whom you must tend for me." The sentence begun in 1462 is not finished, but resumed with a relative clause.

1469 θιγών: conditional, with potential optative ἄν...δοκοῖμ', "if I were to touch them, I would imagine that ..."

1470 σφᾶς: 3 pers. accus. pl. pron.

1471 τί φημι: a cry of surprise ("but what am I talking about?"), as at *Trachiniae* 865.

1472 οὐ δὴ κλύω που: in an incredulous question (*GP* 223), "surely I don't hear...?" For genit. with verbs of hearing see S 1361.
τοῖν...φίλοιν: See on 1462.

1474 τὰ φίλτατ' ἐγγόνοιν ἐμοῖν: For the periphrasis with neut. see on 261-2, and cf. τὰ πικρὰ τοῦ λοιποῦ βίου in 1487.

1475 λέγω τι: See on 1140.

1477 γνοὺς τὴν παροῦσαν κτλ: lit. "having recognized the present delight which used to possess you long ago." Unless πάλαι is used of a recent event (see on 1067) this must mean " since I knew that you used to feel (in them) the joy you feel now."

1478 ἀλλ' εὐτυχοίης: See on 929.
τῆσδε τῆς ὁδοῦ: "because of this trip (by you to see me)."

1479 φρουρήσας: supplementary partic. with τύχοι, "may he chance to have guarded you better than me."

1481 ὡς...χέρας: "*to* (ὡς as if with a person, S 1702) these sibling hands of mine."

1482 ὑμῖν: dat. of feeling (see on 2), not to be translated.

COMMENTARY 127

1483 προὔξένησαν < προξενέω, usually of doing favors: "which have arranged that the formerly bright eyes...see *like this* (not at all)."

1484 ὅς: antecedent τοῦ φυτουργοῦ πατρὸς (1482).
οὔθ' ὁρῶν οὔθ' ἱστορῶν: "since I neither realized nor inquired."

1485 ἔνθεν ἠρόθην: aor. pass. < ἀρόω, "from the place where I myself was sown."

1487 νοούμενος: usually active, "pondering."

1488 οἷον: adverbial, "*how*."
βιῶναι: 2 aor. infin. < βιόω, "live," but a virtual passive, hence πρὸς ἀνθρώπων of agent: "*be treated by* ..."

1490 κεκλαυμέναι: perf. mid., "in tears."

1491 ἀντὶ τῆς θεωρίας: i.e., instead of being allowed to watch.

1492 πρὸς γάμων...ἀκμάς: "to the edges of marriage" = to the age-boundary between being daughters and being wives. (Plural because two of them are involved.)

1493 τίς οὗτος ἔσται: i.e., your husband.
παραρρίψει: of a wager, with λαμβάνων, "run the risk of incurring...?"

1494 †τοῖς ἐμοῖς† makes little sense with the following γονεῦσιν, and indeed the next line may be corrupt also; we might have expected "which will be ruin both for his *children* and *himself* alike."

1497 ἔπεφνεν: 2 aor. 3 sg., "killed," as if from a non-existent verb *φένω (LSJ θείνω II).

1498 ἐσπάρη: aor. pass. < σπείρω.

1498-9 κἀκ τῶν ἴσων...ὧνπερ: allusive plural for singular (see on 1246), "and acquired you (as children) from the same ones (Iokaste) from which he himself was born."

1500 τοιαῦτ' ὀνειδιεῖσθε: internal accus. with passive verb (S 1574), "you will receive such reproaches." ὀνειδιεῖσθε is actually fut. middle, but here equivalent to passive, S 808.

1502 χέρσους: "barren," i.e., childless.
φθαρῆναι: aor. pass. < φθείρω.

1503 ἀλλ': "well" (see on 9; for its postponement after the vocative see *GP* 23).

1504 λέλειψαι: perf. pass. 2 sg., λείπω.

1504-5 νώ...ὤ...ὄντε: duals, of O and Iokaste.

1505 μή...περιίδῃς: "do not (merely) look on (without acting) at them..."

1506 ἀλωμένας: "wandering," i.e., being exiled like me (< ἀλάομαι).

1507 μηδ' ἐξισώσῃς (< ἐξισόω): "do not assimilate them to my misery."

1509 πλὴν ὅσον τὸ σὸν μέρος: "except as far as you are involved" (LSJ μέρος III, Bruhn 247.18).

1510: ξύννευσον < ξυννεύω, "nod," "assent."

1511 εἰχέτην: imperf. dual 2 pers. (with a form usually used for 3 pers., see J): "if you already had sense (i.e., were old enough to understand)..."

1512 μοι: See on 2.

1513 οὗ καιρὸς ἐᾷ: with ζῆν, "where opportunity allows," i.e., in the best place available.

1513-4 ζῆν...κυρῆσαι: infinitives explaining τοῦτ' εὔχεσθε in 1513, "(pray) that you live...and obtain..."

1513 τοῦ βίου: genit. with κυρῆσαι.

1515 ἅλις ἵν' ἐξήκεις δακρύων: lit. "it is enough *where* you have come *in tears*, (see on 1442-3)" = "you have wept enough (so go inside)."

1516 πάντα...καιρῷ καλά: "all things are good at the proper time."

1517 ἐφ' οἷς οὖν εἶμι: "*on what conditions* I will now go" (LSJ ἐπί III.3).

1518 ὅπως πέμψεις: ὅπως with future in an urgent command (S 1920).

τοῦ θεοῦ μ' αἰτεῖς δόσιν: lit. "you ask for the gift of a god" = "what you want (exile), only the god can grant."

1519 ἥκω: "I have come to be..." (LSJ ἥκω I.5).

1519-20 A more explicit version of the argument would be:
(O) I am hated by the gods, so they will not want me to stay in Thebes;
(Kreon) If they hate you they will soon give me sign to banish you;
(O) So, you agree with me?
(Kreon) Do not try to twist my words.

1521 ἀφοῦ: 2 aor. mid imperat. < ἀφίημι, "let go of..."

1522 μηδαμῶς...ἕλῃ < αἱρέω, "don't take them away..." (even though he asked in 1505-7 that they not go into exile along with him).

1523 ἀκράτησας: = ἃ ἐκράτησας, "what you controlled."

ξυνέσπετο < συνέπομαι, "did not follow your life (i.e., continue throughout it)."

1524-30 These lines have been suspected of being a later interpolation (see especially Dawe, *Studies* I. 266-73) on the grounds that they 1) correspond to several lines of Euripidean tragedies; 2) seem to provide a banal judgment of the story; 3) offer linguistic difficulties. But 1) most scholars agree that they are more likely to be interpolated in Euripides than in Sophocles; 2) judgments by the chorus need not always be considered conclusive (see "Topics for Discussion" in Vol. 1, section III.1); 3) unintelligibility is not a symptom of interpolation. See especially Gordon Kirkwood, "Exit Oedipus" (forthcoming).

1524 ὦ πάτρας Θήβης ἔνοικοι: The leader of the chorus evidently addresses the other members of it (a similar "self-address" at *Trachiniae* 1275).

1526 οὗ... ταῖς τύχαις: if the text is correct, a parenthetical rhetorical question, "on whose fortunes who did not gaze with envy?"

1528-9 θνητὸν ὄντ'... μηδέν' ὀλβίζειν: "to call happy no mortal if he is looking at (i.e., still waiting for) his final day." A well-known sentiment, but expressed in a strange form here.

1530 περάσῃ: aor. subj. < περάω, "cross."

GRAMMATICAL INDEX
(numbers refer to verses unless otherwise marked)

Accusative: cognate, 2; internal, 190-3, 419; in apposition to the sentence, 603; of respect, 82-83
Adjective, predicative, equivalent to an adverb: 631
Anaphora: 4-5
Anastrophe: 93-4
Anticipation of subject of indirect question as object of main verb: 15, 224, 302, 740, 926, 1393
Article omitted: with noun in poetry, 4; with generic participle, 516-7.
Attraction: of relative, 148, 350-1, 645, 862, 1416; of nouns, 175, 449-51
Correption: Introd. p. 4
Dative: of feeling, 2; of manner: 10, 405; in -οισι, αισι: 3
Crasis: 6
Enallage-hypallage: 108-9, 480
Future indic. in neg. question = command: 430, 637
Genitive: absolute with subject omitted, 505; introductory with verb of telling "about": 49, 991, 1416; of separation without preposition 24, 97; partitive, of place: 108, 367, 1442-3; predicative: 278-9, 393, 917; with verbs of filling: 4-5, 779; with

alpha privative adjective: 179
Neuter plural, in periphrasis with genitive: 201-2, 1474, 1487
Optative: in indirect statement after secondary verb: 526; potential, for future indicative, 95, 343
Participle: with forms of εἰμί in periphrases: 90, 274, 580, 957, 970, 1146
Pluperfect in contrary-to-fact condition: 261-2, 690, 984
Polyptoton: 100, 284, 479
Plural (poetic) for singular: 237
Prodelision: 112, 215, 360
Relative clauses, incorporation of antecedent: 68
Relative pronoun: attraction into dative or genitive: 119, 148; governed only by participle: 117
Subjunctive with οὐ μή: 771
Synizesis: Introd. p. 4
Variation in construction: 20-1, 477-8.

ἄν repeated: 261-2
ἄρθρα 718, 1270.
αὐτός...αὐτοῦ 137-138, 228, 1237.
γάρ in clause giving information: 277
γνώμη 398

εἰμί + partic. in periphrases: 90, 274, 580, 957, 970, 1146
εἰς in idioms: 516, 519-21, 700, 846-7, 991
ἔχω in periphrasis for perfect: 577, 699, 702
καί adversative, 50, 413, 567; linking alternatives, 539; in comparisons 611-2, 1187-8.
κλῇθρα 1261-2, 1287, 1294-5
κυρῶ + partic.: 258, 362, 594, 985
μή generic in relative clauses and participles, 110, 269, 569, 875.
ὅδε referring backward: 251
οἷός τε: 23
οὐ μή + aor. subjunct. in a strong denial: 328-9, 771
οὔπω "not yet": 105, 594, 1130.
πάλαι of recent events: 1067, 1161, 1477
πρός + genitive of agent: 292, 357, 516, 949, 1488
σαφής: 106
τι adverbial (εἴ τι): 96978i
τρέφω: 356
ὧδ' = δεῦρο: 7
ὡς added to accus. + partic. with verbs of perception: 848, 956